D1201628

12

# THE JAMES

*Books by Blair Niles*

FICTION

    MARIA PALUNA
        A novel of old Guatemala

    DAY OF IMMENSE SUN
        A novel of the conquest of Peru

    STRANGE BROTHER

    LIGHT AGAIN

    CONDEMNED
        A fictional biography of an unknown convict

    FREE
        A novel of exile

NON-FICTION

    BLACK HAITI: A BIOGRAPHY OF AFRICA'S ELDEST
        DAUGHTER

    CASUAL WANDERINGS IN ECUADOR

    COLOMBIA: LAND OF MIRACLES

    PERUVIAN PAGEANT: A JOURNEY IN TIME

    THE JAMES

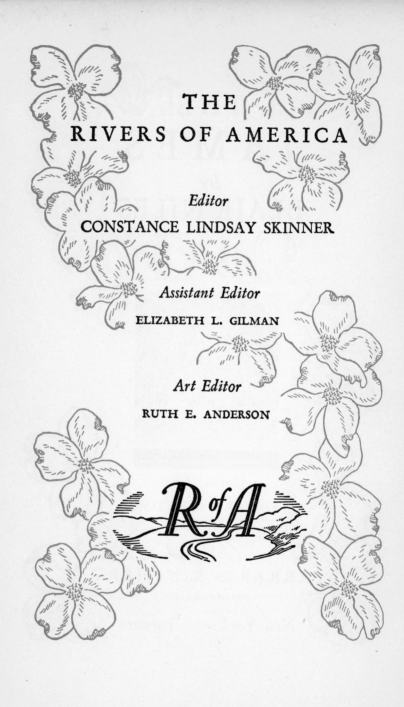

# THE
# RIVERS OF AMERICA

*Editor*

CONSTANCE LINDSAY SKINNER

*Assistant Editor*

ELIZABETH L. GILMAN

*Art Editor*

RUTH E. ANDERSON

# THE
# JAMES

*by*

# BLAIR NILES

*Illustrated by*

## EDWARD SHENTON

## FARRAR & RINEHART
### INCORPORATED
*New York*          *Toronto*

COPYRIGHT, 1939, BY BLAIR NILES
PRINTED IN THE UNITED STATES OF AMERICA
BY QUINN & BODEN COMPANY, INC., RAHWAY, N. J.
ALL RIGHTS RESERVED

DEDICATED

TO MY NIECE

ARGYLL PRYOR RICE

AND

MY NEPHEWS

HENRY GORDON RICE

AND

ROGER PRYOR RICE

# Contents

# CONTENTS

## PART THREE.   ALONG THE ROAD TO APPOMATTOX

## PART FOUR.   OUT OF DEFEAT

# THE JAMES

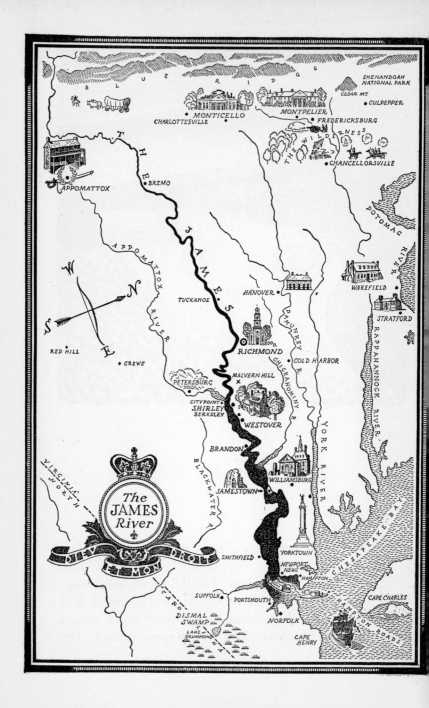

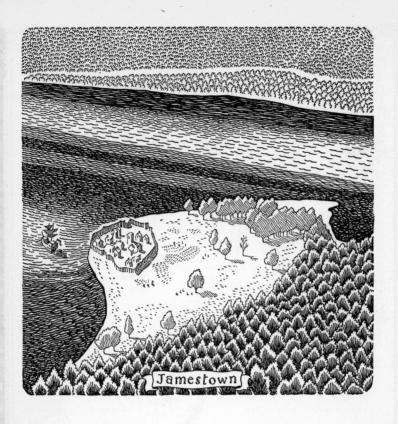

Jamestown

## The Old Muddy Jeems

When you look down from a thousand feet
in the air, you see, not only James River, but a wide
sweep of tidewater Virginia. Parallel rivers flow eastward into Chesapeake Bay. Up from the south and
down from the north lesser rivers pour their waters
into the main streams; into the Rappahannock, the

York, and the James. Creeks contribute to the rivers and brooks feed the creeks. Airplane view establishes each in its place, and relates land and water. You realize why it was that three hundred years ago when the Virginia Venture established the first permanent British colony in the New World, horses played no part in the conquest; for this network of streams formed the only highways; penetrating in every direction the primeval forests of seventeenth-century Virginia. Horses, which on the trails of Mexico and Peru terrified the natives as supernatural creatures, had no value in the conquest of this roadless region of forest and flowing stream, where for a hundred miles inland the tides of the sea ebb and rise in the rivers.

It happens to be a blithe autumn day as you fly over this tidewater country, and in the scene beneath you flaming foliage is mirrored on waters lustrous in the white bright light. The great forests of the past were long ago replaced by plantations, but groves of trees stand about the old mansions, trees march down village streets, and at intervals in the landscape there are areas thickly wooded, painted now in scarlet and gold. Harvest fields lie serene in the sun, dotted with stacks of hay and corn, and strewn with yellow pumpkins, no bigger than oranges as you see them from the plane.

It is a picture of fruition, of fulfillment. Yet it quivers with expectancy, as though, because so much has happened here, surely the future, too, will be vividly alive.

Dropping down to fly low over the James you draw near to the great story of the river; passing over the wide mouth through which sailed the little fleet that brought the first Venturers from England; so "ravished with the admirable sweetness" of springtime on their river that they called it "the famousest river ever found by any Christian"; naming it James River in homage to their sovereign, James I; "Jeems" River in the dialect of their homeland.

Jamestown Island, where they first settled, looks from the air like a great open fan lying upon wide amber waters. A bridge connecting the island with the peninsula forms the handle of the fan; and the fan's decorations are a grove of trees at one end, at the other a square ivy-covered tower, a monument, and two statues set upon velvet grass at the foot of the terraced embankment of an abandoned fort. General Lee had the fort built during the Civil War, the tower was part of the ancient church of old Jamestown, the monument commemorates the founding of the colony, the statues are of Captain John Smith and Pocahontas. Sculptured in bronze the winsome Algonkin princess, her hands outstretched, is moving toward John Smith, who stands looking out over the river. Once he said of the first American colonists, "They have been my Wife, my Hawks, my Hounds, my Cards, my Dice and in total my best content." It is thus that his statue seems forever to dream, gazing out upon the James River.

When your plane again climbs you look beyond the James, across the narrow peninsula, to York River; your eyes pause to dwell upon Williamsburg standing midway between the two streams, and then upon Yorktown where Cornwallis surrendered to George Washington, and the independence of the United States was won; the founding of America and its independence lying within a dozen miles of each other, both visible from the air at the same moment.

Then once more dropping low, you fly above the famous estates which stand upon the banks of James River: Claremont and Brandon, Weyanoke, Carter's Grove, Westover, Shirley, and Turkey Island which was the home of the Randolphs. You see the Chickahominy flowing from the northwest into James River, and from the southwest the Appomattox—the "pleasant Appomattox," John Smith described it. So you arrive at the falls where the river rushes over great boulders; making noise enough, Colonel William Byrd said, "to drown the notes of a scolding wife."

It was this sprightly William Byrd, a grandee in huge curled wig, velvets and brocades, who two hundred years ago founded the city of Richmond.

The James has come far before it reaches Richmond and tumbles over rocks into the tidewater region; for it has crossed the state from west to east. Near the boundary of distant Alleghany country the Jackson River and the Cowpasture River have united, become the James, and started east, forcing a way through mountain ranges and then following a devious route of many windings and bendings, beginning as a clear, little mountain stream which, as it progresses, widens and takes color from the land through which it passes, until below Richmond it is a great copper-hued tidal estuary, in some places as much as five miles across.

The upper James was a wilderness when Byrd went exploring into frontier Virginia two centuries ago; a region of dense forests, of wild life, of Indian tribes pushed westward by the advance of the white man.

Yelling packs of wolves followed in the path of Byrd's expedition. There were herds of buffalo, too, shaggy brown beasts standing on short stocky legs, cocking their little twelve-inch tails, Byrd says, when they were angry, pawing the ground, grunting and snorting with rage when what he expected of such creatures was an echoing bellow. Their flesh was so good that he declared a cardinal legate might have made a comfortable meal upon it in Carnival time. And of the buffalo's horns the Indians shaped spoons which they considered valuable; explaining that they had the remarkable property of splitting into pieces whenever poison was put into them. The expedition had shot so many bear and so much venison that buffalo meat made an acceptable variety in their diet. As for the combination of wild turkey and venison stewed together, it was of so delicious a flavor that they "no more tired of it than a man wearies of an engaging wife because of her being a constant dish." They ate much venison stewed with turkey; to the horror of their Indian guides who insisted that the Guardian Spirit of the forest forbade that the beasts of the earth and the birds of the air should be cooked together.

The buffalo are gone, clouds of migrating pigeons no longer blacken the sky, the Indian is no more a primitive savage.

Today the river in its journey eastward from the mountains to the Chesapeake travels through pasture lands, orchards, tobacco plantations, truck farms, and mining districts; it flows past manufacturing towns; ferries and bridges span its waters, and in every direction there are roads over which flash lines of motorcars.

As you fly through the shimmering light that sparkles over the river, dappling its glistening surface like dancing drops of falling rain, you have spread before you the scene of this story, eternally significant, touchingly human and alive.

And when you come to know it, you no longer think of this river as flowing amber, or copper, but as the "dear old muddy Jeems."

## Plantation Child

TIDEWATER VIRGINIA from the air is a long-shot of the James River story. If you would see a close-up of the setting of the tale your gaze must be focused upon a plantation. For the story is a plantation epic, beginning more than three hundred years ago, with the Venturers who sailed from England in those three little ships—the *Sarah Constant,* the *Goodspeed,* and the *Discovery.*

In that far-off time Virginia itself was just as often called a plantation as a colony.

It was natural that men who had left their homes to sail a wide, fearful sea, and to conquer a savage wilderness, should each look upon his own individual plantation as though it were the world.

This is still the feeling of a child whose home happens to be an isolated plantation; and only in such a child is the plantation magnified to the size and importance which it occupied in the minds of those long-ago men.

And, borrowing this child's eyes, you have your close-up of the Virginia Venture. And, that the child may be definite, as well as typical, she must have a name; whatever name you like—Evelyn or Anne, Ellen or Mary; it does not matter. Mary will perhaps serve as well as any.

The plantation when Mary first knew it was thirteen miles from a railroad station, over a road always bad, often impassable, and so lonely that you might drive the whole way without meeting another human creature; so remote that a child could hardly believe in the existence of anything beyond its horizon.

It is true that when Mary was four years old she had been taken to visit grandparents who had gone to live in a place spoken of as New York. Her grandmother was fond of telling how one day she found Mary standing at the window, looking out into the street weeping. Between sobs she explained that it was because the people in the street did not speak to each other or to her. On the plantation no one ever passed without a greeting.

Of course Mary could not herself remember the incident. New York was vague. The plantation was the world.

Her father's house stood half a mile from the big road. And from the big road a wide driveway, cut through the forest, led to a grove of enormous oaks and hickories. The drive ended in the flourish of a circle, around a plot as grassy as the great trees growing in it would permit. And the drive was of sand, white like the green-shuttered house. A large square porch opened into a hall where a graceful horseshoe staircase mounted to the second floor. At the end of the hall was a library with rectangles of colored glass in the upper sash of its windows, and doors to the right and left of the hall led into parlor and dining room—vast, square, high-ceilinged rooms, with fireplaces. The upper story had bedrooms of the same great size, and since every plantation house sooner or later developed wings, there was at the south a wing with more halls and bedrooms and porches, and at the north a chapel with stained-glass windows. An archway separated the south wing from a long one-story extension so thickly covered with English ivy that its windows seemed to have been cut into a wall of vines. Beside this wall was a walk passing between flowering shrubs and ending at the garden gate.

The extension contained kitchen, storerooms, and a harness room. Its doors, facing the rear of the establishment, opened upon an arcade where on rainy days bedraggled chickens sought protection. At the rear also was a high-roofed smokehouse, and an icehouse sunk into the earth, with its squat roof practically on the ground. A row of white cabins marked the limit of the back yard, and a little distance away were the carriage house and the orchard.

Beyond the garden stretched the fecund low-grounds, to a river whose presence was marked by the willows growing along its banks. On the west pastures rolled to the horizon and black-and-white cattle grazed in the pastures. To the east were cultivated fields, with here and there a tobacco barn or a stable, a clump of trees about a spring, or a little cluster of two or three cabins. To the north there were the woods.

And the plantation with its fields, its river, its garden, its barns, the little whitewashed dwellings of tenants and hired laborers—this was the world, and Mary saw it with the exploring eyes of one newly arrived upon the earth.

The education of a plantation child begins with the dark people of the world. The influence of parents comes later; the earliest impressions are from the more primitive race which thinks in terms of proverbs and drama, the race which, like the child itself, lives close to nature.

"After you, is manners" is the plantation child's introduction to courtesy.

"When the peacock looks at his feet, his tail drops" proves the importance of holding your head high.

"Dogs see spirits" introduces the child to a world beyond the material and the visible.

"When chickens drink they lift up their bills to

thank God" wakes in the child a sense of worship, never achieved by the pompous, catechism demanding:

"*Q.*: What is man's chief end?

"*Ans.*: Man's chief end is to glorify God and enjoy him forever."

And something is born in the heart of any child who has tended a newly hatched chick, or coaxed a wobbly orphan calf to take milk from a nursing bottle.

Mary's first feminine playmate was a small colored girl named Milly. As very little children they would lie for hours at a time beside an anthill, calling softly over and over:

"Doodle-bug, Doodle-bug, yo' house is on fire!"

And then they were fond of snuggling under a snowball bush, and singing:

"Ole Molly har, what you doin' dar?
Setting in de cornder smokin' a cigyar?"

Far off they would hear an older voice singing:

"I looked over Jordan, an' what did I see?
Comin' fo' to carry me home,
A band of angels comin' after me,
Comin' fo' to carry me home.
Oh, swing low, sweet chariot
Comin' fo' to carry me home."

But the little friends under the snowball bush preferred songs of the animal world:

"De coon's got a long-ringed bushy tail,
De 'possum tail is bare,

De rabbit's got no tail a'tall
But a little bush o' hair.

. . . .

Oh, de 'possum is a cunnin' thing
Smilin' in de dark.
Nothin' 'tall disturb his mind,
But to hear my bulldog bark."

Then sliding into another tune, they would sing:

"As I was gwine 'long de road,
'Pon a stump dar sot a toad.
De toad he winked at de tadpole's daughter
An' kicked de big frog in de water."

Later, after Mary and Milly had learned to read, they read *Little Women* together and used to amuse themselves by acting out the story. Milly always wanted to take the part of the blond Amy in the tale. She would dress for the role by pinning to her own black frizzy hair the fragrant yellow pine shavings that fell from the carpenter's bench.

Although the War Between the States was ever so long past, yet among Mary's dark friends there were a few old enough to have known slavery. When the emancipation came Aunt Lethe had remained with the family and later nursed its grandchildren; eventually she helped her aged mistress in the passage from life to death.

Mary's majestic old grandmother was dying. A lamp burned low in the room. Aunt Lethe lay upon a pallet beside the deathbed, her dark skin merging with the shadows. Mary sat beside her in hushed awe.

Aunt Lethe could remember . . . oh, how much she could remember! The war, and how there was so little and you must do the best you could with what you had. The men of the house were gone to fight. Sometimes when you put your ear to the ground you could hear the guns—almost like thunder when a storm is coming up. She remembered that, as the war went on, so many were killed that at last even the boys went off to join the Confederate Army. Mary's father, Aunt Lethe said, had gone before he was seventeen. And when boys like that went into battle, Jefferson Davis said that now Virginia was using up her "seed corn." Then finally there had come what Aunt Lethe called "Lee-Surrender."

After that you didn't hear the guns any more, but a terrible sickness went over the country. It had seized on Mary's father, the fever and ague turning his hair white though he wasn't yet twenty years old.

Outside in the hot August night a whippoorwill was calling. Aunt Lethe broke into her whispered memories to exclaim:

"Listen to dat whippo'will. . . . Listen! De night my ole mammy die a whippo'will call jus' like dat. It call an' it call . . . an' . . . an' I look out an' see it settin' on de chimney . . . callin'.

"When de bref left my mammy . . . den de bird stop callin'. . . .

"An' in de mornin', when I walk out in de yard, dar was dat whippo'will, dead too."

The righteous old lady who died on that August night lives on in Mary's memory. Every day she had been commanded to sit on a hassock beside her grandmother's chair, hemming napkins and handkerchiefs.

Every day she and her brothers must learn a verse from the Bible. On Sundays there were the ponderous questions and answers in the Shorter Catechism. On weekdays they were paid a cent an hour for weeding flower beds or garden walks. There was an obstinate little plant known as the "bluebottle," which seemed to have been created especially that they might understand that in return for money you must work. It was odd to a child that these pennies had a value not possessed by the heaps of Confederate money which would buy nothing, while the pennies, after a tenth had been deducted for the missionaries, might be spent on sticks of lemon, or peppermint candy, kept for the purpose in a glass jar locked in a black walnut wardrobe.

Then, this wise, strict, loving dictator of their early years had died, while out in the night the whippoorwill called.

Spring came early to the garden. On the day when Mary found the first white hyacinth blooming under the shelter of the thick glossy foliage of a tree box, she knew it was spring. The flower was so small, so frail, daring to bloom while patches of snow still lingered in shady spots. She would go many times a day to raise up the low branches of the box and look again at her miracle flower, to convince herself that it was truly there, as lovely and fragrant as she remembered it.

And then almost overnight the garden was a huge bouquet of daffodils, violets, and hyacinths. Every day birds were arriving from the south. It was time to plant and sow, and Mary and her brothers were permitted a part in it all. They cut potatoes into the proper segments: each must contain two "eyes," and the eyes must be so placed in the earth that they faced up and not down. Then when the leaves of the dogwood were as large as a squirrel's ear it was time to plant the corn, four grains to the hill.

> One for the blackbird, one for the crow,
> One for the cutworm, and one for to grow.

It was a season of eager excitement. Suddenly all the trees were in leaf. Birds were hanging nests from their branches, or tucking them away in the shrubbery. And mockingbirds sang all day.

Summer came. Now you must wear your sunbonnet. Cherries were ripening on the garden trees. Sometimes you found pale-blue or speckled eggs in a cleverly hidden nest, and on the ground under one of the tree boxwoods that bordered the flower square a quail once laid a nestful of oval white eggs.

Every day was busy, from the early breakfast to twilight, when it is too dark to tell a hawk from a buzzard. Raspberries, strawberries, and cherries must be canned and jellied for the winter.

So much was going on in so many places at once that Mary fluttered from one event to another; from the garden to the kitchen, from the kitchen to the dairy.

And as her mother went about the duty of supervision, often a pet squirrel sat in the black leather key basket on her arm; and an obese white gander waddled after her wherever she went, even climbing the porch steps into the house.

Mary, too, was always at her mother's heels—a quaint little creature in a sunbonnet of pink or blue.

Summer quickly became midsummer—the hot summertime. Nests squirmed with chirping young birds. All the roses were in bloom; resurrection lilies and tall waxy-white callas flowered; white and yellow jasmine gave the garden a tropic fragrance, and the crape myrtles—pink and white and purple—blossomed above the heads actually of grown people.

And even a child felt the stately repose of the flower square, with its geometric beds edged by hedges of dwarf box, separated by narrow gravel walks; the whole design surrounded by a wider walk shut in by tall tree box trimmed in conical shape.

Early autumn came. The tobacco was cut and hung to be cured in the tall tobacco barns. Wine must be made from the ripe grapes, peaches and figs preserved, pickled and brandied, and both apples and figs dried on long tables in the sun. When a cloud appeared on the fringe of the sky you must hurry to take in the drying fruit before the rain.

And everywhere young birds were practicing for the long migration south.

Frost fell. Trees turned red and yellow. Persimmons ripened. The cider press was busy. Hickory nuts and walnuts were gathered. Apples were stored in barrels, potatoes filled the bins, and beets were put into kilns. The squirrels scampered about the grove, hiding away nuts for the winter.

All day geese in V-shaped formation flew honking high overhead; such of the garden birds as planned to go south had departed; and all but the cedars and holly trees now lifted bare branches to the sky. Crows gathered in flocks and flew cawing from tree to tree.

Mary's father got down his gun, and taking the dogs, went to hunt quail. The children loved to follow, tramping all through golden afternoons in field of yellow broomstraw as high as their heads. When the sun dropped behind the cow pastures they came home to lamplit suppers of broiled quail and hot beaten biscuit.

And fires crackled on the hearths, while outside in the early night the quail were calling to each other as the scattered coveys reassembled.

The great festival of the winter was hog-killing time. It began in the cold of dawn before Mary was out of bed, and she would pull the covers over her head and put her fingers in her ears, for she dreaded to hear the far-off squeals of the doomed pigs. But when the slaughter was over, she, like the others, would heartlessly scurry with excitement to the scene.

A great fire blazed outdoors, as well as in the kitchen fireplace. And every child—black or white—roasted pigs' tails over the flames. Lard was tried out in enormous caldrons suspended over the fires. The sausage grinder was turning all day. Fragrance of thyme and sage filled the kitchen, and laughter took material form in the condensation of breath in the chill air.

The revelry of hog-killing time lasted for days. And then there was Christmas! If you heard a rooster crowing in the night you knew he was "crowin' fo' Christmas." At other seasons he would be merely "crowin' fo' day," but in the weeks before Christmas it was for Christmas that he crowed. On the great day, at the crack of dawn, Negroes waited at the door crying, "Christmas gif'! Christmas gif'!" Then there were firecrackers and Roman candles. After Christmas the cold weather set in. The house was heated only by its open fires. Long sandbags were laid on the doorsills to keep out drafts. The opening of a door automatically produced the caution: "Put the sandbag back." But of course it must be cold, or there would be no ice for the hot summer which was coming.

Thus the cycle of the year revolved until again the pale frail white hyacinth bloomed under the tree box.

❁

The big road passed in front of the colored church. The road was of brilliant red Virginia clay and the church was a small rectangular wooden building showing white against the pine forest which on three sides stood close about it. And a narrow sandy road through the trees connected the plantation and the church.

It was along this road that Mary and her brothers once walked in a funeral procession.

Matilda had died. She had been a servant in the house before her marriage to one of the tenants on the place, and her dying request had been that her white folks should go to her funeral. In after years Mary's mother told her that Matilda had died in an unearthly ecstasy, but that, naturally, a child could not appreciate.

Mary was impressed only by the details of death, the sound of old Uncle Thomas, the plantation carpenter, sawing the planks for the coffin, and then a visit to Matilda's cabin where she lay dressed for the grave, appallingly motionless upon the best bedquilt. And there was a saucer of salt on her chest.

Those things which are odd to an adult are seldom the things which appear strange to a child. Mary did not wonder about the presence of the salt in the stranger presence of death, and she cannot now explain it, except as one of those dark superstitions imported in slave ships from Africa. With many such superstitions plantation childhood had made her familiar. She knew that the evil forces of the invisible world haunted crossroads, but that by whistling or singing as you passed you might protect yourself from them. She knew that you need not fear witches if before you went to bed you laid a broom across the doorsill, for the witch must count every straw before she can enter the room. By that time it will be morning, and with the coming of day witches lose their power. And of course she knew of the good magic of a rabbit's foot and of the evil that might come through conjuring. But she never understood the placing of a saucer of salt on the body of the dead. She had never seen it before and she never saw it again.

When Matilda's coffin was ready they put her in it, and an oxcart bore it through the forest to the church, where under the trees the empty grave waited; the cart wheels creaking as the oxen moved with slow solemnity along that narrow road between walls of trees.

With the exception of her mother, her brothers, and Mary herself, those who followed were black. And from time to time they broke into song:

"Asleep in Jesus, blessed sleep
From which none ever wake to weep."

Quiet words . . . yet as they were sung on that slow procession through the forest they might have been the wild wailing of a savage world. And it was strange to Mary that among the singers were friends who laughed with such abandon about the kitchen fire.

At the grave those who came to mourn Matilda stood like a black curtain hung close about the coffin.

The coffin, decorated with a wreath made from flowers gathered in the garden, was ready to be lowered. And Uncle Abel, the colored parson, stood at its head lining out the hymn:

"How blest the righteous when he dies!"

Suddenly he stopped and handed the hymnbook to Mary's mother. "You all know," he said, "I ain't got but one eye, an' de sweat is runnin' down in de yuther, so I can't see. I gwine ax Mis' Gordon to line out de hymn."

There was a moment's silence, with no sound but the soft mourning of the wind in the pines.

Mary's mother stood straight and slender, her face strangely white against that human curtain of black; black unbroken even by the whites of eyeballs, since the gaze of all was lowered to rest upon the coffin. And after an instant of shy hesitation, her voice clear as the sweet·notes of a flute lined out the words:

"How blest the righteous when he dies . . ."

And the swelling roll of many voices sang:

"How blest the righteous when he dies . . ."

At long-spaced intervals, usually in the late summer and early autumn, when the harvest was over and before the roads became impassable, the plantations exchanged visits, often all-day affairs with imposing midday dinners.

In the kitchen it would be said, "Today we gwine put de big pot in de little one," which meant that the feast was to be as grand as it was possible to make it. The children must have been exasperatingly underfoot on those occasions, for they were in and out of the kitchen and dining room, or under the trees helping to turn the crank of the ice-cream freezer, their mouths open like those of a nestful of young birds, eager for a taste of everything.

Then, by the time the company had driven down the long approach to the house, and around the circle to the door, the children were freshly washed and combed, feeling elegant because their feet, accustomed in summer to running bare all over the grove and garden, were now so wretched in the confinement of patent leather pumps. The children were shy, wild creatures, congealed into solemn silence by the presence of the guests, by the company magnificence of the table, and by the fact that two little colored children, instead of the everyday one, were waving beautiful peacock feather brooms above the table to shoo flies away from the feast.

When the guests said good-bye and drove away, leaving the prints of their horses' hoofs in the driveway, the plantation returned to the busy tranquillity of its way; the drive so undisturbed by carriage wheels or horses' hoofs that the "frogs' houses," which the children were fond of making in the sand, patting each into shape over a bare foot, and then carefully removing the foot, remained intact until there came a rain to wash them away.

When her children arrived at an age to require lessons, their instruction was added to the many duties of the plantation mistress. Also she had formed a class of the sons of white "sharecroppers," which met at the house several nights during the week. The young men had worked all day in the fields. Then they washed off part of the odor of toil and of earth; they plastered their hair close to their heads, and walked, often several miles, to be taught by the woman who so eagerly gave her time to them.

Mary was permitted to sit up on these school nights and to take part in the lessons. It was these toilers on the land who first impressed upon her the meaning of chivalry. They liked to stand in line for the game of spelling. And she would stand too, a small figure in a homemade sateen frock of bright blue. Flushed with pride she would spell her way to the head of the line. And then one night she overheard her mother say that the young men must not deliberately miss the words so that a little girl might reach the top.

This discovery was disturbing, touching Mary's heart in a new way, and yet spoiling the fun. "I *did* spell the words!" she thought. But somehow the fun was gone.

Mary wonders now how one woman accomplished all that her mother did; and yet there was never a sense of haste. On the plantation there seemed always time for everything; people were no more hurried than nature; they lived in its rhythm.

The traditional picture of an indolent South was not true of the plantation. Everyone worked, whatever the sex or color or age. Laziness was so unusual as to be a matter for comment. "Ez lazy ez a dawg dat leans against de house to bark" was applied to the loafer.

Perhaps it is the gift of tranquillity in toil that has established the myth of an idle South. Because you never see the hurrying pace that kills, the conclusion is —a lazy people.

Though much was done on the plantation, it was done without drive and bluster. The work of that world proceeded as bees make honey, or spiders spin glistening webs on the tree box, or ants construct tunnels, or birds build nests, feed young, and twice a year perform great journeys of migration. Like the industry of nature, the plantation was never at high pressure; song and laughter, relaxation and worship were as essential and as much a part of living as work.

In the faded ink of an old recipe book you may find proof of the manifold activities of a plantation mistress of the long ago. There are the directions for the making of candles: "Those who make candles will find it a great improvement to soak the wicks in lime-water and salt-petre . . . the flame will be clearer and the tallow will not run." Among the recipes are all sorts of remedies— a cure for sick headache, for toothache and sore throat, remedies for scalds and burns, for felons and warts and corns, for distemper in cattle, for wounds in cattle, directions for fattening fowls, for making blacking, for a cement which resists fire and water, and an "everlasting fence post, so that there is not a man who will live long enough to see it rotten," instructions for mulching the melon patch, for stopping leaks, for cleaning wallpaper, marble, and matting, for making various wood stains—black walnut and mahogany—and many recipes for dyes. Elderberries, copperas, and alum produce a "beautiful blue," cochineal gives red, hickory bark and red oak provide yellow, sassafras bark is used for brown, red-oak bark and maple for black.

There are recipes, too, for preserving beef in brine, for curing bacon and hams, for making cooling summer drinks, for wines and cordials, for making vinegar and yeast and soap, preserving fruits and vegetables in bottles, for making "ising-glass jelly," and every sort of hot breads and desserts.

Like other children, Mary realized something of the past before she comprehended the future; for the past is like a story, beginning "Once upon a time."

To that long ago belonged the arrowheads so often turned up in plowing the fields along the river. There must once have been a great battle on the river lowgrounds. And along the river Indian canoes must have glided under the willows, and in the woods they must have hunted deer and wild turkey. The arrowheads made little Pocahontas a real person.

Because Pocahontas was real, so was Captain John Smith, and those other Venturers who, risking their lives, came from England to found a colony in the wilderness of the New World.

VENTURERS

# CHAPTER ONE

# "To Overcome Is to Live"

Y<small>OU</small> loved John Smith or you hated him. No one was ever indifferent where he was concerned. And though he has been nearly three hundred years dead, his robust personality has come striding down the centuries, still winning devotion, still making enemies, still living. The echo of his voice seems never to die away, nor his brave eyes to dim; and he remains confident, arrogant, daring. He proclaims a philosophy of strength, he is impatient with the slothful and the futile. "To overcome is to live"—that is the motto on his coat of arms. From time to time in the world there appear such men; and inevitably they are hated as well as loved.

John Smith was born in England of respectable yeoman parents, but at an early age he became a soldier of fortune, traveling up and down the continent of Europe. His adventures seem as incredible today as our winged journeys would have appeared three hundred years ago. But Smith lived in that fabulous age when life itself was melodrama, so that such exploits did not then appear too extraordinary. In the James River story they have a place only because they show the *Arabian Nights* quality of one phase of his mind, and in that quality lay much of his gift for dealing with the aboriginal Indians in whose land the British sought to establish a colony.

According to Smith, he was for a time soldier in the service of Prince Sigismund of Transylvania. The armies of the prince and of the Turks were encamped outside the town of Regall when a challenge announced that, "in order to delight the ladies who did long to see some court-like pastime," one of the Turkish captains defied any captain to combat with him for his head. And Smith took up the challenge. Both armies then assembled in battle regalia to look on, and veiled ladies crowded the city walls. At the very first thrust of the lance the Turkish captain was unhorsed, whereupon Smith cut off his head. On the next day the Turks dared Smith to a second combat; again the armies assembled and veiled ladies watched from the city walls. They saw both lances shattered, saw the combatants turn to pistols to decide the issue, and saw Smith behead his foe. Now—ever in the tradition of gallantry—Smith offered the Turks yet another chance, giving them the choice of weapons. They selected battle-axes, and in the struggle Smith's ax fell to the ground, but at once he drew his sword and a third Turk lost his head.

Some time later Smith was taken prisoner in battle, and in the market place of Axopolis he was sold into slavery. His purchaser was, as is fitting in such a story, a prince, who sent the new slave to his wife, the Lady Charatza Tragabigzanda in Constantinople. This princess became so much interested in the new slave that, fearing he might be resold, she sent him away to her brother, the Pasha of Nalbritz, begging the pasha to treat him kindly. The pasha did not spoil the story by obeying her, and Smith received from him no more consideration than the most wretched slave; even to the degradation of having an iron collar put about his neck. Finally Smith murdered his tormentor, dressed himself in the garments of the dead man, and mounting his master's horse, rode away; far out into the Scythian desert, for he must put himself beyond the reach of any who might identify the mark on his collar. So he rode for many days until at last he arrived at a Russian stronghold, where he was able to free himself from the damning evidence of the slave's collar. He traveled then safely and with much enjoyment through Russia and Poland to Leipzig, where providentially he found Prince Sigismund. It was then that the prince granted him a coat of arms, bearing three Turks' heads and the motto "Vincere est vivere": "To conquer—to overcome—is to live."

How much of all this is true?

Well . . . there is in London, officially registered in the College of Arms, a document in Latin wherein Sigismund gives Smith safe-conduct to his own country, and grants him a "shield of arms, the figure and description of three Turks' heads, which, with his sword before the town of Regall, in single combat he did overcome, kill, and cut off, in the Province of Transylvania." It is all written out by hand, and in the upper left-hand corner of the page there is a copy of the crest granted to Smith by Prince Sigismund. At the bottom of the page there is a certificate, dated August 19, 1625, and signed by Sir William Segar, Garter King at Arms, stating that the above is a true copy of the original document.

❁

Being the sort of man he was, Captain John Smith, when he arrived in England, joined the group of ad-

venturers who sailed with Christopher Newport to
found a colony in Virginia. The enterprise had limitless
possibilities. It might even carry a man eventually to
the court of the great Kubla Khan; for Newport's instructions read that when it should please God to bring
the voyagers to the coast of Virginia they were to settle
upon a river, and the river they selected must bend
toward the northwest; for thus they would soonest find
the other sea.

*The Other Sea* . . . it was in those times always
the passage to the rich, fabulous Orient that adventurers
sought.

Newport was to choose a stream bending to the
northwest. And the new settlement must be located
well inland from the river's mouth; since if they should
sit down near the sea they would be more open to attack.
For a colony formerly planted in that part of the world
under the patronage of Sir Walter Raleigh had disappeared so completely that it was never known whether
its members lived or had all perished. They had been
established upon an island called Roanoke, and some
years later a ship had been sent seeking news of them.
Arriving near to the island in the darkness of night, and
waiting there until the morning should break, those on
board the ship had played upon trumpets and sung
familiar songs of the homeland, hoping for response to
their serenade from those on the island. But there had
come no answer, and with the dawn they had discovered
the island to be deserted.

Because of this singular tragedy, Captain Newport
was cautioned to select for the new colony a place easily
defensible. His instructions concluded with the admoni-
tion that the settlers were not to offend the natives, and

that in none of their letters home were they to write of anything that might discourage future colonists. A strange circumstance of the undertaking was that Newport carried a sealed box containing the names of those on board who were to act as a governing council in the new land. The box was not to be opened until their arrival, and of course throughout the voyage there was much speculation as to which men were to rule.

The voyage was long. For six weeks adverse winds kept the three little ships actually within sight of England, and it was five months before they finally arrived on the Virginia coast. Even before they reached the Canaries, where they took on water, John Smith had contrived to make for himself enemies who charged him with plotting to be king of the colony which they were to establish. And for the remainder of the way he journeyed as a prisoner.

But he had won devotion as well as hatred among the voyagers. "It is because they envy his reputation," his friends said, "that this scandalous accusation has been made against him."

As for Smith, it did not matter that he voyaged as a prisoner in irons; for there flowed strong in him the vigor of a young body, disciplined to hardships and accustomed to danger. He was as sturdy of body as of mind, a muscular bronzed man with a light beard, and horizontal mustaches, like a line drawn to underscore the bold strength which looked out of his eyes. And did he not believe that to overcome is to live?

# CHAPTER TWO

# Beads to Make Her a Chain

A GREAT storm blew Newport's little fleet toward the shore of Virginia. Sailing between the capes which stand watch at the entrance of Chesapeake Bay, they explored a river flowing through so pleasant a land that with great admiration they praised God. It was spring, and the forests rising in lofty majesty on the banks were freshly green. Flowers bloomed and birds sang; new songs and unfamiliar flowers.

Even the fact that on the night of their first landing they had been attacked by savages did not dishearten them; after all, the fellows had run howling before British guns.

The colonists named their beautiful river for King James, and the capes they called Henry and Charles in honor of his two sons. On the north bank of the river, about eighty miles inland, they selected a peninsula as the spot where they would settle, and they christened it Jamestown. Between two trees they stretched a canvas sail and there good Master Robert Hunt, who had come on to look after their souls and to convert the heathen, conducted their first religious service.

Newport had already opened the sealed box containing the names of the Council. When the prisoner, John Smith, discovered that he himself was among those appointed he demanded a trial of his case, and since his

34

enemies were unable to prove the charges against him, he was triumphantly acquitted.

Then, before going back to England to secure supplies and additional colonists Captain Newport explored their river as far as the falls, taking with him a selected number of men.

Along the way a chief came to greet the explorers, carrying in one hand his bow and in the other a pipe of peace, that they might choose whether they would have peace or war. At another point a chief met them marching at the head of his people, playing as he came upon a reed flute, and wearing a crown of deerskin dyed red, with two long feathers in his hair placed like horns on either side of his crown. "His body was painted all with crimson, and his face blue, his ears all behung with bracelets of pearl, and in either ear a bird's claw." This man, they said, received them in a "modest, proud fashion."

There was much banqueting with music and dancing, because it was thought that the strangers were come merely as guests, and it was not yet suspected that they intended to make permanent settlement in the land.

Everywhere along the river they heard of the great chief Powhatan whose name people spoke with awe; and when they returned to Jamestown they found that in their absence a large company of Indians had attacked their settlement, wounding many and killing two. In spite of this, when Newport sailed away to England he carried to the London Company an enthusiastic letter bearing the signature of all the members of the Virginia Council:

"We are set down," they wrote, "within a River, for breadth and sweetness of water . . . as no man's fortune hath ever possessed the like. And as we think, if more may be wished in a River it will be found."

The lovely Virginia spring passed and there fell upon Jamsetown a withering heat, as strange to Englishmen as the brilliant unfamiliar fireflies which pricked the hot darkness of the night. August came and with it a strange new disease, a fever which they called the "country sickness."

The river shimmered in the summer heat, the tides rose and ebbed. Sometimes there was no sound but the soft lap of the water, the buzz of the mosquito, and the groans of the dying.

England must have seemed to them as far away as the stars. Their minds must have gone back to her; remembering only what was happy; remembering tunes played on the viol and the virginals, remembering the boisterous life of the taverns, the strength of old liquor strong enough "to make a cat speak," the baying of hounds, the huntsmen's horns, the flight of falcons, and the bagpipes and drums of Christmas festivities; forgetting how rich were the rich and how poor the poor, forgetting the sharpers and the moneylenders, the "roaring boys and roysterers" who made the streets a peril, forgetting the beggars, forgetting the power of a monarch who could keep even the great Sir Walter Raleigh a prisoner in the Tower.

But Smith's spirit never faltered though, looking

out over the broad deserted James, England seemed far away. . . .

For, as he once said, "Who would live at home idly, or think himself any worth, to live only to eat, drink and sleep, and so die?"

By the autumn only thirty-eight of the hundred and four that had come out of England remained alive; weakened now by sickness and by their scanty diet of barley, sodden in the river water.

It was Smith who would go trading with the Indians. No one else had his gift for dealing with them. From the beginning he had set himself to learn their language, but there was more in it than that. It seemed as though this man possessed some secret understanding of the inner mind of the savage.

Those who lay at Jamestown alternately shaken with chill and scorched with fever begged him to explore further. Only a little distance away, they hoped, everything might be better. Smith might even come upon the passage to that other sea, and so they would all arrive at the riches of the East.

Thus he took the barge and eight men and went to discover in the region drained by the Chickahominy: to discover and to trade for corn.

Forty miles up the Chickahominy, he left the barge to await his return, and proceeded by canoe with two of his own countrymen, and a couple of Indian guides. By the time they had gone twenty miles they were wearied with dragging the canoe over fallen trees and submerged logs, so that Smith with one of the Indians set out to see what might be observed on foot.

He soon heard a whoop and at the same time felt

that he had been struck by an arrow. Indians poured out of the forest and Smith fired, killing two of them. But all at once he realized that he and his guide were standing on a quaking bog into which they were fast sinking. He threw away his weapons and surrendered himself to Indian mercies, hoping that by the time they had helped him to dry ground, he would have thought of some trick by which he might gain his life. Suddenly he remembered his pocket compass; if he could make this appear to them as a magical thing he might divert their attention from the amusement of murdering one John Smith.

As soon as they were safely out of the bog he produced his compass, and the warriors crowded close to see the mysterious little needle which, however you turned the compass, pointed always in the same direction. And while they stared, Smith's Oriental imagination spun for them a discourse upon the movement of the stars, on how "the sun did chase the night round about the world continually, how great was the Land and the Sea, how diverse the Nations," and other important matters.

Not that he expected them to comprehend, but because he understood the effect of sonorous phrases, of the influence of many words, and of a bold confidence shown by those in peril. Still, in the end they bound him to a tree as though they intended to begin the torture.

Yet they hesitated. For this man had the manner of an important—perhaps a magical—person. It might, after all, be unwise to kill him, at least just yet. . . . The chief among them, who was Opekankano, brother to mighty Powhatan, gave the order to unbind him.

Also Opekankano would further examine the marvelous instrument and learn more about it.

It was winter, the season of hunting when great circles of fire were lighted in the forest and Indians killed the beasts trapped within the rings of flame.

From hunting camp to hunting camp, from village to village Smith was marched through the country, and everywhere crowds gathered to gaze at the bearded captive who seemed not at all to understand that he was a prisoner to be delivered into the hands of mighty Powhatan.

Finally Smith was conducted into the presence of Powhatan, lord of the land. The chief received him lying proudly on a bed a foot high, upon which were spread ten or twelve mats. A young woman sat at his head and another at his feet; surrounding him were many warriors, and standing back of them other young women, all with chains of beads about their necks, their heads and shoulders painted red. And among them was little Pocahontas, Powhatan's favorite daughter, the child of his old age.

Smith sent home to England a *Relation* of this interview with the Indian king, though all that happened did not appear in his account as it was first published in London; for it had been forbidden to write anything which might discourage future colonists. But at any rate, Smith arrived at an understanding with Powhatan, since he was permitted safely to return to Jamestown.

And in the Indian vocabulary which he compiled, there was this sentence: "Bid Pocahontas bring hither a little basket, and I will give her beads to make her a chain."

# CHAPTER THREE

## "If the Little Ant and the Sillie Bee . . ."

FROM that interview with Powhatan, Smith returned to Jamestown to find himself accused of murder. The same enemies who had charged him with intriguing to make himself king of the colony now declared that he had led his companions into a trap and was responsible for the fact that two of them had been slain by the Indians. So on the very day of his safe return to Jamestown he was tried, convicted, and sentenced to be hanged. Although men like the knightly Percy and the saintly Robert Hunt protested, Smith's enemies were determined. In the morning he was to hang.

But on the tide, flowing full and strong up the James, Captain Christopher Newport was arriving from England. His return had been so long delayed that in Jamestown men had begun to think he had perished on the wintry Atlantic, like Sir Humphrey Gilbert who had gone down with his ship in a tempestuous sea, while in the darkness his confident voice had shouted to the sailors: "Be of good cheer, my friends! We are as near to Heaven by sea as by land!" In the same fashion perhaps Newport had perished. Or, it might be that he had been captured by some roving pirate, or by the Spaniards.

Yet here he was again, borne up on the swelling

tide. Thus the James River brought rescue to Captain John Smith.

A few days later the frail, reed-thatched village that was Jamestown burned to the ground.

A greater misfortune still was that somebody discovered yellow earth which was eagerly pronounced gold. Hadn't Cortez found gold in Mexico, and Pizarro in Peru? Why, the very cooking utensils of those countries were of solid gold! Therefore there must be gold also in this bright yellow Virginia sand.

After that there was no more rebuilding of the burned houses and no one could be made to take an interest in planting corn. Jamestown was gold-crazy. Newport, who was due to return to England in a fortnight, remained fourteen weeks, loading the yellow dirt into his ships, his crew consuming most of the food sent out for the colonists.

"There was no talk," Smith said, "no work, but dig gold, refine gold. . . ."

Before sailing for England with his yellow dirt, Newport went with Smith to pay a ceremonious visit to old Powhatan, who set them forth a banquet of wild fowl and venison, corn bread, nuts and persimmons. When they had feasted, and had been entertained with dance and song, Smith would trade English gewgaws—bells and mirrors and beads—for the corn which he knew Jamestown was soon to need desperately.

Powhatan was haughty. He would not condescend to peddle, he said, trifle by trifle. If the English would lay out their goods, he would offer what he thought suitable.

Newport fell unsuspiciously into the trap and for the whole collection Powhatan gave only four bushels of corn. But there remained, by accident, a few blue beads not included in the transaction. With Oriental subtlety Smith suavely explained that they had not been offered because blue beads might be worn only by royalty. Then away skyrocketing went the value of blue beads. The royal must have blue beads. A chief's wife felt herself disgraced without a few of the royal blue beads. In the end the blue beads brought more than two hundred bushels of corn. But Powhatan scored at the last by giving Newport only twenty turkeys in exchange for twenty swords.

Of course after Newport had departed for England, Powhatan wanted to continue trading turkeys for swords on the same terms. But Smith would not trade swords at any price; from the beginning he understood that the English could not trust the friendship of men whose land they were appropriating for themselves. No, he would not sell swords at any price.

Then Indians, visiting the fort at Jamestown, tried to sneak off with some of the coveted weapons. Smith captured and imprisoned two of them. And Powhatan sent his craftiest ambassador, accompanied by the little Pocahontas, to intercede for their release. They brought gifts, venison, and pones of corn bread baked in the ashes.

So it happened that Pocahontas visited the settlement at Jamestown; a gay child, turning cart wheels in the square before the fort. She was still too young to have put on the apron of the Indian woman, or the mantle prettily fashioned of feathers which she would wear when she was grown-up. She was just a child, delicately made, graceful and merry whirling naked in the square.

Smith called her the "Nonpareil." For among the Indians, he said, there was never anyone that could compare with Pocahontas, Powhatan's "dear and darling daughter, who exceeded all; not only in her feature and countenance and proportion, but in her wit and spirit." Truly the Nonpareil.

Pocahontas easily won the release of the captive Indians, and for herself whatever might please a little girl.

After that, throughout the hard hungry winter she would cross over her father's river and walk twelve miles through the woods to Jamestown, bringing corn and game; over and over saving the colony from starvation.

Whenever Smith felt that he could safely leave Jamestown he explored one by one the tidewater rivers; seeking always that passage to the other sea and that mine of gold for which the early London backers of the Virginia Venture clamored. He found no gold and no sea, but he mapped the country and made a record of its plants and animals and of the customs of its people.

❀

In the September following their second summer on James River, Captain John Smith was elected president of the Governing Council. And a month later the river tide again brought a ship.

One Thomas Forrest, gent, was aboard and with him his wife, Madam Forrest, and her little fourteen-year-old serving maid, Ann Burras; the first English-women to arrive at Jamestown.

And while Ann was smiling upon the womanless men, knowing in her feminine heart that almost any one of them was ready to make her Jamestown's first wife, Smith was reading the ultimatum sent by the London Company. The company found itself displeased with the colonists; their quarrels and intrigues were not to be tolerated. Also, the company demanded practical results. The settlers had produced none. The shipload of yellow sand had proved to be merely yellow sand: "A drunken ship," Smith had called it, "freighted with so much gilded dirt." The passage to the other sea had not been found, and there was no news of the lost colony. One at least of these three things, the company insisted, must be accomplished; otherwise Jamestown would be abandoned, no more supplies would be sent out, and no more colonists.

As if that were not ironic enough, Captain Newport brought with him a copper crown: it was the fancy of King James that Powhatan should be crowned as a great foreign potentate with whom he, James, was allied. It was fantastic . . . unbelievable. Smith, as president of the colony, must go to Powhatan and invite him to Jamestown for the ceremony of coronation.

The monarch was away, but while Smith waited the Indians made a celebration in his honor. They built a great fire in the forest clearing and spread mats for their guests to sit upon. It was night and the autumn foliage flamed red and gold in the flashing firelight, when out of the shadows a troupe of thirty young girls came dancing into the light. Their bodies were painted, some red, some black, some particolored. The girl who was their leader wore a pair of "fair stag's" horns on her head, and an otterskin at her girdle. As they danced singing about the fire, the flames illumined their figures.

They danced in a narrowing circle close about Smith, singing over and over: "Love you not me? Love you not me?"

And it was Pocahontas who led those singing dancers.

The firelight shone on her sleek young body, on her long braids of black hair, on the stag's horns she wore, and on the otterskin at her girdle. She was all of the forest, with the bright eyes of its creatures and their silent, agile movements; she was a little wild thing, incredibly supple and swift, with an Indian girl's dainty hands and feet, and the beautifully sculptured body of her race. And this little princess of the wilderness sang: "Love you not me? . . . Love you not me? . . ."

On the following day Powhatan arrived.

No, he would not visit Captain Newport at Jamestown. "I am a king," he said, "and this is my land. If your Father Newport would see me, he can come to me here in my own house."

And because Captain Newport must carry out the royal orders from London he came, Indian prestige triumphing over British. But he had difficulty in placing the crown on Powhatan's brow, since the Indian would not lower his head to receive it. For here was a man so full of majesty that as long as he lived every Englishman admitted into his presence felt his regal dignity. "He is but a naked savage," they would say bewildered, "yet how proudly majestical."

When the gifts were presented and the crowning over, John Smith sat down and wrote to the London Company: a "rude answer," he called this letter in which he put before the company just what were the conditions in a colony fighting the cruel wilderness battle. "As for the coronation of Powhatan," he wrote, "by whose advice you sent him such presents, I know not, but give me leave to tell you I fear they will be to the confusion of us all."

Smith sent the letter by the hand of Captain Newport when he sailed for England.

Among the new immigrants come out to colonize Virginia many had been booked as "gentlemen," and in addition the passenger list had included a perfumer, two goldsmiths, a jeweler, and six tailors; very few were sturdy laborers. With such men Smith must clear the land of primeval forest that corn might be planted and houses built; with such men he must maintain a colony on the banks of a wilderness river, menaced continually by savages who at one moment seemed friendly, at the next were treacherously hostile. And he could not appeal to the motive of private gain, for the colonists were at that time allowed no individual stake in the enterprise.

But Smith would not tolerate idlers living upon the toil of the industrious. "No empty porringers," he decreed, "will be filled from the common kettle unless the owner has by toil earned his meal, or has been prevented by illness. . . . He who will not work shall not eat."

Out of Jamestown's bitter struggle for survival in Virginia, John Smith thus grew in stature, from the

mere soldier of fortune to the pioneer planting a colony
in the wilderness. He had begun to think and to evolve
a philosophy. "If the Little Ant," he thought, "and the
Sillie Bee seek by their diligence the good of their commonwealth; much more ought man."

❈

In December, not three months after her arrival
at Jamestown, little Ann Burras married John Laydon,
one of the first settlers. And already fear of that famine
which Smith had foreseen was in every man's eyes.
What were they to do in the months before another
ship could return with supplies?

But Smith thought: *Perhaps there will be no other
ship*. For he had not forgotten the London Company's
threat of abandonment and he remembered his own
letter to the company, that letter which he had called
a "rude answer." Altogether, it might very well be that
Newport would never return. And Jamestown must
have food. Somehow he, Smith, must get corn for
Jamestown. It was his responsibility. If the Indians
would not trade of their own will, they must be made
to trade.

"No persuasions," as his friends expressed it,
"would persuade him to starve."

He took the barge and sailed up and down the
river from one village to another. But Powhatan had
commanded his tribe to barter no more with the English. Even that tribe which had contracted to deliver to
Smith four hundred bushels of corn would now part
with only a hundred. . . . And Jamestown must have
corn or perish.

It was at this time that Powhatan sent a messenger to say that he would like to see Smith; also he wanted men sent to build him an English house: he wanted a rooster too, and a hen, strange new creatures in his country; and he desired swords and guns and a grindstone. In exchange for these things he would give corn.

Smith dispatched men to build the house, and then, taking along a group of dependable colonists, he sailed the barge and the pinnace down James River and into the bay. It was Christmas, and in the Chesapeake they were delayed by a blizzard. While it lasted they were the guests of a small tribe of Indians unfriendly to Powhatan. They sat together around a cheerful fire in the smoky wigwam and ate oysters. "Powhatan has sent for you," the Indians said, "to murder you. He will seem to show you kindness, but do not trust him."

With these warning words in their minds the English sailed out of the bay, and into that river on whose bank the great chief had his headquarters. When they arrived at his landing they found the river frozen far out from shore, but they broke their way through ice to the bank and established themselves in a vacant house, Smith then sending to Powhatan to say that they were come.

On the following day the king received them, and what happened at that interview has been told by certain of the men whom Smith took with him:

"Corn?" Powhatan had no corn for anyone. What made them think he had corn to trade?

"Powhatan"—Smith was stern—"I am surprised you have forgotten that we are here at your own invitation . . . you must have a short memory."

The Indian laughed. There might perhaps be a

little corn, but only in exchange for swords and guns. There would be no corn to barter for other things.

("Do not trust him," the Indians on the Chesapeake had said, "for he plots to murder you.")

"Powhatan," Smith continued, "to testify my love I sent you men for the building of your house, neglecting mine own. You have returned my friendship by forbidding your people to trade with us. As for swords and guns, I told you long ago I had none to spare. You must realize that those I have can keep us from want . . . yet steal from you, or wrong you, I will not. Nor will I break that friendship which we have mutually promised. Not unless you force me to it by bad usage."

Powhatan listened. He would spare Smith what corn he could.

"And yet . . . yet, Captain Smith, yet some doubt have I of your coming to my country . . . that doubt makes me not so kindly to receive you as I would. For many do inform me that your coming is not for trade, but to possess my country. For this reason my people dare not bring you corn. They see you and your men armed. And so they dare not bring you corn. If . . . if you would free us of this fear, leave your weapons on board the boats in which you have come. Here they are needless, for we are all friends, and forever Powhatans."

("Do not trust him. Have no faith in him, for he plots to destroy you." Was this, perhaps, why he was so eager to have the weapons left aboard the boats?)

"Seeing you thus armed, Captain Smith, my people dare not bring you corn—"

So the old Indian chieftain and the young, florid-bearded British captain, talked throughout that day, and again on the following day.

"To free us from fear, leave your weapons aboard the boats in which you have come—"

This great ruler over thirty tribes, feared up and down the tidewater rivers, actually pleaded with John Smith. Both were making a desperate fight: the old chief seeking a way to save his land from those who would possess it; the young captain, with equal desperation, fighting for corn to save Jamestown from starvation.

"To free us from fear, leave your weapons. . . . Why are you jealous of our loves? . . . Come in friendly manner to see us, and not thus with your guns and swords."

"Powhatan, the vow I made you of my love, both myself and my men have kept. As for your promise, I find it every day violated by some of your subjects. Yet we have no desire for revenge. Else had your people known the cruelty we use to our enemies, as well as our true love and courtesy to our friends. . . .

"Your people, when they come to Jamestown, are received with their bows and arrows. And, as is the case with you, so it is our custom also to wear our arms . . . as for provisions, do not imagine that we shall starve without your aid."

(Yet in only a few days Jamestown would be without food. Corn . . . corn . . . he *must* have corn for Jamestown!)

"Do not think, Powhatan, that we shall starve without your help."

Powhatan sighed.

"Captain Smith, I have never dealt so kindly with any chief as with yourself. Yet from you do I receive the least kindness of any. Captain Newport gave me swords, a bed . . . what I desired, ever taking what I offered."

("By whose advice you sent him such presents"— Smith had written to the London Company—"I know not, but give me leave to tell you I fear they will be to the confusion of us all.")

"Captain Newport gave me what I wished. Only you refuse to do what I ask. Only you. Yet you would have from me whatever you desire. You call me father, as Captain Newport is your father . . . but if you intend so friendly as you say, send away your arms that I may believe you."

(Was he trying to prolong the talk until his warriors had assembled? And would the men on the barge and the pinnace arrive before that happened?)

"You must know, Powhatan, that as I have but one God, I honor but one king, and I live here not as your subject, but as your friend. . . ."

Leaving some of his women in talk with Smith, Powhatan went out of the room and fled secretly away, and while they talked Indian warriors surrounded the house.

Then, so Smith's friends tell the story, "with sword and pistol, he made such a passage among the naked Devils that those next him tumbled one over another, and the rest made haste to escape."

He gathered his followers together in that house on the riverbank where they had lodged. In the afternoon a messenger came to Smith, with Powhatan's excuses and the gift of a chain of pearls. Also corn was provided with men to carry it down to the boats, but as it was low water the boats could not then get away.

Waiting in the house on the river for the tide to turn, the English heard the Indians making merry, with music and dancing and games. But still the ebb tide kept them waiting. Darkness fell. And Pocahontas came softly through the night. Smith was in danger and Pocahontas, Powhatan's favorite daughter, came to warn him.

Those who were present have told the story.

"Pocahontas," they say, "Powhatan's dearest jewel and daughter, in that dark night came through the irksome woods and told our captain that great cheer would soon be sent us . . . but that Powhatan and all the power he could make would then come and kill us all . . . if we would live, she wished us presently to be gone.

"Such things as she delighted in, we would have given her, but with the tears running down her cheeks, she said she durst not be seen to have any, for if Powhatan should know of it, she were but dead.

"And she went away by herself as she came.

"Then within less than an hour, eight or ten lusty fellow came with platters of venison and other victual . . . but the captain made them taste every dish, which done, he sent some of them back to Powhatan to bid him make haste, for he was prepared for his coming."

Thus warned, the English could not be taken by surprise; and at high water they sailed away.

Captain Samuel Argall was a young man with a reputation for getting what he went after. He was just the man, the London Company thought, to undertake the finding of a more direct route between England and Virginia.

The company was disturbed about the Venture. Much money had been spent and there was nothing to show for it. Yet that fellow John Smith was writing arrogantly, actually calling the company to task. And certain of the colonists who had returned to England were spreading talk of Smith's cruelty to the Indians, which was embarrassing, because from the beginning it had been understood that converting the "Naturells" to Christianity was a prime object of the enterprise. Clearly something must be done about all this or the whole investment would be lost.

If the length of the voyage could be cut and Virginia brought nearer to England—that would make supervision of the colony easier. A straight route would save a thousand miles over the roundabout West Indies voyage. Let young Captain Argall take his ship out and see if it might not be possible to make a direct and clear passage in the eye of the wind.

At the same time the company secured a new charter from King James; with the object of reorganizing the whole method of governing the colony. This charter would abolish the office of a president elected by the local Council, and substitute a governor appointed in London.

Such was the news that Argall brought to Jamestown when, after a voyage of nearly ten weeks, he arrived in the eye of the wind.

But Captain Smith—people said—his term as president had not expired . . . what of Captain Smith?

Oh, all that was changed . . . everything was

changed. The company itself was reorganized, and many great men added to its directors. Virginia, the new charter declared, extended for two hundred miles to the north and to the south of Point Comfort, while to the west it reached to the other sea, though how far that was nobody knew. The company was raising new funds. Broadsides had been written and sermons preached about Virginia. London had gone quite wild, and everybody was buying shares in the Venture. Lord Delaware was to be the governor and already a great expedition of nine vessels, with supplies and five hundred settlers, was ready to sail: with Sir Thomas Gates coming out on the *Sea Venture* to represent Lord Delaware.

Smith was no longer president.

That might be, Smith said, but until he had official orders he would continue to govern. In the meantime he was anxious to move Jamestown to a more healthful location: to that end he made excursions up and down the river.

In August part of the expected fleet of nine ships arrived. They had passed through a hurricane which had lasted two days and two nights, and the *Sea Venture*, bringing Sir Thomas Gates, had disappeared, lost perhaps in the tempest. And Smith, though he had found so lovely a site that he called it "Nonesuch," was unable to move the colony, for he had been seriously burned in a gunpowder explosion and was forced to go for treatment to London in one of the returning ships.

He left ten weeks' provision in the storehouse, and there were hogs and goats and sheep, and ever so many chickens, a horse too, and six mares. The colony now numbered nearly five hundred, among them women and children. More than fifty houses had been built, and a good palisade to protect the settlement from attack. So things were when Smith said farewell to Jamestown.

And seeing him go, his friends mourned: "thus we lost him that would never send us where he would not lead himself, that would never let us want what he could by any means get us. . . . 'Seeing,' as he once said, 'that we are not born for ourselves, but each to help the other.' . . ."

"Each for the other" and, like the "Little Ant and the Sillie Bee," each for the "good of the Commonwealth."

# CHAPTER FOUR

# Pocahontas

It seemed to Pocahontas very long ago that the white man had come. In actual time the dogwood had bloomed but twice, and but three times, high in the golden autumn haze, the geese had flown south. But so much had happened that surely it was long ago, for the whole world was altered since the day Captain John Smith had been brought a prisoner to her father.

Before that she had been just a merry little girl. She had known, of course, that one day she would be a woman: then she would paint her body a lovely red, she would hang pearls about her neck, and put white aigrettes in her hair. She would have a husband too; he would be a chief, perhaps as great as her father. And she would have children. From the time her son was born she would plunge him each day in the river, in order to harden his soft body, and so soon as his hands could hold them he would have a bow and arrow, and she would not give him his breakfast until he had succeeded in hitting the target she set up for him.

One day her father would die, and according to custom, his brother, Opekankano, would rule. But always there would be Indian villages along the riverbanks, with houses made of saplings woven together, and mats hanging at the doors. Inside there would be the fire that must never be allowed to go out. Always people would light the darkness with burning torches of pine, and when it was cold they would dress in skins. These things had always been, just as the rivers always flowed, the sun always rose and set, and the summer followed the winter: the happy summer when wild roses and sunflowers bloomed in the village, and women were busy in the cornfield and the garden: cultivating the corn in rows, with beans and peas, pumpkins and cymblins between the rows; and in the gardens growing muskmelons, passion-vines, gourds, and tobacco.

It was in the season when the trees were green and strawberries ripe in the forest that news reached her father that white men had landed in the next river. But no one had been alarmed; the older people remembered that white men had come before, but they had never stayed long. These men also would not stay. . . .

The spring passed. The rains of early summer fell upon the crops. As usual, in the morning the breeze was sweet but with the day it died away. Then the hot summer came when the heat was heavy and the air still. Often in the late afternoon thunder rolled and boomed and fire flashed in the sky. Sometimes there was heard the great crash of a tree falling in the forest.

And people said that in the next river the white men were dying. Soon there would be none left. Perhaps by the time the northwest winds spread frost upon the ground and the geese flew south all the white men would be dead. It might easily be that that would happen.

But it was not so.

Frost powdered the earth. Chinquapins and persimmons ripened. Cranes in vast numbers passed over headed south, and darting like arrows high across the sky flocks of geese called *Cohunk! Cohunk!* They, too, were going south. But the white men remained, though scarcely fifty of them were left alive.

Cold winter came. The snowbirds arrived, fluttering black and white in the low bushes. In the far depths of the forest bears went into their holes, so fat with the small sweet wild grapes of autumn, and the honey of wild bees, that they waddled when they walked. The trees were naked, and it was not easy for the woods creatures to hide. It was winter and still the white men had not gone.

It was the season of hunting. Wild turkeys with wings outstretched ran in terror from the hunters' fires, and with stricken eyes the deer fled. But it was of no use; they might as well have stood still, smiling like the opossum; for in the end the hunters killed them.

From such a hunting party Captain John Smith had been brought to Powhatan.

It was a beautiful thing to see how he scorned danger, almost as though he did not know that Powhatan was famed for his cruelty, that men had not only death to fear from him, but a death of hideous agony.

Often Pocahontas had seen her father sitting in the door of his house directing the torture. Oh, many times she had seen that happen. Surely this white man with the big light beard must have heard of Powhatan's cruelty. Yet he seemed so careless of his danger that he could entertain them all with marvelous tales; such tales as Pocahontas had never heard. He could laugh and tell tales. Then what pains he took to learn the words: "Bid Pocahontas bring hither a little basket, and I will give her beads to make her a chain." . . .

All that had been when she was still a little girl.

It did not seem possible that he was dead. But that was what people were saying. Captain Smith, they said, was dead. Pocahontas could not believe it. For a long time even Powhatan did not think it could be true.

Yet Captain Smith did not come to trade, insisting that he must have corn. Corn for Jamestown seemed always more to him than his own life, for he so often risked his life for corn.

Now nothing was any longer as it used to be. Her happy visits at the place they called Jamestown . . . her visits, too, were past.

There was no one like Pocahontas, Captain Smith used to say: he had given her the pretty name "Nonpareil," and that meant that there was no one like her. And he had taught her to call him "father." But all that was over, like her childhood.

Perhaps it was on the night when she had bound the antlers to her forehead, put on the otterskin apron, and painted her body; perhaps it was then that her childhood was finished; that night when in the torchlight she had danced, singing "Love you not me?"

Now people were saying, "He is dead. He was burned with their gunpowder, and he is dead."

Everything was changed; even the songs people made up were different. They used to sing about love and about hunting, making the words as they sang. Now they made up songs about the white men, songs of scorn and hatred.

"Ho," they sang: "see how in spite of their guns we kill these men."

And a chorus jeered: "Whe! Whe! Yah, ha, ha!"

"As for their Captain Newport, he never deceived us by his gifts or by the crown for Powhatan."

"Whe! Whe! Yah, ha, ha!"

"For all the white man's guns he can be killed, he can be killed by us."

"Whe! Whe! Yah, ha, ha!"

But her father had fallen into deep melancholy. Above every other village in his kingdom, he had loved Werowocomoco, that village to which Smith had been brought prisoner. Now everyone could see that Powhatan took no more pleasure in his village: so long as there were white men in the next river, he could not know peace.

Lately the white men's ships had brought women as well as men; it was plain, therefore, that they had come to stay.

Pocahontas saw her father sit brooding in fear.

Everywhere in all the villages of his kingdom there was fear. The whisper of fear was on all the rivers.

And now again the geese flew south, calling *Co-hunk!* just as though the world were as it used to be. So winter was come. The Indians talked of dreadful things happening at Jamestown. The colonists were starving and in their despair thirty of them dared to come to Powhatan. And Pocahontas had never known her father to condemn men to a slower horror of torture.

After that no more white men came to the village. Before the winter was over it was known to the watchful Indians that in Jamestown they were too weak from hunger even to seek acorns in the forest, and that they were burning the timber from their houses because they lacked strength to cut firewood in the forest.

"Whe! Whe! Yah, ha! ha!"

The Indians sang in exultation. It was only a matter of time now—a very little time—and the white men would be gone.

Then news came that once more the tide bore ships up the river. . . . But to the mournful beat of drums the ships took on board the starving colonists. Guns were fired in last salute, and the ships dropped down the river.

For three days Jamestown stood, deserted.

"Whe! Whe!" . . . at last the white men were gone.

But again there were ships in the river. The two so lately sailed had returned, and with them were three more. The three had brought food in abundance, and many colonists. A new chief, too, had come; a great man gorgeously arrayed, quite different from Captain Smith who had had no such glory of dress.

Indians went to Jamestown to stare, and to trade. Pocahontas was not among them. For it must be true that Captain Smith was dead.

# CHAPTER FIVE

# A Princess for a Copper Kettle

THE news brought to Powhatan was quite true: the terrible Starving Time in Jamestown, the two ships which had rescued the survivors, and the abandonment of the settlement with melancholy salute of guns. It was true also that within three days the ships had returned with three more.

The first two ships were the *Patience* and the *Deliverance,* built in Bermuda by the shipwrecked men of the *Sea Venture* which had foundered on the rocks of that island. With the three new ships came Lord Delaware himself, arrived in the mouth of the river at the melancholy moment of Jamestown's abandonment. His fleet brought salvation; abundant provisions and colonists, among them, in addition to "knights and gentlemen of quality," many artisans and laborers.

Crops were immediately planted, new buildings begun, and old ones repaired. Lord Delaware loved flowers and he had the church "kept passing sweet" with blossoms: When he went on Sunday to service he was escorted by all the councilors, captains, and other officials and gentlemen . . . with a guard of fifty halberdiers in livery of bright red cloaks. The lord governor himself sat in a velvet chair, with a velvet cushion before him upon which to kneel. All very different from plain John Smith in his heavy breeches and leather jerkin, with his own hands felling forest trees and building houses.

But for all its new prosperity the men of Jamestown suffered, and often died from the baffling country sickness. Lord Delaware himself became so ill that he went home to England, and now it was Sir Thomas Dale who was to govern in his name.

John Smith had had no authority to alter the system under which he ruled. All supplies and all products of work had been held in common. Governor Dale, with his greater power, allotted each man a plot of ground for his own personal use. The chroniclers of the day recorded the effect: "Formerly," they say, "when our people labored jointly together, the most honest would hardly take so much true pains in a week as now for themselves they will do in a day." And of the New England Pilgrims, William Bradford later recorded that not until the plan of holding property in common was abolished did the colonists become thrifty and industrious.

Jamestown began to thrive, but Indian raids increased: they stole cattle, hogs, tools, guns and ammunition; whenever possible they took prisoners whose fate was often a death of lingering horror.

Then Argall, trading in the Potomac for corn, chanced to hear that the princess Pocahontas was there visiting friends. This gave Captain Argall (described by those who knew him as an "ingenious, active and forward-looking young fellow") a shrewd idea; he would abduct the princess and take her to Jamestown. With Pocahontas in their possession, he reasoned, the English could force Powhatan to restore their stolen property and to free those white men who were his prisoners.

Argall's first move was to win the chief, Japazaws, in whose family Pocahontas was a guest. He invited Japazaws to visit the ship; and among the things he showed him there was a beautiful copper kettle.

The more Japazaws thought about that kettle, the more he coveted it.

Ralph Hamor, who was at the time secretary for the Jamestown colony, tells the story:

Japazaws desired the copper kettle.

Very well, Argall would let him have it, on the condition that he persuade Pocahontas to visit the ship.

Japazaws hesitated.

Argall promised that no harm should come to the princess.

The kettle was beautiful and shining. Japazaws would see what he could do, provided that Pocahontas was not to be harmed.

Argall repeated that assurance.

Japazaws confided the scheme to his wife. It was a lovely kettle.

Mistress Japazaws then told Pocahontas how greatly she longed to visit the white man's ship. Actually she had never been aboard a ship. If only Japazaws would permit her to visit this one! The lady played her part well; she pleaded and cajoled. Japazaws was obstinate. Mistress Japazaws wept. Japazaws conceded that if it pleased the princess Pocahontas to accompany his wife he would consent.

Pocahontas agreed.

Supper was served them on board. Captain Argall was entertaining, and Pocahontas suspected nothing, so that it was a simple matter for Japazaws and his wife, after supper, to slip away with the bewitching kettle.

"As for Pocahontas," Hamor writes, "much ado there was to persuade her to be patient . . . and with extraordinary courteous usage to Jamestown she was brought."

The English at once sent a messenger informing Powhatan that his daughter was in their possession and that they would hold her until he was willing to ransom her in exchange for the English prisoners, the stolen swords and guns and tools.

Three months passed without a reply from Powhatan, and then seven of the prisoners, a few muskets, and some corn were returned.

Another messenger was dispatched to say that Pocahontas was well and kindly treated, but she would not be freed until the remainder of the prisoners and the goods were received.

Again months elapsed with no word from Powhatan.

Governor Dale himself then went into Powhatan's river with such vessels as happened to be anchored at Jamestown. The governor equipped these ships with armed men, and he took with him also the princess Pocahontas.

If the Indians were so bold as they pretended, let them fight for her; or let them return the men and the stolen articles which they were holding. Otherwise, he declared, the English would burn their houses, take away their canoes, break their fish traps, and do whatever damage they could.

At Powhatan's headquarters Dale found that the

chief had gone inland, and men had to be sent to present to him the governor's ultimatum.

Powhatan's reply was that the prisoners had all run away; but on the following day he would return the guns and the tools. Meanwhile, instead of keeping his word, he sent four hundred armed warriors, daring the English to come ashore.

Then, since it was April and the season for planting corn, Governor Dale went back to Jamestown, announcing that he would give the Indians until harvesttime to meet his demands. If they failed, he vowed to return and destroy them utterly.

And little Pocahontas grieved. If her father had loved her, she cried, he would not value her less than swords and guns and axes.

She was learning the old truth about eating cake and having it.

Her heart had put Captain John Smith's safety before everything else. Now it appeared that her father valued stolen goods above his dear and darling daughter.

John Rolfe was fond of smoking, and while he smoked he thought. He thought about tobacco. In England and all over Europe more and more people were smoking; even if the clergy did oppose the habit and King James called tobacco a "filthy weed." People were smoking. The trouble was, they preferred the tobacco grown in the Spanish colonies; something would have to be done to improve the Virginia product. Rolfe pondered while he smoked.

After a while he began to experiment in growing

and curing tobacco. All his interest centered upon this problem; for during the months in Bermuda, while the *Patience* and *Deliverance* were being built, his child had been born and died, and in a short time his wife, too, was dead. Arrived in Jamestown, Rolfe could give his undivided mind to the cultivation of tobacco.

And then Captain Argall brought Pocahontas a captive to Jamestown. She was a young woman now, and still the Nonpareil that John Smith had christened her when she was a child; still gentle and tender and small of stature.

Governor Dale put her in charge of the Reverend Mr. Whitaker to be educated and converted. There was at the time in Jamestown a certain Don Diego de Molina, a suave Spanish official who, coming in a small coasting boat to the mouth of the river, had permitted himself to be taken prisoner in order that he might report to the King of Spain precisely the condition of the British colony in Virginia. Molina must have looked with some amusement upon the deliberate fashion in which the Reverend Whitaker went about converting Pocahontas. The Spanish conquistadores would have baptized and christened her at once; the British method must have appeared a tedious matter to Molina.

But that was not, of course, Molina's concern; his business was to smuggle out of the country those reports which he sent back to his sovereign; concealed in the soles of shoes and in coils of rope.

Meanwhile something other than conversion or spying or experimenting with tobacco was happening in that settlement on the north bank of the James where the tides rose and fell and men toiled to found a colony in the wilderness. For not all the attention of John Rolfe, "honest young gentleman of good behavior," was now devoted to tobacco.

There came a day when he put into the hands of Governor Dale a long letter. The letter opens with an involved preamble, as though its writer hesitates to arrive at the real purpose.

"Did not my case," he says, "proceed from an unspotted conscience I should not dare to offer to your view and approved judgment these passions of my troubled soul. . . ."

(You cannot help wondering, as you read, whether Governor Dale already knew what Rolfe was so reluctant to put into words, or whether it would come to him as a surprise.)

"Let this," Rolfe continues, "this, my well advised protestation which I have made between God and my own conscience be sufficient witness at the dreadful day of judgment . . . to condemn me if my chiefest interest and purpose be not to strive with all my power of body and mind . . . for the honour of our country, for my own salvation and for the converting to a true knowledge of God and Jesus Christ, an unbelieving creature, namely Pocahontas! . . ."

(Poor little Pocahontas! So it is you who are the cause of this fearful day-of-judgment matter!)

"Pocahontas," the letter continues, "to whom my heart and my best thoughts are and have a long time been entangled and inthralled in so intricate a labyrinth, that I was even awearied to unwind myself there-out."

(Suddenly the words ring with a sincere passion. "I was even awearied to unwind myself there-out.")

"To you, therefore, most noble Sir, the patron and

Father of this country, do I utter . . . this my long
continued affection which hath made a mighty war in
my meditations. And here do . . . truly relate . . .
that I forgot not to set before mine eyes the frailty of
mankind and his proneness to evil . . . nor was I igno-
rant of the heavy displeasure which Almighty God conceived against the sons of Levi and Israel for marrying
strange wives . . ."

(You can picture Rolfe busy about his tobacco, and
all the time torn by this battle between his heart and
his tradition.)

He tells the governor how he has prayed to be preserved from sin, fearing that his love was but the wicked
instigation of the devil.

"But," he laments, "when I thought I had obtained
my peace, behold but more temptation . . . besides the
many passions and sufferings which I have daily and
hourly; yea, and in my sleep, endured, awaking me to
astonishment . . . pulling me by the ear and crying:
'Why dost not thou more endeavor to make her a
Christian?' "

Then his heart again cries out above all other con-
siderations, and he speaks of the great appearance of
love which Pocahontas shows toward him, and of the
"capableness of her understanding, her aptness to receive
any good impression . . . besides her own incitements
stirring me up . . ."

What then should he do! he exclaims. Should base
fear of displeasing the world influence him, when perhaps this is a task God has set him to do?

The letter concludes, complacently remarking that
Rolfe does not so undervalue himself as not to believe
a more worthy match possible for him.

But, in spite of that, and in spite of the suggestion that his alliance with Pocahontas would be of value to the colony, love shines through the lengthy pompous letter, breaking forth now and then into a genuine cry from the man's heart.

So it came about that Pocahontas was baptized—christened Rebecca, the Lady Rebecca—and married to John Rolfe.

It is said that Don Diego de Molina, the Spanish prisoner, was among those of quality present at the wedding. Whether or not that was the case, he was at the time in Jamestown. And again he must have wondered at the difference between Spanish and British conquerors; for without scruple the conquistador took the aboriginal woman, by marriage or otherwise, as the case might be.

It was the marriage itself that was of real concern to Molina, and to his sovereign, Philip of Spain. For the marriage made peace between the colony and the Indians. Actually two of the bride's brothers and an uncle came to the wedding. Jamestown rejoiced, and Governor Dale wrote home to London that Pocahontas lived lovingly with her husband. Others who knew her say that "by the diligent care of Master Rolfe, and his friends she was taught to speak such English as might well be understood . . . that she was instructed in Christianity, that she was become very formal and civil after the English manner . . ." And that she had by Rolfe a child whom she loved most dearly.

# CHAPTER SIX

# Letter to the Queen

ABOARD the ship *Treasurer,* Rolfe and his lady
sailed for England. Other passengers were Governor
Dale and the Spaniard Don Diego de Molina, whose sovereign had at last negotiated his release from captivity
in Jamestown. And when the *Treasurer* had safely arrived, there was Captain John Smith returned from a
voyage to New England. So it came about that Pocahontas, who had thought him dead, met once more the
hero of her childhood.

In a letter to Queen Anne, John Smith describes
the scene. He is writing because he would have the
queen understand how much the Virginia colony owed
to the princess, Pocahontas. He goes back to the day
when he was brought before Powhatan for judgment.
There was present, he says, Powhatan's beloved daughter, Pocahontas, then but a child—a child of "compassionate and pitiful heart," who "hazarded the beating
out of her own brains" to save him from the death to
which her father condemned him. And in that hard
winter of famine Jamestown would have starved but
for Pocahontas, who "with her wild train, came to
Jamestown as freely as to her father's house," bringing
corn and venison. Again a year later she risked her life,
he says, coming unaffrighted through the dark woods
to warn him of danger.

And, "humbly kissing her Majesty's feet," Smith
begs that she will do some honor to so great a spirit as
Pocahontas, cannily adding that such attention on the
part of the queen will be to the advantage of England's
colony on James River.

He himself, he explains, cannot do for Pocahontas
the service she so well deserves, since he is about to sail
again for New England. But, hearing that she was at
Branford with some of his friends, he went there to see
her, and he describes how, when he saluted her as "Lady
Rebecca," she turned from him without a word, hiding
her face and remaining thus for some hours.

When at last she spoke, it was to reproach him:

"You did promise Powhatan that what was yours
should be his, and he the like to you. You called him
father, being in the land a stranger. By the same reason,
so must I do to you."

When Smith explained that his formality came
from respect for her position, she cried out: "Were you
not afraid to come into my father's country, and cause
fear in him and all his people but me? And fear you
here that I should call you father? I tell you that I will.
And you shall call me child. And so I will be forever
and ever your Countryman. . . ."

Pocahontas has forgotten nothing. All is remembered: the stones upon which Smith's brains were to
be beaten out; the release from that death which she
won for him; the pretty new name that he had given
her—the Nonpareil.

And, remembering, she turned away in silence,
covering her face.

Unless he had forgotten all, how could he greet her now as the Lady Rebecca!

Surely he, too, remembered; he could not forget the wide shining river and the slender body of a little savage princess glistening in the sun.

Then you seem actually to see her as she lifted her head again to exclaim: "They did tell us that you were dead and I knew no other 'til I came to Plymouth!"

Lady Delaware herself presented Pocahontas to their Majesties, and all agreed that by the "Decency and Grace of her Deportment she charmed the whole Court. . . . Persons of Quality took her up, and she was guest at Masks, Balls, Plays and other Public Entertainments, all of which wonderfully pleased and delighted her."

An artist painted a portrait which represents her with brilliant crimson lips and skin of a faint copper hue. He shows her with huge thoughtful dark eyes, set beneath straight black brows and above high cheekbones. She is wearing a dark hat so banded in gold as to give the effect of a coronet. A mantle of brocaded red velvet embroidered in gold gives only a glimpse of her gown with its rows of gilt buttons up the front. Above the scarlet mantle flares a stiff ruff of white lace, and white lace cuffs finish the sleeves. In one hand—a small, beautifully formed hand—she is carrying a little fan of ostrich plumes.

The great historian, Purchas, met her and she made a deep impression upon him. "The Indian princess," he says, "did not only accustom herself to civilization, but still carried herself as the daughter of a King. . . . I was present when my honorable and reverend patron, the Lord Bishop of London, entertained her with festival and state and pomp beyond what I have seen in his great hospitality afforded to other ladies."

What Pocahontas herself thought of London can never be known. But surely she compared James I with her father. King James must have been a shock to one whose people held a high standard of physical perfection and of prowess; for the legs of this king appeared too weak to carry his body; his tongue was too thick for his mouth; his puffed lips never quite closed over his teeth; his protruding eyes rolled in a vacuous stare; and his gaudy clothing was seldom clean.

It was strange that such a man as James should be king of the English, and that they should have given his name to so noble a river as the Powhatan.

The English visit came finally to an end. The last splendid entertainment was over. A London gentleman, writing to Britain's ambassador at The Hague, related what there was of court gossip. The "Virginia Woman —Pocahuntas," he said, had been most "graciously used" by the king. There had been recently a gorgeous masque at which she had been present, and "greatly pleased."

But now the "Virginia Woman . . . was upon her return, though sore against her will. . . ."

Pocahontas had had her glittering hour, and Rolfe was taking her back to his plantation on the James.

It was March and at home in Virginia there would

be spring in the air. Fish would be running in the river, and bears coming out of their holes, and turkeys gobbling. In sheltered spots flowers dared to bloom, people would be planting corn, and sowing tobacco seed. The white magic of dogwood would soon gleam in the forest and all the trees would unfurl their leaves. Then before you knew it the hot summer would come, with buzzards soaring high in the lazy heat, while on the plantation everybody was busy ridding the tobacco of the big green caterpillars.

The years would pass, with her baby son growing into a small boy and then into a man.

And always there would be the river flowing deep and strong.

The ship which was to take Rolfe and Pocahontas to Virginia dropped down the Thames to Gravesend. Suddenly then Pocahontas fell desperately ill. . . .

"And it pleased God at Gravesend to take this young Lady to His Mercy, where she made not more sorrow for her unexpected death than joy to the beholders to hear and see her make so religious and Godly an end."

In these words Rolfe and Captain Argall recorded her death.

And when news came to John Smith that Pocahontas was dead and buried at Gravesend on the Thames, he must have remembered how she had cried out: "I tell you I will call you father, and you shall call me child, and so I will be forever and ever your Countryman."

The tender tale of little Pocahontas and her hero shines like a personal memory out of the old records; so vivid that it seems strange its truth should ever have been doubted.

You wonder that anyone could question that she saved Captain Smith from death. Such a rescue was in keeping with an established Indian custom. And without admitting the child-worship which Pocahontas felt for Smith, how is it possible to account for her coming a year later through the "dark irksome woods" to warn him of her father's plan to massacre him and his companions?

Smith himself alludes only casually to this, but it is related in detail by several of the Englishmen present when it happened. And it is Smith's companions, not Smith himself, who describe that dance in the autumn forest when Pocahontas sang: "Love you not me?"

For more than two hundred years the famous episode of the first rescue was accepted; never questioned even in attacks upon Smith by personal enemies, eager to make a case against him because they considered him vainglorious and unjust in his criticism of them.

Then an American historian observed that this rescue was not mentioned in that brief *True Relation* which Smith sent back from Virginia to a friend in England and in the summer of 1608. And ever since this discovery historians have argued, disagreeing about the truth of the rescue.

It must be remembered that Smith was writing under the ban which commanded the colonists to record nothing which might alarm possible settlers, and that even after his manuscript reached England it was censored before publication; for in a foreword the editor explains: "Something more was by him written, which being (As I thought) fit to be private, I would not venture to make public." Also the Pocahontas incident is not the only event thus omitted from the *True Relation*.

All this seems to answer those who have thought the rescue invented by Smith at a later date in order to exploit himself when Pocahontas was the popular sensation of London. But if that were the case, why didn't his letter enlarge upon the story? It had immense romantic value, yet his letter to Queen Anne tells it in the fewest possible words: only one short sentence is devoted to it. And in his subsequent works, though free from censorship, Smith mentions it but briefly.

When you add together every line written of Pocahontas by those who actually knew her, though their words are few, she comes convincingly to life in their pages. No one writer tells the complete story, so that, in order to get the whole picture you must assemble what each has contributed: Anas Todkill, the soldier; William Phettiplace, captain of the pinnace; Wyffin and Pots, who wrote "gentlemen" after their names; Hamor, who was secretary of the James River colony; Rolfe, her husband; Governor Dale, the Reverend Mr. Whitaker; Purchas, the historian, who knew her in London, and—Captain John Smith.

In what these men have written there is no conflict in opinion, or in any fact, except a slight variation in their estimate of her age. Out of this eyewitness testimony the girl Pocahontas emerges lovely and tender and human, while the story itself is a tale of timeless beauty.

# CHAPTER SEVEN

# Immigrants

ROLFE left his little son to be brought up in England and sailed alone to James River.

He was now become a great man in the colony. With Pocahontas he had been entertained by persons of quality, actually received by their Majesties; he was secretary of the colony, and he had developed a Virginia tobacco which could compete with the Spanish product.

Even the London gallants who had refused to smoke any but the "right stuff" were now willing to use Virginia tobacco. There was comfort for Rolfe in the knowledge that it was he who had done this for Jamestown. What was needed now were laborers. That was the problem upon which Rolfe—the original of North America's founders of industry—must meditate as he smoked.

At that time in England the poor were so poor that if an entire family toiled from morning until night throughout all the days of their lives the most they could hope for was to live on brown bread and cheese. There were many who must starve for lack of work, and the horde of vagabonds was so great that people were forbidden to move from one parish to another without official permission, and destitution had driven homeless children upon the streets.

In Virginia Rolfe was thinking that the tobacco plantations needed laborers; not skilled workers, but merely hands.

Meanwhile the city of London gathered together a hundred homeless children and shipped them to James River, to be bound out as apprentices to serve the planters; the boys until they were twenty-one, and the girls for an equal period, unless in the meantime they married. At the expiration of their service they were to be placed as tenants on the public lands, and provided with houses, cattle, and a supply of corn—free men with a chance to make a life for themselves.

Talk of opportunity in the New World went back to England. And those who found it difficult to earn even brown bread and cheese began to think of that waiting opportunity. But how were they—the poor—to get to Virginia? There was but one way: they could voluntarily bind themselves out for a term of years, going as indentured servants. They might trade four years of liberty for this opportunity. Tobacco . . . tobacco, people said, was gold: men could buy anything with tobacco.

Thus many sailed as indentured servants, and many others took their all and bought passage to Virginia. The gentry, too, and younger sons of the nobility left the past and sailed away into the future.

Destitution had filled the jails of England, and it was decided to permit certain prisoners to go out to Britain's New World possessions under sentence to serve from seven to fourteen years on the plantations.

In the English seaport towns kidnaping became all at once a flourishing business: youths and children were lured aboard ships and dispatched to America to serve terms of apprenticeship. People spoke of the kidnapers as "spirits," and whenever anyone mysteriously disappeared it was whispered that they had been "spirited away."

So it was that Rolfe saw the forest cleared and plantations opened up and down the river. At Jamestown wooden houses stood in two neat rows; there were three stores framed together and Mrs. Jane Pierce was boasting of the fine figs in her garden.

In England King James had beheaded Sir Walter Raleigh. But for Raleigh there might have been no Virginia colony, yet he had been beheaded. People said he had asked to smoke a pipe of tobacco in that last terrible hour before he went to the block. In the same year old Powhatan died and Opekankano succeeded him, but his death seemed not to affect that peace with the Indians which had scarcely been disturbed since the day Rolfe married Pocahontas. Still it was necessary to maintain a strong palisade around Jamestown, and in case of need guns might be fired from the church tower.

In this period of hopeful prosperity Rolfe let his eyes dwell upon Mrs. Pierce's young daughter Jane. She would be a worthy match, for no man was more respected in the colony than her father; her mother was a notable housewife, and of all the houses in Virginia none compared with the Pierce house in Jamestown. Rolfe had something new to dream of while he smoked; Jane would make some man a good wife.

For Rolfe to dream was to act.

Then in the year 1619 much of importance happened in Virginia. In July the first legislative body ever assembled in America met in the Jamestown church: it consisted of a Council appointed in London, and a

House of Burgesses made up of elected representatives from boroughs which extended now for seventy miles along both banks of the James. So was democracy born in the British New World.

And John Rolfe, secretary of the colony, was elected a member of the House of Burgesses; an important personage in his starched ruff and bright-hued coat, and worthily married to Miss Jane Pierce.

It was in the same summer that, as secretary, he recorded the arrival of a Dutch ship bringing twenty Negroes who were sold in the colony. Captain Pierce, Jane's father, had one—a woman who was called Angelo.

Also, there arrived from the London Company a shipment of young and handsome girls, destined as wives for the colonists. The company wrote that these girls had been selected with extraordinary care; testimonials to the character of each being enclosed.

"We are all desirous," the letter ran, "that marriage be free according to the laws of nature"; no girl was to be married against her will and no husbands were to be considered except such as were free men, or tenants, with means to maintain wives; and upon marriage each husband was to pay to the London Company a hundred and twenty pounds of tobacco to meet his wife's passage money. Truly, tobacco was gold. And it was Rolfe's experiments that had made it so.

One day in the spring of 1622 Rolfe, like other men, was busy on his plantation. It was the season when a planter must be preparing the ground for tobacco. And no one had any reason to feel anxiety. Only the week before, the king, Opekankano, had sent a message saying he held peace between the English and the Indians to be so firm that the sky should sooner fall than their accord be broken.

Then suddenly the dreadful thing happened.

The tale is related by one of the survivors. On the fatal morning, he says, Indians came into the plantations in the manner of friendly visitors, coming unarmed. And some among them sat down to breakfast with the white men; suddenly, all fell upon the colonists, murdering them with their own weapons or with whatever tools happened to be at hand. They butchered the old and the young, the men and the women. None was spared, either in the houses or in the fields. Three hundred and seventy-four were slaughtered.

But Jamestown escaped. An Indian boy called Chanco lived at the time in the home of a colonist whose plantation was across the river from Jamestown. The night before the massacre, Chanco's brother came and lay with him. In the quiet dark he told his news: command had gone forth from Opekankano that in the morning every Indian was to rise up and slay the white man; not one white man was to be left alive.

Chanco waited until his brother slept, then crept stealthily out of his bed. He had decided to warn that white man with whom he lived, for, he said, the man had used him always as a son. And in the first light of dawn this man rowed across the wide river to give the news to Jamestown.

But there had been no one to warn John Rolfe away on his plantation . . . and after that day nothing was ever again heard of him.

Undismayed, immigrants continued to flow westward across the sea, to New England now, as well as to Virginia. The massacre had temporarily set back such matters as the building of a university on James River, but colonization proceeded as though there had been no catastrophe. A quarter of Virginia's little population had perished, but more hurried to take their places.

Back in England, Parliament and James I were quarreling and there was intrigue within the London Company itself. James revoked their charter and took over Virginia as a royal province, with its governor appointed by the crown but its House of Burgesses remaining an elected body. James then died. Charles I succeeded him. Captain John Smith died, unmarried to the end; he was buried on the south side of the choir, in the Church of St. Sepulchre in London, and upon his tomb was engraved his coat of arms, with the three Turks' heads and the motto "Vincere est vivere": "To conquer—to overcome—is to live." Cromwell came into power. Charles I got his head cut off. Royalists fled to Virginia. Cromwell died. The crown was restored and Charles II came to the throne. Now it was the turn of Roundheads and Dissenters to be persecuted, and if possible to escape to America. Charles II died and his brother, James II, became king. Rebels were hanged or sold into service on the plantations of the West Indies and America.

James II was forced to leave his throne, and England invited his daughter Mary and her Protestant husband, William of Orange, to reign. Half a million Huguenots fled from persecution in France and some of them found a haven on James River. And at intervals through the years ships had brought Africans to America to be sold into slavery, but for sixty years after the arrival of that Dutch boat with the first Negroes the number of slaves increased so slowly that in Virginia a slave might actually have grown to old age and died without ever seeing another of his kind. It is no wonder that there was born in the heart of the race the lament:

> Sometimes I feel like a motherless child,
> A long way from home.

In those years more than fifty thousand whites finished their terms of indenture and became free citizens, able in a short time to become the owners of small farms.

In addition to immigrants, ships now brought out furniture and finery, seeds and pigeons, beehives and mastiffs and occasionally horses, though the highways of Virginia long remained its rivers and its creeks. Now quinine had been introduced from Peru; and at last the colonists had a cure for that country sickness which had cost so many lives.

It was out of these varied elements that Virginia became a flourishing colony in whose making each played his part; merchants and seamen, yeomen, gentry, and nobility, political and religious fugitives, Englishman, Scotchman, Welshman and Frenchman, and the black man out of Africa; the jungle savage, the unlettered peasant, university men of Edinburgh, Cambridge, and Oxford.

The new land they made cost them toil and pain and death, massacre and starvation; often the ache of homesick hearts and of great loneliness. But in the presence of a gallant courage obstacles fell like wheat before the scythe. And of such buoyant spirit were they that, even in that first hard perilous century, they were so given to elegant dress that, in order to discourage too great finery, a law was passed, providing that each Sunday at church every man should be assessed according "to his own and his wife's apparel."

# THE WORLD THEY MADE

# CHAPTER EIGHT

# Young New World

CAPTAIN JOHN SMITH used to say that it was not for everyone to plant a colony, though it was easy enough to live in the house after it was built.

The pioneers who planted Virginia passed. John Smith, whose genius had kept Jamestown alive, was gone; Pocahontas, who had brought food to the starving colonists; Rolfe, who had made a tobacco which could compete with the Spanish product; Governor Dale, who had understood that private ownership of property is a spur to industry; Chanco, the Indian boy whose grateful loyalty to the man who "used him as a son" had preserved Jamestown from massacre—these were gone.

In the tidewater region the battle with the wilderness was won. Nathaniel Bacon led his attack against the Indians and launched his famous "rebellion" against Governor Berkeley's tyrannical rule. He burned Jamestown. And then he died; the rebellion collapsed; whereupon Berkeley hanged so many of Bacon's men that in England Charles II exclaimed: "That old fool has hung more men in that naked land than I have done for the murder of my father!"

Jamestown was rebuilt, but accidentally caught fire and was burned again. And in 1699 the capital was

moved from malarial Jamestown to Middle Plantation
on the peninsula between the James and York rivers.
Connected with both streams by creeks, it was a satis-
factory location for the center of a plantation civilization which still traveled largely by water.

They called the new capital Williamsburg, and
among the acts early passed by the Assembly meeting
there, was a heavy duty on the importation of slaves;
for already in Virginia certain men saw its danger and
their hope was to put an end to traffic in human beings.
But the African Company had made it so profitable a
business that the crown vetoed the bill, and the slave
trade increased.

The new century which inherited the colony was
too young and buoyant for gloomy foreboding. It had
an immense zest for living. So had its Governor Alexander Spotswood. Under his enthusiasm Williamsburg
was developed and made beautiful, so much money
being spent on his house that Virginians ironically
named it the "palace."

And Spotswood was ambitious to discover what lay
beyond the high blue mountains. On a certain day in
August the governor, with a group of gentlemen, their
horses and servants, two companies of rangers, and four
Indian guides, went exploring.

John Fontaine of the famous family of Huguenot
refugees was one of these gentlemen explorers. His journal describes how at night they supped and drank good
punch before great campfires; it tells of the snakes they
killed, the deer, the wild turkeys and the bear they shot,
the fish they caught, and how at the mountaintop, look-

ing out over the beautiful valley of Virginia, they toasted King George in champagne, and fired a volley of guns in his honor; how they then drank to the princess in fine Burgundy, and fired a second volley; how there followed toasts to the royal family in claret, with still another volley; and finally how all drank the very good health of their governor and saluted him also with guns. There were other drinks—red and white wine of Virginia, Irish Usqubaugh, brandy, shrub, two sorts of rum, canary, cherry punch, and cider. "We were very merry," John Fontaine says, "and diverted ourselves with our adventures."

When he returned to Williamsburg Spotswood gave each of the gentlemen on this joyous expedition a miniature horseshoe of gold set with diamonds. Upon it he had engraved in Latin: "Thus it is a pleasure to cross the mountains." This the Reverend Hugh Jones—long ago chaplain to the House of Burgesses—says was done to "encourage gentlemen to make new discoveries and new settlements."

In the year after this adventure with the knights of the Golden Horseshoe, Governor Spotswood was concerning himself with the matter of pirates. Everybody expected pirates out in the open sea; but to have them hovering like hornets about the Capes, that, people said, was too much.

Especially to be feared was the bold Blackbeard with his headquarters in Ocracoke Inlet on the Carolina coast. Blackbeard had been formerly a sailor out of Bristol, but now he was a pirate with a reputation that not another sea robber could equal. His right name was Teach; his huge black beard had given him the nickname. He wore the beard immensely long, and it grew, people said, to his very eyes. He was fond of plaiting it in two long braids which he tied about his ears with the prettiest pale blue ribbons. And he liked to terrify his victims by fastening slow-burning matches under the brim of his hat. You could die of terror merely to see Blackbeard with the matches burning on either side of his head, and his beard tied up with blue ribbon. He carried always on his person as many as six pistols, and he was so cruel that actually, they said, one night aboard his ship, when he sat about the table with his crew, suddenly he blew out the light and began shooting; shooting at the legs of his own men under the table: "just," he explained, "to let them know he was there."

And in the matter of women—well, Blackbeard had had thirteen wives, and nobody knew how he got rid of one to make way for another.

Spotswood was determined to put an end to this Blackbeard and his raids upon vessels off the Virginia Capes. As it happened, two of his Majesty's ships-of-war were then lying in the Chesapeake, and a certain Lieutenant Maynard, aboard one of them, offered to lead an expedition against Blackbeard. If the governor would give him a couple of sloops, Maynard would challenge Blackbeard where he lay on his schooner in Ocracoke Inlet.

"Bring him back," Spotswood said, "dead or alive, bring him back."

With this Maynard sailed away, headed for Ocracoke; and no one thought he would return.

An old ballad tells the story of what happened. It is said that Benjamin Franklin wrote it when he was thirteen years old:

Valiant Maynard as he sailed
Soon the Pirate did espy
With his Trumpet he then hailed
And to him they did reply,
Captain Teach is our Commander,
Maynard said, he is the man
Whom I am resolved to hand, Sir,
Let him do the best he can.

Teach replied unto Maynard,
You no quarter here shall see,
But be hanged on the Main yard
You and all your company. . . .

Then Blackbeard called for wine and drank damnation to Maynard and his crew.

In the battle which followed, men on both sides were killed and wounded until at last Maynard and Blackbeard fought it out on the deck of the pirate schooner.

Maynard boarded him, and to it
They fell with Sword and Pistol too;
They had courage and did show it . . .

But in the end Maynard sailed back to Virginia, with the frightful head of Blackbeard nailed to his bowsprit and fifteen of the pirate's crew aboard in irons, to meet their end on gallows set up for the purpose outside the town of Williamsburg.

When the Reverend Hugh Jones came out from England to teach mathematics in the College of William and Mary, and to act as chaplain of the House of Burgesses, he was delighted with Williamsburg. He considered the palace a magnificent structure, beautified with gates, fine gardens . . . and a good cupola illuminating most of the town on Royal Birthnights. As for the Virginians themselves, he was charmed with their "good diversion and splendid entertainments. Actually," he said, they lived "in the same neat Manner . . . dressed after the same Modes, and behaved themselves exactly as the Gentry of London." And Governor Gooch, who followed some years after Spotswood, boasted that there was not an ill dancer in his government.

Though the little village of Williamsburg was gay the year round, the season was during the meeting of the Assembly, usually in autumn and spring. The normal population was not more than two thousand, but when the Assembly met the burgesses moved their families in from the plantations. Town houses were opened, taverns crowded, and the streets lively with the coming and going of chariots, coaches, chaises, and horsemen.

By this time there was a theater in Williamsburg, the first in the colonies. Visiting professional companies gave *Othello* and *Romeo and Juliet,* as well as the comedies and drolls of the day. When there were no professionals in town the gentlemen and ladies of the country put on plays themselves, such as *The Busy Body, The Recruiting Officer,* and *The Lying Valet.*

People were so fond of music that through the open windows of Williamsburg's houses came the sound of harpsichord, harmonica, guitar, German flutes, fortepianos, and voices singing. In the season there were horse races, cockfights, and contests of every description. A number of "brisk young men" would wrestle for silver buckles; dancers would compete for a pair of handsome shoes; fiddlers would enter a contest for a violin; a hat to the value of twenty shillings would be cudgeled for; a pig would be the prize won by whoever succeeded in catching and lifting it by the tail made slippery by soaping; a pair of elegant silk stockings would be awarded to the prettiest young country maid present; and a quire of ballads would be sung for by a number of songsters, all of them to have "liquor sufficient to clear their Wind Pipes." This was also the profitable season to hold slave auctions and auctions of land, for merchants to bring in their wares and hairdressers and wigmakers to open shops.

And there were, of course, continual balls and dinners, the most brilliant being at the palace and in the beautiful Apollo Room of Raleigh Tavern.

It was in this gay century of colonial Virginia that Philip Fithian, a very young divinity student, came from New Jersey to act as tutor to the children of one Robert Carter, master of Nomini Hall, a famous estate in tidewater Virginia. Fithian was an earnest, observant young man and in his leisure hours kept a journal, purely for his own pleasure, with no idea of publication.

Fithian is far from home—a seven days' journey on horseback. His diary is his companion; he sets down his memories of home, his devotion to the faraway girl whom he calls "lovely Laura," and he records every detail of life on Robert Carter's plantation as it appeared to his theologian's eyes.

He is shocked that Sunday should be a day of diversion as well as of churchgoing. Actually everyone is in a happy mood, and by Saturday night the faces of the slaves shine already with festive smiles. Sometimes Fithian comes upon them in the stable fighting cocks. There is a strange air of jollity about Sunday to which Mr. Fithian is not accustomed. The river is alive with sailboats and canoes. True, some are going and coming from church; but others are fishing. And church itself has the genial air of a club. Horses and carriages stand under the trees; beaux buzz about the local belles; older men gather in groups discussing politics and farming, actually until the service begins, when the men enter the church in a body.

Conviviality extends even to worship, and this is most surprising to Mr. Fithian. And he himself begins to thaw, recording not only the text of a sermon, but the dinner which follows, the invited guests, and the elegance of the food—beef and greens, roast pig, oysters, fine boiled rockfish, puddings and cheeses and fruits, and brandy toddy, in which they drank to the king and queen, the royal family, the governor, and finally to the young ladies of their acquaintance.

Among the sermons Fithian records one preached from the text, "He that walketh uprightly walketh wisely." And slowly, as he comes to know these people, at first so alien to him, he seems to realize that they, too, endeavor to walk uprightly. His friends had warned him of the danger of going to live among a people exceedingly wicked and profane. "You'll have no Calvinistic books to read," they said, "and hear no Presbyterian sermons, and you must keep much company."

Now, little by little, the pages of his journal warm,

as though the life in which Fithian finds himself cast upon them a faint rosy flush.

Nomini Hall appears to the young tutor majestic and agreeable: looking down the avenue of poplars—an avenue three hundred yards long—the house seems most romantic, gleaming white through the trees, its many windows catching the light; a truly elegant building, with stately white columns on its south side.

Mr. Carter, whom he had been prepared to find a wicked and bitterly swearing person, he analyzes as "sensible and judicious, given to much retirement and study" . . . Law is this gentleman's chief study; music is his "darling among amusements"; and he and his children are constantly practicing on a great variety of instruments. Mr. Carter has a "vastly delicate ear," his conversation is "always profitable," and nowhere is swearing so excessive as Mr. Fithian had feared.

The Carters take their tutor to visit other plantations, and he becomes familiar with talk of breeding horses and dogs, talk of fox hunting and horse racing. Occasionally, with a certain reluctance, he is persuaded to go to a ball. There is a ball at Squire Lee's that lasts four days. The ladies "dress gay and splendid"; when they dance their skirts and brocades rustle and trail behind them.

But Mr. Fithian does not forget the beautiful "Laura" he has left behind him in Jersey. "Keep her, kind Heaven," he prays, "and in her friendship, make me happy . . . Good and benevolent Laura" for whom he has the "highest esteem."

You feel this girl's presence on every page of the journal, yet happily Mr. Fithian has an eye for the plantation young ladies, describing their clothes, their persons, and their characters.

Miss Jenny Washington impresses him with her propriety and her easy winning behavior. When she dances a reel or a country dance it is without any "flirts or vulgar capers." She dresses richly and in good taste: her light-brown hair is "craped" high with two rolls on each side, and topping the whole a small cap of beautiful gauze and lace into which is woven an artificial flower.

Little Miss Priscilla Carter—one of his own pupils —he praises for her sweet obliging temper, for the fact that she never swears, that she dances finely and plays well on keyed instruments.

Miss Betsey Lee sits erect, placing her feet with great propriety, and letting her hands lie carelessly in her lap, never moving them but to adjust her dress or to perform some exercise of her fan. Brilliant earrings sparkle in her ears. Her dress is rich and fashionable, but Mr. Fithian, divinity student, finds her "pinched up rather too near in a long pair of new-fashioned stays," which, he comments, "I think are a nuisance both to us and themselves. For the late importation of stays, said to be most fashionable in London, are produced upwards so high that we can have scarce any view at all of the Ladies Snowy Bosoms; and are extended down so low that Walking must cause a disagreeable friction on some parts of the Body."

As for the gentlemen, the great wigs of William Byrd's day had gone out of style, for the time is just before the Revolution. Shorter wigs have come in, and men are beginning once more to wear their own hair, but powdering it and combing it back into a queue, which is tied with a black bow, or confined in a black silk bag. They are still wearing knee breeches, clocked silk stockings, lace ruffles, and gold and silver laced cocked hats. Breeches, coats, and waistcoats are of plush and satin and broadcloth, in black or blue, green, scarlet, or peach color.

And Fithian finds it "beautiful to admiration to see a number of such persons set off by dress to the best advantage, moving easily to the sound of well-performed music."

"Blow high, Blow low," he exclaims, "these Virginians will dance or die!" He himself, of course, cannot dance, but he can play a game called Button, and in redeeming his pawns he has several kisses from ladies.

The country as a whole he declares delightful, and the Virginians so sociable, "so kind, one can scarce know how to dispense with, or indeed accept their kindness."

You feel that Mr. Fithian is melting; actually, when expected letters do not arrive from his Laura, he speaks of her as "that vixen, Laura." He may yet know the contentment of a balance between the gay and the serious. He has seen that those Virginia girls, so bewitchingly frivolous, marry early, bear huge families, bring up their children well, manage the complicated domestic machinery of big plantations, and yet at a moment's notice gaily throw on a scarlet cloak, tie a crimson kerchief over their hair, mount a horse and gallop off to a neighbor to dance all night. He has noted to his amazement the planters' understanding of agriculture and of the many industries practiced on estates, maintaining their own blacksmiths, brickmakers, masons and carpenters, breeding livestock, training horses for the races and dogs for the hunt. It is a life fresh, vigorous, zestful, beyond anything Fithian has known before.

More than a hundred and fifty years ago (and some six years after Fithian had married his "Laura") Lucinda Lee is making visits to her plantation kin, and in odd moments writing letters to her friend, Polly Brent.

These letters were found, torn and discolored, lying forgotten in an old desk. Polly had married into a Maryland family, left Virginia, and taken Lucinda's letters with her. Ninety years passed between their writing and their publication. But their irrepressible youth, their femininity sparkle as newly as spring water.

Lucinda is having a gay time. She has just come in from a ride on a hardgoing horse. There is company for dinner and she must smart herself. She has to have her hair "craped" which, she thinks, is of all things the most disagreeable. The house is full of guests. Two new beaux have come. One is homely but is a mighty worthy man. There is going to be dancing. She has met a Mrs. Pinkard —the best Creature about lending you anything. Really she is among the finest women Lucinda has ever seen, and is thought very handsome. She always chooses which headdress Lucinda shall wear.

It is September and a quantity of delicious peaches are ripe. The garden is the most beautiful place. Lucinda walks there with Nancy and Milly Washington. Milly is a thousand times prettier than Lucinda at first thought. They all cut thistles to try their sweethearts. One of the gentlemen catches them at it, and "you can't conceive how he plagued us."

Cousin Hannah wears a blue lutestring habit, with a "taffety" apron and the most "butiful little hat you ever saw on the side of her head." When Hannah's young husband is away in Fredericksburg the poor girl is dejected, and rejoices when he returns. "You may depend on it, Polly, this said Matrimony alters us Mightily, I am afraid it alienates us from everyone else. It is I fear the bane of Female Friendship. Let it not be with us Polly, if we should ever marry."

On another day Lucinda writes all about a great frolic:

"After we went to our room we took a large dish of bacon and beef; after that, a bowl of sago cream, and after that apple-pye. While we were eating the apple-pye in bed—God bless you, making a great noise—in came Mr. W. dressed in Hannah's short gown and petticoat, and seazed me and kissed me twenty times in spite of all the resistance I could make; and then Cousin Molly. Hannah soon followed wearing his coat. They joined us in eating the apple-pye, and then went out.

"After this we took it into our heads to want to eat oysters. We got up, put on our rappers and went down to the cellar to get them; do you think that Mr. W. did not follow us and scear us just to death. We went up tho, and eat our oysters. We slept in the old lady's room too, and she sat laughing fit to kill herself at us."

Lucinda is reading *Lady Julia Mandeville.* "The stile is beautiful but the tale is horrid . . . I think I never cried more in my life reading a novel." She reckons that Polly must have read it. Lucinda confesses herself too fond of novels but in reading other books she is becoming less so. All one morning she is entertained by reading *Telemachus;* really delightful and very improving.

Frequently she mourns being separated from Polly's dear company, but such, she says, "is the fate of Mortals . . . never to be perfectly happy." But it must be right, "else the Supreme Disposer of all things would have not permitted it. . . ."

So, in the gay century, they ate and drank, were merry, danced and rode, had their hair "craped" . . . and did not forget the "Supreme Disposer of all things." All this necessarily accents the life of those with the leisure and the ability to express themselves in writing. On the wilderness frontier there were no tutors to set down their observations, and why write letters when there was no post to deliver them? But in his account of surveying the Carolina boundary line William Byrd records the Spartan frontier existence. There were no servants; every woman was her own cook, washerwoman, weaver and seamstress; when necessary she defended her children against the Indians, or went with her gun into the forest, killing deer and turkeys for the family; she shot wild cattle, she could catch hogs or knock down a beef with an ax. Yet, Byrd comments, "she shews nothing of ruggedness or immodesty in her carriage."

England was "home." Even those Virginia colonists who had never seen it—and probably never would—thought of England as home. The ships' captains were a personal direct link between the river plantations and London: the plantations had their own docks where ships came to load tobacco for the London merchants. In return for the planters' patronage the captains undertook a vast amount of shopping in London. Those captains seem to have been endlessly kind. They looked after women and children who might be voyaging alone. When colonists sent birds or squirrels as presents to friends in England, the captains saw that they were cared for aboard ship. News of what was going on traveled by way of the captains between England and Virginia. To their responsibilities in the matter of navigation and pirates, they added all this.

Much of the colony's business passed through the firm of John Norton & Sons, merchants with headquarters in London and ships plying between Virginia, the West Indies, and England. Quantities of letters were exchanged between the colonists and John Norton. The correspondence abounds in personal messages, in items of news and gossip. Everybody knew everybody else, and many were more or less related. It was a time when handwriting was as fine as copperplate, when letters and books were profusely splashed with capitals, and abbreviations were popular. Tobacco appears in these letters as tobo; hogshead is hhd; Humble Servant is Hble. Servt.; opportunity is oppy; Dear is Dr, and there is much individuality in the matter of spelling and punctuation.

These letter writers are, of course, greatly concerned with tobacco:

"Tobo never so plenty since Before I knew the Trade. . . .

"Sorry to hear from all hands that the Price of Tobo is so low. . . .

"This serves to convey a Bill of Lading for 6 hhds. of Tobo."

Notices of shipments of tobacco are often accompanied by orders for goods desired from London: for medicines, garden seed, tools, lottery tickets, clothing, thoroughbred horses and dogs, elegant sets of table and tea china, decanters and drinking glasses, table silver, painted chariots, music and books—Shakespeare's *Works* in eight volumes, Pope's *Essay on Man,* Locke's *Essay Concerning Human Understanding,* Yorick's sermons in seven volumes, and Sir James Stewart's *Political Economy,* a "Book much celebrated by the Reviewers."

A Mr. William Reynolds sends a bill of lading for eleven hogsheads of tobacco, and asks Mr. Norton to send him a tailor, indentured to serve four years. Mr. Reynolds begs that the tailor be not so old, as he has seen some that have "brought their spectacles with them" and were "fitter for a hospital than a shop board."

Catherine Rathell, who has a shop in Fredericksburg, brings her wares over to Williamsburg when the Assembly sits. She is always imploring Mr. Norton to hurry with the goods she orders. Writing in November, she says that the Assembly meets in March. Therefore she must request "of all things on Earth You will by the very first ship that sails out of London send me these goods."

She has taken a store exactly opposite the Raleigh Tavern, the best situation in Williamsburg. She "piques" herself on having the very best and most fashionable goods in Virginia. In one letter her distress for gentlemen's shoes is very great, and she would call Mr. Norton's attention to the fact that gentlemen now call frequently for shoes with long hind quarters that buckle low on the foot.

And she needs immediately three dozen sword canes; 6 neat Newest fashioned falling necklaces; 6 nice white silver papered Wedding fans with pierced Ivory Sticks; essence of Pearl for the Teeth; and 3 doz. of thread hair nets such as gentlemen sleep in.

If these articles are not shipped by the very first opportunity without fail, it will be a disappointment which Mrs. Rathell insists will totally ruin her.

A certain Mrs. Martha Goosley, mother of the ship captains, Cary, George, and William Goosley, writes Mr. Norton that the marriage of one Mr. Cramm "has made a great noise here. But Pray why may not an old Man afflicted with the gout have the pleasure of a fine hand to rub his feet and warm his flannels? Comfortable amusement you will say for a girl of fifteen, but she is to have a chariot and there is to be no Padlock but upon her mind."

Mrs. Goosley expresses herself as glad that Mrs. Norton has grown so fat. "If," she says archly, "you had not told me, it was by Drinking Porter, should have suspected it was owing to some other cause which commonly had that effect upon her in Virginia" . . . "I wish," Mrs. Goosley continues, "I could get some Porter. Would try the effects upon my thin Carcas. It might perhaps plump my face a little which at Present is almost as sharp as a Hatchet. Am very careful of myself for this spring has been as fatal to old women as to old cows. There is four gone off, within these six weeks."

When Mr. Norton invites her to make a visit to London in a ship of which one of her sons is captain, she replies that she is obliged for his kind invitation and

will, some day or other, surprise him. So—she adds—
"Pray have the Mill got in order that grinds old women
young."

In many of these letters there is talk of taxes, especially of the hated Stamp Act; and there is comment
upon William Pitt's and Edmund Burke's defense of the
American colonies.

People are concerned about smallpox, so prevalent
in London. It is too bad that Aunt Turner is suffering
from "St. Anthony's Fire," and what a misfortune that
Colonel Tucker's six warehouses and his wharf were
struck by lightning and burnt down.

Occasionally the letters contain good wishes on the
occasion of a marriage: there is comment that "A vir-
tuous woman is ever a blessing to a Man. Others are
nothing better than a Moth in a garment."

And these letters never forget the perils of the sea.
Bills of lading declare so many hogsheads of tobacco,
"Shipped by the Grace of God." Captains are listed as
"Master under God for this present Voyage . . . bound
by God's Grace for the port of London." The documents conclude, "And so God send the good ship to her
desired port in Safety. Amen."

The *Virginia Gazette,* printed in Williamsburg,
made its first appearance in August, 1736, and for years
it was the only newspaper south of the Potomac. It was
a weekly, representing itself as containing the "Freshest
Advices Foreign and Domestick." The foreign advices

mean nothing now. But the pages devoted to domestic affairs reflect the current of human living.

Births are recorded, and marriages. A young gentleman of fine Estate is wed to a young Lady of Beauty. A gentleman of twenty-three marries a "Sprightly old Tit of eighty-five, possessed of a fortune of three thousand pounds." A grey bobtailed horse, branded on one buttock "XX" and on the other "R" has disappeared, and along with him a white flea-bitten mare, with switch tail and long mane. Runaway slaves and fugitive indentured servants are advertised, with reward offered for their recovery.

A group of such indentured servants escapes in a longboat; among them a man wearing a dark wig, a red Daffil coat and blue cloth breeches; a lusty fat Englishwoman in gold-laced hat and brown Holland gown." There is missing also a convict servant man, bowlegged, with the "Picture of our Saviour on the Cross" tattooed on one of his arms. This man's apparel is said to be uncertain, as he has stolen various sorts of clothing. His name, too, is uncertain, since he has the habit of changing it. Also he is a "sly subtle fellow who pretends to be a Scotchman, but *is* an Irishman."

Among the missing slaves is a Negro called Cajar, a man with a "downcast look and a voice that sounds as if coming out of a tree." And there is an "outlandish negro named George who plays exceedingly on the banjo." There are occasionally even eloping wives, whose husbands place announcements in the *Gazette* to the effect that said husbands will pay no debts of said wives' contracting.

The owners of stallions advertise largely in the *Gazette*, for Virginia is interested in the breeding of horses. One such notice reads: "Merry Tom stands at my house, and covers mares at a guinea the leap, or five pounds the season." Turning the pages you see these advertisements appearing over and over; then suddenly ceasing. And you wonder . . . was that servant man of uncertain name and clothing who pretended to be a Scotchman but was really an Irishman, the man with the picture of Christ on the Cross tattooed on his arm, was he caught and returned to his master? And what happened to the longboat in which the lusty fat Englishwoman was escaping? And that white flea-bitten mare with the switch-tail, what became of her? The Negro whose voice sounded as if coming from a tree? The outlandish George who played exceedingly on the banjo? And how many pedigreed colts were sired by Merry Tom?

The advertisements appear, reappear in several issues of the paper, and then are seen no more.

It records also the passage of laws, and the meting out of punishment for crime: hanging is the penalty for housebreaking, horse stealing, and murder; for felony men and women are burnt in the hand. And it lists arriving and departing ships: sometimes a sinister slave ship has come from Guinea, or a sloop from the West Indies, with a cargo of rum, sugar, and tropical fruits.

In the columns of the *Gazette* you read, too, the disasters of the day: how, in the absence of the master of a house, three Indians came and killed his wife and children and set fire to his home. You read of the loss of ships at sea. Poor Catherine Rathell, who piqued herself on carrying goods of the Newest Taste, sailed for England upon a ship which never reached its haven.

# CHAPTER NINE

# Duke of Gloucester Street

IT was when the New World was still young that a youthful giant rode into Williamsburg. He was only twenty-one, and Governor Dinwiddie had sent for him.

Although he had been to Williamsburg before, he was not a familiar figure in the capital, for his home was on the Potomac. Yet because he was so immensely tall and because, even in a country of fine horsemen, he stood out as a magnificent rider, people must have gazed admiring, curious perhaps to know who was this young centaur with the frank cheerful face who rode down Duke of Gloucester Street.

The street runs almost due east and west, with the College of William and Mary at its western end and three-quarters of a mile away, at its eastern end, the Capitol. It is a wide gracious street with a sweet dignity all its own. Midway between Capitol and college is Raleigh Tavern, and beyond, on the other side of the Palace Green, Bruton Parish Church lifts a high spire, while facing the green, imposing and stately, the Governor's Palace stands among its gardens.

And the governor had sent for this young giant who came now riding down sandy unpaved Duke of Gloucester Street upon that long-ago October day. Out of all Virginia the governor had selected George Washington to execute a difficult and dangerous commission.

And since each of us is inseparable from what has gone before, this young man's past rode with him into Williamsburg.

He was only eleven when his father died, and he had early understood that he must support himself. Lawrence, his stepbrother, who was the eldest of the family, had been sent to England for his education, but after the father's death there had been no money for such advantages; not even enough for the college at Williamsburg. Therefore, if young George Washington was to have an education he knew that he must make the most of every chance that came his way. Thus he studied hard when there was opportunity for schooling.

At fourteen he was filling his copybook with whatever appeared to him desirable knowledge: geometrical definitions, the form for a promissory note, for a bill of exchange, a tobacco receipt, a bail bond, a servant's indenture, a deed of gift, a land lease, a Virginia land patent, a will, exercises in surveying, and one hundred and ten "Rules of Civility and Decent Behaviour in Company and Conversation"—all set down in a small, neat, round hand.

"Associate yourself with men of good quality . . . for 'tis better to be alone than in bad company. . . . Undertake not what you cannot perform . . . be careful to keep your promise . . . be not hasty to believe flying reports to the disparagement of any. . . . Let your recreations be manful . . . when a man does all he can, though it succeeds not well, blame not him that did it. . . . Keep alive in your breast that little spark of celestial fire called conscience."

These were among the Rules of Civility, carefully copied in Washington's notebooks.

He copied also a poem called "True Happiness."

> These are the things which once Possess'd,
> Will make a life that's truly bless'd.
>
> .        .        .        .        .
>
> Round a warm Fire, a pleasant Joke
> With chimney ever free from Smoke.
>
> .        .        .        .        .
>
> A quiet Wife, a quiet Soul,
> A mind as well as body whole,
> Prudent simplicity, Constant Friends,
> A diet which no art commends.
>
> .        .        .        .        .
>
> Possess'd of these all else defy,
> And neither wish nor fear to Die.

The contents of the youthful Washington's note-books are the essence of his personality and his philosophy.

In his early life he spent much time with his step-brothers, Lawrence and Augustine, on their plantations, and he apprenticed himself to the official surveyor of the county. Lawrence gave him practical experience in surveying his own property on the plantation, which he had named Mount Vernon, in honor of Admiral Vernon under whom he had fought at Cartagena. And when George was sixteen he went with his friend, George Fairfax, over the Blue Ridge and into the Shenandoah wilderness, to survey part of that vast tract of some five million acres which had descended to Lord Fairfax as a grant made by Charles II to his grandfather.

And none of all this would have come about but

for Lawrence who was married to a cousin of his Lordship. Lawrence gave him his opportunity; George himself won the friendship of the observant worldly-wise old lord.

Looking back at them across the years they make a charming picture, the old lord and young George Washington. They were both tall, both with a natural majesty of bearing, both bold horsemen, both devoted to hunting. But George was a slender, callow, chestnut-haired youth, with steady blue-grey eyes spaced far apart, and looking at you straight; his Lordship, aquiline-nosed, mature, and experienced, and the finished product of London society in the eighteenth century. People said Lord Fairfax had come out to Virginia to remain a bachelor through life because of a woman who on the eve of marriage had cast him off for the glittering prospect of a ducal coronet.

This Lord Fairfax was part of George Washington's education, as his brother Lawrence was part of it, and the surveyor with whom he had worked, and the Rules of Civility, and the friends he made when he stayed with Lawrence at Mount Vernon; among them his Lordship's Fairfax cousins, living near by on their estate, Belvoir; especially his friend was George Fairfax and the eighteen-year-old girl he had just married—beautiful gay Sally Cary, whose father had a plantation on the lower James and a house in Williamsburg.

When George Washington was nineteen he went with Lawrence to Barbados. Lawrence had consumption, and a winter in Barbados was recommended. But there George came down with smallpox, while Lawrence realized that for himself death was so near that he was beyond being benefited by climate. And since he must die, he would die in Virginia.

Before George was twenty-one he had inherited Mount Vernon, and had been appointed adjutant general of northern Virginia, with the title of major.

This was the past that rode with him into Williamsburg on the last day of October in the year 1753.

Out of that past, like fixed stars, stood the memory of Lawrence, the figure of his old Lordship, and of Sally Cary, wife to George Fairfax; Sally with dark hair brushed back from her long slender face, and her straightforward eyes looking from beneath eyebrows drawn with unfaltering precision; Sally Cary Fairfax, slim, aristocratic, brilliant, presiding with wit and grace as the young hostess of Belvoir.

All this made up the past, and now George Washington, riding down Duke of Gloucester Street in obedience to a summons from Governor Dinwiddie—was riding into the future. . . .

There was trouble, the governor told him, on Virginia's Ohio frontier. Yes, everyone knew that. Virginia claimed the territory. So did the Ohio Company, in which the Washingtons and Dinwiddie were shareholders. So also did France. The fur trade with the Indians of the region was immensely profitable, and Governor Dinwiddie would send a letter to the French commander on the frontier, three hundred miles away through wilderness, warning the French not to encroach upon Virginia's possessions. The messenger who was to carry this letter must bring back a reply; he must also win the friendship of the Indian tribes of the district.

And stout, red-faced, white-wigged Governor Dinwiddie put into young George Washington's hands that letter, written in the name of his Majesty, the king.

In January—two months later—Washington rode again into Williamsburg, bringing to Governor Dinwiddie the French commander's reply.

He had journeyed through trackless wilderness in freezing rain and snow. When his horse was too exhausted any longer to carry a rider, he had traveled on foot, gun in hand and a pack on his back, adapting himself to forest life, wearing a hunting shirt and moccasins. Along the way he had made speeches to the Indians on behalf of the British king. He had met the savage queen, Aliquipa, winning her with gifts of a matchcoat and a bottle of rum. She preferred the rum. This queen, he says, was "old and fat, as wrinkled as a frosted persimmon. She smoked a pipe and had a tomahawk in her belt . . . I did not think that she would be a comfortable partner in the marriage state."

Washington made notes and maps of the region which he delivered to the governor in Williamsburg, together with the French commander's letter which stated emphatically that France claimed the Ohio frontier as her own territory to which the British had no right.

And in April Governor Dinwiddie dispatched Washington again; this time at the head of a detachment of soldiers.

When he returned once more to report to the governor at Williamsburg he had experienced victory and defeat.

From New England to Virginia the colonies were alarmed by the defeat. Benjamin Franklin's *Gazette* published a cartoon of a rattlesnake cut into segments, with the caption "Join or Die." And General Braddock came out from England to Virginia with an army of British regulars; the French and Indian War was launched. In London General Braddock's frivolous set were saying that the general's only qualification to conduct a war against American aborigines was that his bald head prevented his being scalped.

But Braddock was to accomplish one great thing: under him the colonies were to act in unison; he was to join together the pieces of the rattlesnake. As for victory, he believed it to be certain. The scarlet coats of his regulars were bright, they maneuvered with military precision, scorning to fire, like Indians, from the shelter of tree or rock. Of course victory was certain: he had no doubt of that. Still, he would take George Washington, as his aide-de-camp: the young man knew the territory and might be of use.

Before his departure for the frontier a dinner was given to General Braddock in Williamsburg. One of the men present wrote of meeting there a certain Major Washington; about twenty-three, "comely and dignified," possessed of "wit, judgment and self-reliance . . . He strikes me as of an extraordinary and exalted character . . . destined, in my opinion, to make no inconsiderable figure in the country."

In early June Braddock led his army northwest, and from camp along the route Washington sent back a letter to Sally Fairfax—Mrs. George Fairfax of Belvoir. It is a winning letter of humility.

When he last had the happiness of seeing her, he says, she had spoken of wishing to hear of his safe arrival, charged with the responsibility of a trunk of money. But she had added that this information might be sent to her in a letter to someone else. Washington writes that he has inferred this to be a "gentle rebuke," a polite way of forbidding his correspondence with her. He could but think this, remembering that he had not found it possible to "engage one moment" of her attention. If it were true that she did not wish to correspond with him, then she must forgive his writing, must excuse it, on the ground that he was so elated at his successful arrival. But if, after all, he had been mistaken in his "fearful apprehension" . . . how easy it would be for her to remove his suspicions and make him "happier than the day is long" by honoring him with a correspondence, which he feels she had once partly promised to do.

In July he sent to his brother, John, a letter full of the youthful, impetuous fire of his twenty-three years. "We have been scandalously beaten by a trifling body of men . . . I had four bullets in my coat, and two horses shot under me, yet escaped unhurt, although death was leveling my companions on every side."

And to the governor he wrote that the regulars had stampeded in panic. Their "dastardly behavior exposed their officers and all who tried to do their duty to almost certain death."

But their officers had fought "with incomparable bravery" and the Virginia companies had "behaved like men and died like soldiers . . . of three companies scarce thirty left alive" . . . and General Braddock had been shot through the lung and had died in three days' time.

And those soldiers from the various colonies who were with Braddock took away the memory of the tall young Virginian who had fought so gallantly that lost battle.

It has been written of this phase of Washington's career: "These men were young—many of them of his own age and less—ardent and brave, loving high courage. They had seen a shining valor and honor before which their petty sectional jealousies fled like wraiths. They carried the name of George Washington home with them to every quarter. In their splendid enthusiasm for him was the seed of American unity which would flower about him a score of years later."

The British regulars, too, must have been impressed by Washington the soldier; so that in the American Revolution there were men on both sides who remembered.

It was on a visit home to Mount Vernon that he wrote again to his neighbor, Sally Fairfax. A servant had reported that Mrs. Fairfax was expecting a seamstress, and Washington writes to ask whether, if he sent over some material, "Miss Nancy," the seamstress, would make him some shirts. He will send linen and cambric, with "a shirt to measure by." The shirt fits "tolerably well," but he would have the new wristbands somewhat narrower, and the ruffles deeper by half an inch. He will be obliged if Miss Nancy will do him the favor to get suitable thread and buttons, as he has forgotten to procure them himself. And he is sorry to give Mrs. Fairfax the trouble of directing the making. Evidently his brother's wife is no longer at Mount Vernon, and he is again a womanless man.

So, at intervals, Colonel Washington returned to tidewater Virginia, to his friends at Belvoir on the Potomac, and to the capital at Williamsburg. And then he is again silent in the wilderness.

Finally, exhausted by anxiety and exposure, he comes in the autumn of 1757 to Mount Vernon, and from there he sends a messenger with a letter to Sally Fairfax. He has been three months seriously ill, and he writes to borrow her receipt book that he may instruct his servants to prepare such food as the doctor has ordered; and he would be grateful, too, for materials to make jellies, for a pound of tea, and a bottle or two of wine.

It is a touching letter, from a man alone in his illness.

In the early spring he is able to ride down to Williamsburg. He breaks the journey by spending the night with his friends, the Chamberlynes, near York River ferry. The Chamberlynes happen to have a house guest: the young widow, Martha Custis. Of course, George Washington knows who Martha Custis is; "Martha Dandridge that was," as the Virginians quaintly express it.

Martha Dandridge had been introduced to Williamsburg society at just about the time Sally Cary had married George Fairfax and come to live at Belvoir. The beaux had singed their wings in Martha's dainty beauty as they had in Sally's radiance.

Looking today at the portraits of Martha and Sally, Martha is as quaint and sweet as a faded valentine, while Sally is of that timeless distinction which in every age seems modern, for her beauty is of a rare simplicity, without dated furbelows.

The two women had both been flames, attracting bevies of suitors. Then Sally had chosen young George Fairfax, and Martha had taken Daniel Parke Custis— Evelyn Byrd's cousin—a rich man twice Martha's age.

Now Mr. Custis was dead, leaving Martha a wealthy widow with two small children.

And Martha Custis, like everyone in Virginia, knew about George Washington; that he had had two horses shot under him, and four bullets in his coat; and that, though he was only twenty-six, he'd been made commander in chief of all the forces in Virginia.

He must have appeared hugely tall on that spring day when he greeted the little widow Custis at the Chamberlynes' house on York River; tall in his uniform and his laurels; and she a tiny creature.

Then he had been very ill; surely lonely without a woman to care for him; a lonely great man.

The Martha Custis of the portrait wears her hair combed back from an oddly childish face. It is hard to believe her a few months older than Washington; hard to believe that she had had four children, and known the sorrow of burying two of them in Bruton churchyard. Men undoubtedly found such a woman appealing.

So they met—Washington and Martha Custis—in an hour of mutual need, the lonely soldier and the little widow.

People said that it was love at first sight. Certainly it was need at first sight.

George Washington stayed the night at the Chamberlynes' and rode the next day to Williamsburg.

On his way back to the frontier where he was determined to plant the British flag, removing forever the banner of France, he visited his little widow in her own home—the White House on the Pamunkey River; and when he resumed his journey, soldier and widow were engaged to be married.

Along the way he sent her a letter:

"We have begun our march for the Ohio. A courier is starting for Williamsburg and I embrace the opportunity to send a few lines to one whose life is now inseparable from mine. Since that happy hour when we made our pledges to each other my thoughts have been continually going to you as to another Self. That an all-powerful Providence may keep us both in safety is the prayer of your ever faithful and affectionate friend."

Two months later, in camp at Fort Cumberland, he was writing again to Mrs. George Fairfax. He begins his letter "Dear Madam" (Did he never call her by the fascinating little name of "Sally"?).

"Dear Madam: Yesterday I was honored with your short but very agreeable favor . . . How joyfully I catch at the happy occasion of renewing a correspondence which I feared was disrelished on your part."

Sally Fairfax has written of his engagement to Martha Custis. Alluding to what she has said of this, he writes: " 'Tis true. I profess myself a votary of love . . . and further I confess that this lady is known to you. Yes, Madam, as well as she is to one who is too sensible of her charms to deny the Power whose influence he feels he must ever submit to.

"I feel the force of her amiable beauties in the recollection of a thousand tender passages that I could wish to obliterate, till I am bid to revive them. But experience, alas, sadly reminds how impossible this is. . . .

"You have drawn me, dear Madam, or rather I have drawn myself, into an honest confession of a simple Fact. Misconstrue not my meaning; doubt it not, nor expose it. The world has no business to know the object of my love, declared in this manner to you, when I want to conceal it. One thing, above all things in this world I wish to know, and only one person of your acquaintance can solve me that, or guess my meaning. . . . I dare believe you are as happy as you say, I wish I was happy also. Mirth, good humor, ease of mind, and —what else?—cannot fail to render you so. . . ."

These are the phrases which stand out from the letter. You can picture Washington's tall figure bent over the paper, writing perhaps by a fluttering candle-flame at the end of a day's march; its light touching his chestnut hair, and his skin bronzed by sun and wind; his huge hand grasping the quill with which he tries to set down what is in his heart. He is by nature so straightforward, so simple, and what he would say demands a delicate subtlety. It must have taken long to put it into those hesitant words.

Yet they tell the story.

He is engaged to the little widow Custis. She is vivacious, pretty, and vastly affectionate; Martha, his "dear Patsy," who needs a man to look after her. They have not one material care, he and Martha, for Lawrence has left him Mount Vernon, and since he was sixteen he has earned a living at his trade as surveyor; to that he has now added military distinction. As for

Martha Custis, she is in her own right one of the richest women in Virginia.

His thoughts go continually to Martha, "as to another Self" . . . her life is now "inseparable" from his.

But, an honest realist always, he will not deceive himself. He will not deny that Sally was the bright inaccessible sun in his sky; he will not deny the beauty and charm to which he must ever submit, or the memory of "a thousand tender passages" which, though he would forget, he must remember. He accepts this fate with dignity and sincerity. If his letter means what it appears to mean, it tells a story beautiful and innocent. You feel that if Sally Fairfax had loved him the letter would never have been written, that he felt her so secure in devotion to her husband as to make it possible for him thus to write of a love such as a troubadour might feel for some shining lady forever beyond his reach.

Just what she replied to this letter, no one knows, but two weeks later he is writing again: "Do we still misunderstand the meaning of each other's Letters? . . . I think it must appear so, 'though I would feign hope the contrary as I cannot speak plainer without—

"But I'll say no more and leave you to guess the rest."

Then he leaves the subject, to write of the campaign against the French and their Indians.

George and Martha were married in January of the year 1759, in the bride's home, on the Pamunkey River.

Martha wore white brocaded silk into which was woven a glistening silver thread. The brocade was draped to show an embroidered satin petticoat. Her feet were in purple slippers trimmed with silver lace, and for jewels she wore necklace and earrings and bracelets of pearls. Colonel Washington was in citizen's dress of blue cloth, with an embroidered waistcoat of white satin. There were gold buckles at his knees and on his shoes; his hair was powdered, and he carried a dress sword.

And as you look upon them—the majestic military bridegroom and his pretty little bride in her wedding furbelows—you are convinced that she will be happy in her new life; for a woman—or a nation—might trustfully give her hand into the keeping of George Washington, confident of contentment and security.

The couple went to Williamsburg to spend their honeymoon in Martha's town house.

And when the House of Burgesses convened in the spring, Washington was among its members, elected from the county of Fairfax. When he first took his place in the Capitol at the eastern end of Duke of Gloucester Street, the speaker of the House announced the gratitude of the Assembly to Colonel George Washington "for his brave and steady behaviour, from the first Encroachments and Hostilities of the French and their Indians, to his Resignation after the happy Reduction of Fort Duquesne."

And those who were present say that when Washington rose to acknowledge the honor, he so blushed and stammered that the speaker considerately came to his relief: "Sit down, Mr. Washington, your modesty is equal to your valour; and that surpasses the power of any language I possess."

Thomas Jefferson decided to send himself to college. One of his reasons was that at home there was so much company that it interfered with his studies. He lived with his widowed mother at Shadwell, a plantation on the road to Williamsburg; and people on the way to and from the capital always stopped at Shadwell. And, Jefferson's father being dead, it fell upon him as the eldest son to act as host, and at the same time more or less to bring himself up. Now, at seventeen, he decided to go to college. Study there would not be interrupted by the constant demands of hospitality. Also, he thought, at college he would make "a more universal acquaintance."

So it happened that, some twelve months after George and Martha Washington's honeymoon in Williamsburg, gawky young Jefferson came to Duke of Gloucester Street and entered himself as a student at the College of William and Mary.

On his way from Shadwell he stopped to spend the Christmas holidays in Hanover at the home of Colonel Dandridge. And he met there a strange man who was neighbor to the colonel: a gaunt shabby man, with brilliant eyes, deep set in a thin sallow face. People were never able to agree on the color of these eyes; one saying they were light blue, another calling them hazel, another grey.

The passion of this man's life, as Jefferson saw him on that Christmas holiday, appeared to be for fiddling, dancing, and pleasantry. Jefferson liked all that too, and he, the youth of seventeen, and Patrick Henry, a man some seven years older, immediately became friends. Patrick Henry was in fact the gay heart of the party. His was a spirit that could rise above personal disaster;

he happened to be bankrupt at the time, but what place had bankruptcy at a party?

The small country store in which Henry's father set him up had failed. Then he tried farming, working in the fields beside a couple of Negro slaves. Then he made another attempt at storekeeping. People said the store went bankrupt because Henry couldn't resist giving credit to anybody who wanted it. But what with bad debts, and what with his running off all the time to fish or hunt, how could he have expected to succeed? Henry, they said, seemed to love idleness for its own sake. It was too bad, for no man was fonder of his wife and children than Patrick Henry, but there were times when he couldn't seem to stick by his work. They told how he would lie all day under the shade of a tree overhanging the river. True, he had a fishing rod, but it seemed to make no difference to him whether or not there was a nibble at his line. It seemed enough for him just to be idle. And "his great delight was to put on his hunting-shirt, collect a parcel of overseers and such like people, and spend weeks together hunting in the 'piney' woods, camping at night, and cracking jokes round a light-wood fire."

In the store Henry was more interested in talking to people than he was in selling them goods. He loved to listen and he loved to talk, to make people laugh or cry, to make their blood "to run cold or their hair to stand on end." It was as if the human heart was an instrument on which he played, making it express whatever emotion he liked.

People would come to the store just to hear Patrick Henry tell stories in the deep strong voice which unerringly stirred their emotions.

In that country store, Henry acquired little by little the gift of speaking in such words as could not fail to reach the simplest heart.

Yes, everybody liked "Pahtrick" Henry; so in those days did Virginians pronounce his name.

Thomas Jefferson had reasoned that in going to college he would have a "more universal acquaintance." And already even before he arrived in Williamsburg he had made a friend of Patrick Henry.

Henry confided to his new young friend that he thought he'd be a lawyer. He'd teach himself law; when he felt he was ready for his examination he'd be coming to Williamsburg, and then he'd see Jefferson, he'd look him up.

The second of Jefferson's new friends was Dr. Small, the Scotch professor of mathematics at William and Mary. This man, Jefferson always said, "fixed the destinies of my life." Dr. Small was cultivated, broadminded, and of aristocratic manner. He was at once attracted by his brilliant young pupil and made him his close friend. Through Dr. Small, Jefferson met George Wythe, the great lawyer, and Governor Fauquier, a man distinguished in mind and manner.

These men were young Jefferson's intimate friends, for, like George Washington, he had the power of attracting the best always, and the wisdom to absorb what the best had to teach. They dined familiarly together, Jefferson and his friends.

Then three months after Colonel Dandridge's Christmas party, Patrick Henry came to Williamsburg for his law examination. "I will be a lawyer," he had said, lightly setting his genius to the prodigious task. And now here he was, calling upon Jefferson as he had promised; winning admission to the bar, and then going home with a license to practice.

Jefferson was popular with the young people of Williamsburg, as well as with older men. He became infatuated with pretty Rebecca Burwell, christening her Belinda; and when that young lady married someone else, he set down in his "commonplace book" the cynical quotation: "O Zeus, why hast thou established women, a curse deceiving men in the light of the sun?" He was convinced that his disappointed springtime love was an eternal matter from which he would never recover.

But Belinda did not move him so deeply as to interfere with study, or with reading; for he worked hard and he consumed books like a devouring flame: Tully and Seneca, Epictetus, Euripides, Socrates, Milton, Homer, Shakespeare, Swift, Cervantes, Locke. . . .

He graduated from William and Mary and began the study of law under his friend, George Wythe. For exercise and amusement he was fond of horseback, or at dusk he would lay down his books and run a mile. Then there was always dancing. Young and old danced. When there were balls in Williamsburg everybody went and everybody danced. When the Assembly was in session, if you looked in upon a ball in the long gracious Apollo Room of Raleigh Tavern you might see among the dancers Colonel Washington's tall graceful figure, perhaps shabby Patrick Henry in Williamsburg on law business, Fairfaxes, Blands, Lees, Carters, Carys, Randolphs, and the youth, Thomas Jefferson, tall with thick red hair, and light hazel eyes.

The fiddlers played; such pieces as "Kiss Me Early," "Money Musk," and "The Buff Coat." The dances were courtly minuets, gavottes, the Virginia reel, the hearty jig, and the hornpipe. And the candlelight flickered upon men as gorgeous in color and elegant brocade as their women.

These Virginians loved the gaiety of their young New World; but deeper than that lay their almost mystic devotion to the soil; it was the plantation that was to them the very heart of life, to which they eagerly returned when the Assembly adjourned.

> They loved their land because it was their own,
> And scorned to give aught other reason why.

With this profound love George Washington loved Mount Vernon. "To see plants rise from the earth," he said, "and flourish by the superior skill and bounty of the laborer, fills a contemplative mind with ideas which are more easy to be conceived than expressed."

It was his habit to record in a set of notebooks the details of his Mount Vernon life; setting down the items briefly:

Surveyed a water-course.
Began 'stilling cyder.
Began to cut Timothy.
Put new girders in my Mill where they had sunk.
Rid to Muddy Hole.
Fox hunting with Lord Fairfax.
Home alone all day.
Directed the running of a fence.

Exceedingly hot. Went to Alexandria to see the tragedy of Douglas played.

Colo. and Mrs. Fairfax dined and lodged here.

Rid out with my hounds.

The new negro, Cupid, ill of pleurisy; brought him home in a cart for better care.

Rid round and examined wheat fields.

Mrs. Washington has measles. Mrs. Fairfax called on her. Wind cold and high.

Went ducking. Killed two mallards and five bald faces.

A dance at Gadsby's Tavern in Alexandria.

Fox hunting. Catch'd two foxes.

Dined with the Fairfaxes at Belvoir.

Snowing all day but not very fast . . . played at cards.

Beeves put up to be fattened.

Finished corking my vessel.

The Oyster man behaving in a dastardly manner at my landing.

[What on earth could the Oyster man have done that was so "dastardly"?]

The diaries show Washingtons and Fairfaxes, so frankly, so serenely, happy together, with their visits, their dinners and dances, and their ridings to hounds that you wonder if Washington has forgotten that he once wrote to Sally Fairfax: "I dare believe you are as happy as you say. I wish I were happy also." Has he forgotten? Or is it that through his philosophy that one may not expect "perfection to fall to the share of mortals" he has come to know that, while he cherishes his bright dream-love, he may at the same time live in loyal devoted content with his Martha?

Certainly there is no question of the happiness and devotion of the life he and his Martha lived together.

Through his letters and diaries there runs a constant protecting care of her, and there is a tradition that she would speak of him as her "old man," and when in a coaxing mood she would stand twisting a button on his coat, and looking up into his face. He is concerned with every detail of her life, with the furnishing of their bedroom and with the clothes he orders for her from London—silks and laces, and shoes of the smallest fives. He calls her children the "little progeny," and in his thought for them you see how he yearned for children of his own. He buys "little books for children beginning to read," and for Miss Custis when she is five years old he orders a "fashionable dressed baby doll."

When you see Washington at Mount Vernon you feel that he has achieved all that the poem on "True Happiness" listed, as things which "Once Possess'd, will make a life that's truly bless'd." A "quiet Wife" and a "quiet Soul" are his; and from daybreak to dark he is busy in riding over his lands superintending every detail of the plantation, making improvements, and trying experiments in agriculture. Wearing a big white straw hat, and carrying an umbrella tied to his saddle, he thus rides through his fields.

Reading Washington's own words, the strange sanctimonious haze in which others—never himself— have sometimes enveloped him dissolves, and he stands forth so masculine a man that he comes to you with the smell of freshly turned earth, with the odor of a gun just fired, with the scent of the moist feathers of the bird which a dog brings in his mouth to the hunter. You smell wet wood, smoldering over a forest campfire, and you breathe the new-mown fragrance which a horse exhales in warm summer air.

In his own uncensored speech Washington emerges a man of dynamic vigor.

At the beginning he had to work over his spelling. You see his mastery of it, from the time of that first journal of a surveying expedition when he wrote that they started on "Fryday" and at night they slept under a "thread bear blanket with double its weight of vermin."

Now and then his spelling reveals his pronunciation, as when he speaks of watching the Indians "daunce."

The simple stately dignity of style characteristic of him becomes, when necessary, vehement. There was that "dastardly" behavior of the Oyster man at his landing; and the man whom he calls "a thorough pac'd Rascall." . . . Of another he says that "a damneder scoundrel God Almighty never permitted to disgrace humanity." . . . And "How in God's name did my brother Samuel get himself so enormously in debt?" (That his brother Samuel was five times married may explain it). . . . A sum of money appropriated in wartime Washington describes as "but a flea-bite," compared with what was needed.

An editor of Washington's collected writings, with good but mistaken intentions, cut out such words as he thought unworthy of the colorless paragon he would have this forceful human Washington appear. Washington's "but a flea-bite" he altered to read "totally inadequate." "Rid" the editor changed to "rode," and so on. In the process Washington was denatured.

But now that the diaries and letters have been printed as they were written the man is at last unveiled.

He is not subtle; his humor is rather a sense of fun than of humor; his mind does not flash, it moves with a slow certainty; "the honestest man, I believe that ever adorned human nature," was the opinion of one who knew him well. And he was always human; loving intercourse with people, dancing, hunting, playing cards and billiards, devoted to the theater, and with a nice taste for dress; a man of gusto, with an immense zest for living; yet with a realization of values which made excess impossible. Rarely does a man know himself as Washington did; understanding the strength of his passions, the violence of which he was capable, the necessity for control of his emotions.

Yet for all that he knew of himself Washington had no notion that he was a great man; for his greatness was as the greatness of a mountain, or of the sea; a greatness unaware of itself.

Jefferson is more brilliant, more versatile, more widely cultivated, more charmingly companionable; Patrick Henry can shake your soul as it pleases him; but Washington—well, when quiet Colonel Washington leaves Williamsburg for Mount Vernon, Duke of Gloucester Street seems empty until he returns.

When you come so to know him, the very postage stamps and dollar bills which now perpetuate the modest wisdom of his face strangely quicken your heart, and suddenly he is alive again, the tall, quiet Virginian who fills you with confidence and courage.

In May iris and roses, mock oranges and magnolias bloom in the gardens along Duke of Gloucester Street. And it was in May that news of Parliament's passing the Stamp Act came to the burgesses in session in the Capitol of Williamsburg.

The Stamp Act would tax practically every business transaction. No will or deed, no insurance policy, no ship's clearance papers, would be legal without bearing the new stamps. Even newspapers and advertisements must carry them. The object was to raise money to pay for the costly French and Indian War; to support an armed British force in America; and for the protection of the colonies.

The Stamp Act was, of course, discussed in the House of Burgesses; among those present were Colonel Washington, Richard Henry Lee, Pendleton, Randolph, and Richard Bland, who, because of his knowledge of history, was called the Antiquary. And sitting for the first time was the new member, Patrick Henry, known now as the brilliant lawyer of Hanover County, but still a shabby ungainly figure, conspicuous among the other burgesses in the spectacular costume of their day.

Standing in the doorway listening to the debate was a lanky carrotheaded young man. And so it happened that Thomas Jefferson heard Patrick Henry make his famous speech.

The Stamp Act, Henry thundered, was tyranny: "Caesar had his Brutus! Charles, the first, his Cromwell! And George, the third—"

"Treason!" the burgesses shouted, at such mention of the king's name. "Treason!"

"George, the third"—Henry paused—"may profit

by their example. If this be treason, make the most of it."

He spoke, Jefferson said, as Homer wrote.

The flame of his oratory swept men off their feet. And Patrick Henry had become the Voice of the Revolution that was to be.

Henry had come to protest against the Stamp Act, and now that was done he would go home to Hanover. That same afternoon he was seen on Duke of Gloucester Street. He was dressed in rough buckskin breeches, he carried his saddlebags over his arm, and he was leading his horse, walking slowly as he talked to a friend who strolled beside him.

Then he mounted and rode home through the green forests of early summer.

Four years later it was again May, and again in the Capitol at the eastern end of Duke of Gloucester Street, the Assembly was in session.

Thomas Jefferson was now a practicing lawyer, and a member of the House of Burgesses.

Governor Fauquier was dead and the Right Honorable Baron de Botetourt, had taken his place.

The Stamp Act had been repealed, but Parliament had levied new taxes; taxes on paints, paper, glass, and tea imported into her American colonies.

The burgesses in Assembly now declared defiance of any but self-taxation; reluctantly Lord Botetourt dissolved the House, which proceeded to meet the next day at Raleigh Tavern in that Apollo Room so identified with festivity; and there they voted to boycott British goods so long as the revenue tax was in force.

Meanwhile, far away in Boston British troops were

now quartered on the town. It was told that the soldiers amused themselves by standing outside meetinghouses during hours of service and singing "Yankee Doodle." And that the Boston populace retaliated by shouting "Lobsters for sale!" when the redcoats appeared.

The Virginia burgesses went back to their plantations. Jefferson had begun the building of Monticello from designs which he made himself, and quite as though there had never been a Belinda, he fell in love with the bright auburn beauty and the musical talent of the ardent young widow, Martha Skelton, who lived near Williamsburg. Time passed, and Lord Botetourt died. Lord Dunmore was appointed Governor. Jefferson married Martha Skelton and took her to Monticello; and his garden notebook shows that, like Washington, he had an absorbing interest in agriculture. Martha Washington's daughter, Patsy Custis, died, and soon after George Fairfax went to England to look into property which he had just inherited. His wife, Sally Fairfax, went with him.

And in George Washington's diary there appears this item: "Colo. and Mrs. Fairfax have gone to England. Mrs. Washington and I went to Belvoir to see them take shipping."

That is all.

The next entry reads simply "Rid to Muddy Hole . . ."

Again it was spring, and the Virginia Assembly met in the Capitol at Williamsburg. They appointed the first of June as a day of fasting and prayer to express sympathy for Boston. England, indignant at the famous "tea party," had ordered the port closed. Governor Dunmore retaliated by dissolving Virginia's Assembly, which again moved serenely over to the Apollo Room of gay Raleigh Tavern.

An attack upon one of the colonies, it declared, was an attack upon all. The colonies decided to call a Continental Congress, to meet in Philadelphia, for the purpose of considering their position. A convention was summoned to Williamsburg to elect delegates.

Roger Atkinson, from his home on the Appomattox, wrote his brother-in-law, describing those delegates chosen to represent Virginia in that first Continental Congress:

"Richard Henry Lee," he says, is "as true a trout as ever swam, as staunch a hound as ever ran."

Peyton Randolph has "knowledge and experience. . . . Above all things a man of "integrity and the Roman spirit."

Benjamin Harrison is not described, because so well known to the brother-in-law.

Edmund Pendleton "a humble religious man . . . also a very pretty smooth-tongued speaker."

Patrick Henry, "in religious matters a Saint, but the very Devil in Politicks—a son of Thunder . . . stern and steady in his country's cause."

Richard Bland, "staunch and tough as whit-leather" with "something of the look of musty old Parchments which he handleth and studieth much."

Colonel Washington, "a modest man but sensible and speaks little—in action cool, like a Bishop at his Prayers."

Roger Atkinson, writing freely and familiarly to his brother-in-law, says no word of whether a man was of wealth or of birth; though all the delegates were of fine and sturdy ancestry, and Bland, Randolph, Harrison, and Lee could trace their descent from the Cavalier William Randolph, who had emigrated to Turkey Island in James River, and his wife Mary Isham, back to the baronets of Northamptonshire, the powerful Scotch Earls of Murray, through the generations to William the Conqueror, and further still to the Saxon kings.

Of all this Roger Atkinson said nothing. What he thought important was that a man be true, stanch, stern and steady, learned and modest; that he possess good sense, judgment, experience, and above all, integrity.

And because these qualities were honored on the tidewater plantations of the young New World they were produced, which is not to say that there was no dishonesty, for then as now, mankind was mankind. But it is to say that in every age and place that which is most reverenced comes always into existence; where there is demand for "true trout" there always will be true trout.

# CHAPTER TEN

# New Rights

Normally Patrick Henry's figure slouched, his shoulders stooped, but as he spoke he gradually became erect. His face shone and his eyes. What color were his eyes—green or blue, grey or hazel? Men never agreed upon their color. As for his voice, it was magic in its effect on all who heard it.

So it was when Patrick Henry spoke at the convention in old St. John's Church in the city of Richmond, high on the hill above the rushing falls in James River.

It happened in the month of March, following the famous first Continental Congress. That Congress had sent to George III a Declaration of Colonial Rights, insisting upon a freedom to manage their own affairs which no colonies in the world had ever before demanded.

And now in Richmond, Patrick Henry was speaking in St. John's Church. The tolling bell which had summoned those who crowded the church was silent, and Patrick Henry was speaking:

"The war is inevitable! . . . let it come! . . . Is life so dear or peace so sweet as to be purchased at the price of chains and slavery? Forbid it, Almighty God! I know not what course others may take, but as for me, give me liberty, or give me death!"

There was deep silence when he sat down. Then the cry rose. "To arms!" . . .

"My dearest," Washington wrote from Philadelphia to Martha, "I am now set down to write you on a subject which fills me with inexpressible concern . . . when I reflect upon the uneasiness which I know it will give you. It has been determined in Congress that the whole army raised for the defence of the American cause shall be put under my care, and that it is necessary for me to proceed immediately to Boston to take upon me command of it.

"You may believe me, my dear Patsy, when I assure you in the most solemn manner that, so far from seeking this . . . I have used every endeavor in my power to avoid it, not only from an unwillingness to part with you and the family, but from a consciousness of its being a trust too great for my capacity. . . . It has been a kind of destiny that has thrown me upon this service . . . I shall feel no pain from the toil or the danger . . . my unhappiness will flow from the uneasiness I know you will feel from being left alone."

He wrote also to friends and relatives begging them to do all they could to cheer and comfort this "Patsy" whose well-being was constantly in his heart.

In June of the famous year 1776 Virginia voted herself a free and independent country, electing Patrick Henry her first governor. George Mason presented his immortal Bill of Rights, which was unanimously accepted, and in that same month Virginia adopted a constitution, and sent orders to her delegates at the second Continental Congress in Philadelphia, instructing them to introduce a resolution which would declare all the colonies free and independent.

Between the meeting of the first and second Congresses something had happened in the minds of men. America had begun by fighting for the rights of colonies; now America wanted independence based upon a right new in the world: the right of man to equality of opportunity in the pursuit of happiness.

❁

Richard Henry Lee—he who was described "as true a trout as ever swam"—presented to the Philadelphia Congress the resolution of independence which had been suggested by Virginia.

John Adams, of Massachusetts, seconded it. But, although all favored independence, still might it not be wiser to delay a little? Was it prudent to go so fast? For some weeks the Congress considered and debated.

Then, on the second of July, the resolution was passed.

Already a committee had been appointed, headed by Thomas Jefferson, to prepare a declaration of this independence.

The first three sections of the Declaration, Jefferson based upon George Mason's Bill of Rights—that new right of man to life, liberty, and the pursuit of happiness.

In the second section Jefferson stated America's charges against the British king.

This was followed by the Lee resolution that the colonies "solemnly publish and declare" that they "are, and of Right ought to be, Free and Independent States . . . absolved from all Allegiance to the British Crown."

The document closed with the pledge: "And for the support of this declaration . . . we mutually pledge to each other our lives, our fortunes and our sacred honor."

In the debate on the Declaration which Jefferson had presented, that important sentence was stricken out in which the British king was charged with "violating the most sacred rights of life and liberty in the person of a distant people who never offended him, captivating and carrying them into slavery" . . . suppressing "every legislative attempt to prohibit or restrain the execrable commerce."

Over and over again, ever since 1699, Virginia had tried to put a stop to the importing of slaves, but every attempt had been vetoed by the king.

Five years before the Revolution, a group of Virginia burgesses had resolved: "We will not import or bring into the Colony, either by sea or land, any slaves, or make sale of any . . . or purchase any . . . that may be imported by others . . . unless the same have been twelve months upon the continent." Among the signers of this resolution were the old familiar names of Peyton Randolph, Richard Bland, Edmund Pendleton, Richard Henry Lee, Thomas Jefferson, Benjamin Harrison, and George Washington.

Two years later Virginia once more sent a petition to the throne, beseeching permission to check this trade of "great inhumanity."

And the first clause of Virginia's constitution listed the king's protection of the slave trade as one of the reasons for separating from Great Britain.

But, to placate American shipping interests engaged in importing slaves, and those colonies of the Far South which stood out against its abolition, a similar clause was ruled out by the Congress at Philadelphia, leaving the question to be settled at a future date.

In its final form the Declaration of Independence was put to the vote of the delegates, John Adams, of Massachusetts, pleading eloquently in its favor.

On the evening of July fourth the Congress adopted the document, which in solemn, beautiful cadence expressed what then filled men's hearts. All over the land it was proclaimed with the firing of cannon and the ringing of bells.

And in the James River story this Declaration has a place because of the immortal part played in it by Virginia's sons.

Considering the question of equality, John Adams, ardent supporter of the Declaration, later wrote to his wife Abigail, setting forth his interpretation of its meaning: "By the law of Nature all men are men, and not angels—men, and not lions—men, and not whales—men, and not eagles—that is, they are of the same species; and this is the most that equality of Nature amounts to. . . . Equality is moral and political only, and means that all men are independent. But a physical inequality, an intellectual inequality of the most serious kind is established unchangeably by the author of Nature. . . . The precept, however, *do as you would be done by,* implies the real equality of Nature and of Christianity."

# CHAPTER ELEVEN

# Goody Bull and Her Daughter

IT had been years since he was in tidewater Virginia and now at last he was returning.

"It's General Washington!" people cried, their voices adoring. "It's General Washington . . . and his army."

And they wondered where the battle was to be.

But the passing soldiers could say nothing of the general's plans, for they themselves did not know. Actually they had been kept in such complete ignorance that there had been high betting on whether the general planned a siege of New York or whether he would lead them to Virginia. Yet their trust in him was so deep that wherever he led they would follow. Then they had been marched from New York across New Jersey and down into Virginia. At the same time Count Rochambeau was conducting the French forces, also down into Virginia.

Perhaps they were all going to Yorktown where the British commander, Cornwallis, had established his army. Perhaps General Washington, Rochambeau, and Lafayette would unite against Cornwallis.

Those who watched the marching men did not yet know that de Grasse was bringing up a fleet of twenty-eight French ships from the West Indies to Chesapeake Bay. For only bit by bit was Washington's scheme unfolded. Deep secrecy was necessary in order that de Grasse might shut off any aid to Cornwallis by water, while the combined armies joined in attacking him by land.

If this succeeded . . . But it must succeed!

Then—it was Washington's hope soon to go home, to return to the quiet pastoral plantation life which he so loved.

There would be no more the heartbreaking sight of Hessians, fat, fed mercenaries putting to the bayonet his ragged, hungry troops; no more treason; and no longer the ordeal of that propaganda by which the Tories had tried to poison the North against the South, forging letters containing insults to New England; letters hinting at a personal scandal so foul that he could not stoop to defend himself.

Every charge could be proved false, was one day to be proved false; yet the whispering campaign had continued.

In accepting the command of the American forces Washington had insisted upon serving without pay. And once, in the torment of what he had been made to suffer, he had exclaimed that not for fifty thousand pounds would he again subject himself to such an experience.

Yet he had gone on with a courage constant under every adversity, a man incapable, people said, of fear; "in action cool, like a Bishop at his Prayers," just as Roger Atkinson had written to his brother-in-law.

But when independence was won, how Washington would rejoice to return to the tranquillity of Mount Vernon; where he might dwell upon such memories as that Christmas night of snow and sleet, when in the floating ice crossing the Delaware he had led his soldiers to victory; to remember the great hour when news came that France had recognized the independence of the United States, and had signed the treaty of alliance. He would remember young Lafayette's delight. "We must have a grand noisy feu de joie!" he said. Thirteen thundering guns had made the feu de joie, and the soldiers had shouted lustily for the King of France.

Lafayette—the Marquis de La Fayette. As long as he lived Washington's heart would go out to Lafayette in affection. He had come full of impetuous faith in the American cause; a redheaded, blue-eyed boy, not yet twenty. He had bought a ship and fitted it out himself. He had left his little seventeen-year-old wife whom he adored, and she was expecting a baby. He had left also wealth and position. "The moment I heard of America," he cried, "I loved her. The moment I heard she was fighting for freedom, I burnt with a desire to bleed for her."

And General Washington had learned to love him. They had met at a dinner in the general's honor, and Lafayette had not needed to be told which was General Washington; he knew him at once, he said, by the majesty of his face and figure, and by his kindly high-bred manners.

Washington in his simplicity wrote to this ardent boy that "It will ever constitute part of my happiness to know that I stand well in your opinion."

And Lafayette loved him, revered him, writing home to France of the "beauty of his character and his soul. No one else could keep the army and the revolution for six months."

The boy had been in every way a comfort, an officer whose courage and prudence could be relied on.

Yes, Lafayette was a memory to cherish in the sweet retirement of domestic life for which Washington longed.

When you see them together—General Washington and young Marquis de La Fayette—you are reminded of Lord Fairfax with his friend, the boy George Washington.

In the peace of that yearned-for retirement, Washington would not forget that every year when the army went into winter quarters his wife—his "dear Patsy"— had come to cheer him with talk of Mount Vernon, and of Jack Custis's wife and babies, sitting placidly knitting while she talked; knitting socks for his brave barefoot soldiers.

Memory of these soldiers would never pass; ragged, hungry regiments of men; with "Liberty or Death" embroidered on the hunting shirts which were their uniform, and on their banners the device of a coiled rattlesnake and above it the words "Don't Tread on Me." The slogan which, at the time of the French and Indian War, had been "Join or Die" had become "Don't Tread on Me."

Washington, on his way to Yorktown, marched through a land laid waste by the enemy.

Virginia's manhood had been fighting with the armies in the north and in the Carolinas. And how they had fought, how they could shoot, those men bred on the plantations and the frontiers of that Virginia which the tutor Fithian found a land of such gay good cheer. They had left Virginia defenseless when they went to join Washington's army. The British found her thus helpless when they sailed up James River to Westover, and thence proceeded overland to Richmond, burning and raiding as they went.

Jefferson had followed Patrick Henry as Virginia's governor and because Richmond, seated upon the navigable James River, was more central, more easily defended than Williamsburg, the capital had been moved to that city. But with the British invasion, the government had been forced to flee temporarily to Charlottesville, and then from Charlottesville to Staunton. And Richmond had been burned, as formerly Dunmore had burned Norfolk.

At last Lafayette had been sent to the protection of the stricken state. "The boy cannot escape me," Cornwallis said, marching fast upon his heels, and as he marched he also ravaged the land.

Now here was General Washington himself. "It's General Washington," people cried as he passed.

Since the Americans had taken the British "Yankee Doodle" for their own, making up verses which told the tale of the Revolution as it progressed, the British had abandoned it for a song called, "The World's Turned Upside Down." The words describe a quarrel between Goody Bull and her daughter. "Goody" was the name for a housewife, whose rank was not high enough to entitle her to be "Madam." And Goody Bull was, of course, England; her daughter represented the revolted American colonies.

> Goody Bull and her daughter together fell out,
> Both squabbled and wrangled and made a—rout.
> The daughter was sulky and wouldn't come to,
> And pray what in this case could the old woman do?

To the rhythm of drum and fife the American troops marched swiftly through Virginia to Williamsburg. And "Yankee Doodle" was their tune:

> Cornwallis, too, when he approached
> Virginia's Old Dominion,
> Thought he would soon her conqueror be;
> And so was North's opinion.
>
> .    .    .    .    .
>
> Yankee Doodle, keep it up,
> Yankee Doodle, Dandy. . . .
>
> .    .    .    .    .
>
> But our allies, to his surprise,
> The Chesapeake had entered
> And now, too late, he cursed his fate,
> And wished he ne'er had ventured.

For now at last all knew that de Grasse had arrived with his fleet in the Chesapeake, blocking the entrance to York River.

The general's plans were working out. When the allied forces marched from Williamsburg to Yorktown they outnumbered Cornwallis two to one, and there was no escape for him by water. He had fortified Yorktown, but it would not be possible for him to hold out long.

> And now too late he cursed his fate
> And wished he ne'er had ventured.

The drums and fifes were jubilant. The combined troops now surrounded Yorktown. Silently in the dark of night the soldiers threw up breastworks. At dawn they were cannonaded from the town, but with each day they moved nearer.

Within the little town there was smallpox and

fever. Cornwallis lacked fodder for the horses, which as the days passed were led one by one into the river and shot, their carcasses drifting down the stream.

And steadily the American line advanced; finally within six hundred yards. Now they were ready to begin the bombardment, and General Washington himself set off the first gun. Then for eight days and nights Yorktown was besieged.

Thacker described the scene as he saw it from the trenches: "bombshells were incessantly crossing each other's path in the air . . . clearly visible in the form of a black ball in the day, but in the night, each like a fiery meteor with a blazing tail . . . brilliant, ascending majestically from the mortar to a certain altitude, and gradually descending to the spot where they were destined to execute their work of destruction." Some of them "over-reaching the town fall into the river, throwing up columns of water like spouting monsters of the deep." Four British ships lying there were set on fire, their flames lighting the dark night.

At length Cornwallis sent out a white flag requesting a parley.

It was very quiet now that the delirium of bombardment had ceased. In this quiet Cornwallis prepared the terms of his surrender. And on the morning of October nineteenth Washington submitted those to which he would agree; on condition that they were signed by eleven o'clock, and that by two o'clock the garrison was surrendered.

In an avenue of men a mile long the allies waited, the French on one side, the Americans on the other; General Washington on horseback heading the Americans; Count Rochambeau heading the French. With the Americans were those three young men so loved and trusted by Washington—Lafayette, Hamilton, and Light-Horse Harry Lee.

Washington had named General Lincoln to receive the surrender. And at two o'clock the garrison came out, with General O'Hara at its head, representing Cornwallis, who was said to be ill. The procession moved slowly with colors furled and cased; marching to the time of the familiar song "The World's Turned Upside Down"; that song whose words tell the story of how Goody Bull and her daughter fell out. . . .

That "sweet retirement to domestic life" for which Washington longed seemed now soon to be his. But his glad triumph was saddened by the death of Jack Custis. Within a few days after the surrender Jack died, a victim of the hard conditions of the siege. He was Martha Washington's only remaining child, the only one left of the "little progeny": since he was six years old he had been as a son to Washington. "Dear Patsy" . . . she had been always such a fluttering nervous mother. He remembered how he had kept Jack's smallpox inoculation from her until he had recovered, so that she might not be anxious. And now he must go to her with the news of Jack's death. The general's greatest victory had come; come leading Sorrow by the hand.

But Mount Vernon was never to be childless, for Washington at once determined to take two of Jack's children—little Nelly Custis and George Washington Custis—to comfort the heart of his "Patsy."

# CHAPTER TWELVE

# "It Squints Toward Monarchy"

IT happened in a long drought which had parched and killed the young tobacco plants. The day was Sunday, the first of June; a hot bright day. The delegates who were to debate the Federal Constitution arrived in Richmond thickly powdered with the dust which their horses' hoofs had raised in clouds along the way. The dust was white, grey, or red, according to the section of Virginia from which the men had come. All day they had been arriving; on horseback, in gigs or phaetons.

One of those who had journeyed by gig came up from south of the James. He was driving himself. And this man, they say, was dressed in the homespun of his own loom, and the dust which covered him was brick-red.

They say, too, that as he drove his tall spare figure leaned forward in the gig, and that he seemed worn with travel; perhaps also worn with the anxiety concerning that battle which he was come to fight.

At the same time, from north of the James, another man was approaching, driven in a well-turned-out phaeton, and the dust which lay upon this man, upon his vehicle and his horse, was grey. Even before the phaeton stopped at the steps of Swan Tavern, and the traveler got out, you could see that he was lame, for he had crutches beside him. He was a tall man but his body was shrunken with age. Yet neither his age nor the fall from a horse which left him a cripple had taken from him the distinction of his bearing.

It was a little before sundown when these two men arrived at Swan Tavern, and on its steps met and greeted each other. The man who had arrived in the gig was Patrick Henry, the "Son of Thunder," come to oppose the Constitution. The man helped out of the phaeton and assisted up the steps was Edmund Pendleton, its ardent supporter.

Ever since Henry's speech against the Stamp Act, both he and Pendleton had played a great part in the momentous history of their time. Now they were come to Richmond as delegates to the Convention which was to decide whether Virginia would accept the Constitution which would change the United States from a mere league of independent states to a Union. Before the Revolution the American colonies had been isolated, one from another. The war had temporarily related them, and they had then formed themselves into a confederation of separate states. But their league had been a ship without a captain, for the confederation had no president, and no real power. It could make laws but could not enforce them. It was helpless before the problems which crowded upon it. The states must pay off their debts, must establish credit, must have treaty relations with the rest of the world. Without any central authority this was impossible and in many parts of the country liberty had become license. Europe laughed at the chaos in America.

"Let us act as a nation!" Washington cried. "Let

us have a government by which our lives, liberties and properties will be secured."

Then, in that year when in England his friend George Fairfax died, and Sally wrote her sister-in-law that weeping had destroyed her sight—in that year a Congress met in Philadelphia to discuss what could save the new states from ruin. Washington had presided at that Congress and a Constitution had been drafted which was now to be discussed in Richmond.

In all the states opinions were divided. Men had fought for liberty. Many had died. Whatever Constitution was adopted must preserve the liberty so hardly won.

The Congress was creating something new in the world. Its difficulties had been great. There was the question of abolishing the slave trade. Washington had long said he was "principled against slavery," that he wanted to see it abolished, but that the "one proper and effectual mode by which this can be accomplished is by legislative authority." And George Mason, author of Virginia's Bill of Rights, called it a "diabolical trade . . . a disgraceful thing in America." Virginia delegates to the Congress voted the immediate abolition of foreign slave trade. New Jersey, Pennsylvania, and Delaware voted with her. The other states all voted no. In order to get consent to the Constitution there had to be compromise. And at any cost the new system must quickly be adopted, for the captainless ship was fast running on the rocks. The compromise was made. The importation of slaves might continue for twenty years more. This contented the rice and cotton planters of the deep South and those New England shippers engaged in importing slaves from Africa. But of all the difficulties before the Congress, the greatest had been the problem of combining States' Rights with a strong central government.

Now at last the work was done. The Constitution was ready to be submitted to the states. Eight had already accepted it, though in Massachusetts it had won by a narrow margin. One more state was necessary for ratification. In that June when on the plantations drought was killing the young tobacco plants, New York, New Hampshire, and Virginia were also to make their decision.

Patrick Henry, though his affection and regard for Washington were "unalterable," was determined to fight with all the power in him against this system of government which Washington thought held the only salvation for the states.

When Henry had gone home to Hanover, after the first Continental Congress, the neighbors crowded about, asking who was the greatest man at the Congress, and Henry replied that for wisdom and solid judgment George Washington was the greatest man on the floor. Yet now Henry could not follow the judgment of this man whom he so admired.

Of the Virginians who had been delegates to that first Congress, Peyton Randolph, of the Roman spirit, and Richard Bland were dead. Of that group, all of them over six feet tall, who had ridden up to Philadelphia to represent Virginia at the first Continental Congress, three more did not appear at the Convention in Richmond which was to vote on the new Constitution. Jefferson was in Europe, Richard Lee remained on his plantation, and Washington awaited the result at Mount Vernon.

Of the original group only Henry, Pendleton, and Harrison were in Richmond now, but George Mason was there, and the great lawyers, George Wythe and John Marshall. Light-Horse Harry Lee was present, and two young men—James Madison and James Monroe.

The Constitution was debated for three weeks. Patrick Henry spoke almost every day; often two or three times a day.

"I am but a poor individual," he said, "but I speak the language of thousands." To Henry's mind the new system would rob the states of their rights. "You will sip sorrow," he said, "if you give away your rights. . . . It is said that this Constitution has beautiful features, but . . . they appear to me horrible, frightful. Among other deformities is an awful squinting. It squints toward monarchy. Your president may easily become king . . . He will be a man of ambition and abilities, how easy for him to render himself absolute . . . we shall have a king. . . ." Yes, the Constitution "squints toward monarchy."

During this speech Henry's eyes swept the crowded hall, fell upon his son. Henry knew that he must have come with news from home, and he paused to ask a friend seated near him to take the boy out and question him. The boy's news was that his father's second wife had just given birth to a son. The cradle, as Hugh Grigsby has said, began to rock in Henry's house when he was eighteen; it continued rocking until his death at the age of sixty-three. So this latest birth was not startling news to Patrick Henry, and he continued his impassioned plea to "preserve the poor commonwealth of Virginia . . . to preserve," he told his audience, "your liberty and mine."

Day after day the debate went on. George Mason and James Monroe backed Henry. Madison, Marshall, Wythe, Light-Horse Harry Lee, and Edmund Pendleton argued for the Constitution.

And Washington waited at Mount Vernon.

It was a choice, he felt, between anarchy and a "union under one federal head." The people must choose "whether they will be respectable and prosperous, or contemptible and miserable as a nation."

There came the last day of the debate before the vote was to be taken.

"The gentleman," Henry said, speaking of Madison, whose part in the drafting of the Constitution had been great, "the gentleman has told you of the numerous blessings which he imagines will be the result of this system. I see the awful immensity of the dangers with which it is pregnant. I see it. I feel it. When I see beyond the horizon that bounds human eyes . . . and see those intelligent beings which inhabit the ethereal mansions . . . I am led to believe that much will depend on what we now decide. . . ."

A violent storm, ending the long drought, broke into Henry's speech. One who was present says that it shook the whole building, and that the spirits Henry had called seemed to come at his bidding. "It grew dark. The doors came to with a rebound like a peal of musketry. The windows rattled. The huge wood structure rocked. The rain fell from the eaves in torrents which were dashed against the window panes. The thunder roared, the lightning flashed."

But the Son of Thunder did not pause in his eloquent pleading. . . .

The next day the vote was taken. Henry had spoken with all his old magic. He had carried men on the tide of his profound sincere feeling. But he had been answered. And over the Convention there had hovered the spirit of the man who waited at Mount Vernon.

"We are either a united people, or we are not," Washington had insisted. "If the former, let us in all matters of general concern act as a nation which has a national character to support."

When the vote of the Richmond Convention was counted, the majority was not large; it was only ten.

But that majority agreed with Washington that the world must not think that "we are a nation to-day, and thirteen States to-morrow. For who would treat with us on such terms?"

Patrick Henry, for the first time, had lost. But now that it was settled, he said, all must cherish the Constitution and give it a fair chance.

Yet he had not entirely lost. For certain amendments safeguarding the liberty of the individual states were to be added. And Virginia had still further qualified her vote by declaring the right to secede if ever she should feel her liberty to be threatened.

Pendleton, rising on his crutches, dissolved the Convention. "We are brothers," he said, "we are Virginians. Our common object is the good of the country. . . ."

Men hid their faces in their hands and wept when

they heard these final words, uttered in that aged voice, tremulous with emotion.

And before sunset many were on their way home; by horseback, gig or phaeton they were gone, the dust now laid by the heavy rains which had fallen the day before.

❁

They made Washington president, and he saw with terrible clarity how vast a task it would be to guide the toddling steps of the new Republic. The hard years of war had told upon even his superb physical body. He had hoped, he said, to spend his remaining days in the "sweet retirement of Mount Vernon; in the practice of the domestic virtues, in cultivating the affections of good men . . . with a glass of wine and a bit of mutton always ready for a friend."

His spirit shrank from the presidency. Yet duty was become the habit of his life.

As you see him setting out from Mount Vernon, words spoken long ago came back to you; the words of Captain John Smith, coming from far off like the voice of the bellbird heard in the distant depths of the jungle. The voice is saying, "If the Little Ant and the Sillie Bee seek by their diligence the good of the Commonwealth, much more ought man."

It was with that feeling of obligation that George Washington left Mount Vernon for New York to be inaugurated as the country's first president.

When he had accepted the post of commander in chief of the Revolutionary Forces he had said to the Congress: "I beg it may be remembered by every gentleman in this room, that I this day declare with the utmost sincerity, that I do not consider myself equal to the command I am honored with."

Now at his inauguration, people say that he trembled with the same modesty. His journey to New York had been a triumphal progress. The adoring people had worshiped him as he passed. Yet when he came to make his speech of acceptance, those who heard it say that he could scarcely read the paper which he held in his hand; and emotion shook his voice when he declared the "magnitude of the trust" to be overwhelming to one "inheriting inferior endowments from Nature, and impracticed in the duties of civil administration."

He realized that untrodden ground lay before him. He had to make a country; a democracy of a pattern never before seen in the world. Lawlessness, which in many parts of the land had followed the Revolution, must come to an end; it must be possible for the good to live in safety. Financial honor must be established. Arguments in favor of the cancellation of debts must be opposed. Peace must be preserved between states which had not yet learned to co-operate with one another.

Washington was eager, too, for expansion, for the opening up of the West. And from the beginning he felt that it was important to lay down a code of behavior. Had he not as a boy copied carefully the hundred and ten "Rules of Civility and Decent Behaviour"? He must now formulate rules for the conduct of a Republic.

He had lived at Mount Vernon in the unassuming dignity of a country gentleman, but he considered that there should be a certain ceremony in the life of the president. He explained that if there were rules of proceeding which had originated in the wisdom of nations, it would not be prudent for a young country to dispense with them altogether. He decided that the president could not make visits. On Thursdays he would give official dinners. On Tuesdays from three to four he would hold a levee; and on Friday afternoons Mrs. Washington would receive. When they drove out it was in a cream-colored coach drawn by six perfectly matched bay horses. He had always understood the value of outward forms in the life of a gentleman. He would establish them in the life of the nation. In all things the young Republic must be respected; by the world and by its own citizens. Such ceremony was not to his own taste, nor to Martha's. She called it a dull life and said that she felt like a prisoner of state.

Yet many cried out that all this "squinted toward monarchy."

The French Revolution brought Washington his most troubling problem. He was horrified by the extremes to which it went. He saw a people tearing each other to pieces in the name of liberty. When Lafayette was imprisoned he sent money to Madame Lafayette and later took into his home her son, young George Washington Lafayette. But when England went to war with Revolutionary France he insisted that the United States must be neutral. The country, he said, was still convalescent. He would not permit it to go into a disastrous war. It needed twenty years of peace before it could stand on its own feet. The sentimentalists cursed him for ingratitude to France. His enemies multiplied; and he wrote brokenheartedly to Jefferson that he would not have believed that while he was doing his utmost "to establish a national character of our own" his "every act would be tortured," and that, too, in "such exaggerated and indecent terms as could scarcely be applied to a Nero . . . or even to a common pickpocket."

When his first term was over he longed to go back to Mount Vernon; longed for its tranquillity, and realized that with every year of his absence his plantations were literally going to destruction. Still he could not refuse to act again as president. Even his enemies begged him, realizing that without him the Republic would collapse.

And so he took on once more the burden.

In these bitter years little Nelly Custis was growing up in the Washington home; a laughter-loving, vivacious, sunnyhearted girl, a clever mimic, a talented musician, adoring the man she called "grandpapa," and he delighting in her gay beauty. Perhaps . . . it is possible . . . that she reminded him of Sally Fairfax. Yes, she is like Sally Fairfax.

They were close friends, President Washington and little Nelly Custis, who was granddaughter to his Martha. When Nelly happened to be away from home, Washington, in all the stress of the presidency, found time to write to her; interested in everything that concerned her.

She has written him describing a ball in Georgetown, and he replies: "Let me touch a little now on your Georgetown ball and happy, thrice happy for the fair . . . that there was a man to spare." Nelly has evidently declared that she never intends to give herself a moment's uneasiness on account of any man. Of this, Washington says: "A hint here: men and women feel the same inclinations toward each other now that they have always done . . . and you, as others have done, may find perhaps that the passions of your sex are more easily raised than allayed . . . In the composition of the human frame there is a good deal of inflammable matter, however dormant it may lie for a time, and like an intimate acquaintance of yours, when the torch is put to it, *that* which is *within you* may burst into a blaze. . . ." He goes on to explain to this adopted child whom he loved so well that "love may and therefore ought to be under the guidance of reason." And he concludes: ". . . Every blessing, among which is a good husband when you want and deserve one, is bestowed on you by yours affectionately—"

When you read, you feel the tenderness and the depth of Washington's emotions. And you understand how removed he was from that "squinting toward monarchy" of which many were afraid.

# CHAPTER THIRTEEN

# Farmer Washington

He had a hundred cows, yet now he had to buy butter. While he had been teaching the infant Republic to walk, his plantations, without his supervision, had little by little become so disorganized that when he at last came home to live he discovered that he was keeping a hundred cows and buying butter.

In all his years of absence as general and president he had insisted on weekly reports from his overseers, and had written instructing them about the crops, advising them about the sale of farm products and of fish caught at his landing. But with all his care the plantations brought in no profit, and it was even necessary to buy butter!

But now he had made his farewell address as president, said a cordial good-bye to John Adams, his successor, and was at last come home. Nelly Custis wrote to a friend: "Grandpapa is much pleased with being once more Farmer Washington." And Martha described herself as happy as a cricket to be again just an old-fashioned Virginia housekeeper; returned to the gracious informality of plantation life.

No more Friday At-Homes, no more official dinners at four o'clock on Thursday afternoons, with Black Sam, the steward, dressed in small clothes and wig, marshaling a corps of gloved servants in resplendent livery.

And no more ceremonious levees on Tuesday afternoons, with the president receiving in black velvet, holding his cocked hat in hands which wore yellow gloves; at his side a sword in a glistening white leather scabbard; his hair snowily powdered, with its queue tucked away in a black silk bag.

All that was over, and such ceremony no longer necessary. In the simple dignity of a gentleman's plantation, Martha was happy; and Washington, who had said that he would rather live quietly at Mount Vernon than to be emperor of the world—he, too, was content.

He rose at sunup, and on his white horse rode throughout the morning over his fields, watchful of every detail.

The old familiar entries appear again in his diary: the weather and the crops. He draws up a new contract with a new gardener to the effect that the man is to have four dollars at Christmas with which he may be drunk for four days and four nights. Two dollars is to be allowed at Easter, and two dollars at Whitsuntide, on which occasions the gardener may be drunk for two days and two nights. At other times he is to be limited to a dram in the morning and a drink of grog at dinner.

Washington was still exacting no more of human nature than he thought could be fulfilled; and he was still of that inflexible justice which insists that promises must be kept and contracts observed. That had been his policy as general and as president; as farmer, he ran his plantations on the same principles.

But there is less in the diaries now about the hounds, Mopsey and Tartar, True-love and Music-bell, less about litters of puppies and their ancestry. There is much about the Federal City growing up on the banks of the Potomac, where in the first year of the new century the government of the United States is to be located. Washington is building himself a house in the Federal City and often goes with Mrs. Washington to watch its progress. And he has become too famous to find at Mount Vernon that retirement of which he so often spoke; for all the world comes to him there. His diary records daily visitors, to dine and often to spend the night; the Spanish minister, the British envoy and his lady, a Polish gentleman, a gentleman from Demerara. . . .

There came one day two decorous judges to pay a visit to the great man of Mount Vernon. The road had been dusty and these gentlemen decided that they would stop in a near-by wood and make a complete change of clothing before presenting themselves. They dismounted, and gave their horses to the colored servant to be tethered. The gentlemen then undressed. The servant opened his masters' portmanteau, but instead of the seemly raiment of a gentleman of that day, he found the bag filled with the wares of an itinerant peddler.

At the tavern where they had spent the night there had been a Scotch peddler; their bag had been exchanged for his by mistake.

The decorous garments—the broadcloth coats, the black silk hose, fancy waistcoats, the clean underlinen—which they expected were not there, but in their place such goods as a peddler carries, fancy soaps, scissors, lengths of ribbon and calico, imitation jewelry.

The nude gentlemen laughed, the colored servant laughed, and Washington, happening to be strolling about his grounds, heard this laughter coming from the wood, and went to investigate.

He saw two gentlemen, standing stark naked before an open portmanteau filled with a peddler's gear. They were an absurd spectacle. And Washington, too, laughed. It was impossible not to laugh. He laughed until actually he rolled on the ground in his merriment.

In the year after Washington retired to Mount Vernon, the Reverend Bryan Fairfax made a trip to England, and Washington entrusted him with two letters to be delivered to Sally Cary Fairfax, who was living as a widow at Bath.

It was said that for financial reasons she had been forced to "lay down her carriages," but that she was living in a "private and genteel manner."

One of the letters given into the hands of Bryan Fairfax was from Martha Washington and the other was from Washington himself. It was dated Mount Vernon, May 16, 1798.

It began thus: "Five and twenty years have nearly passed away since I have considered myself as the permanent resident of this place, or have been in a situation to indulge myself in a familiar intercourse with my friends by letter or otherwise."

Five and twenty years had passed since that day when he had put down in his diary the fact that Colonel and Mrs. Fairfax had gone to England, and that he and Mrs. Washington went to Belvoir "to see them take shipping."

The Washington who sat writing the letter which Bryan Fairfax was to deliver, was sixty-six. His eyes had somewhat failed, he was slightly deaf, and the false teeth of the eighteenth century were not so satisfactory as those of the twentieth.

The woman to whom he wrote was some two years older than himself, and as age came upon her suffered greatly from gout. But, writing to her, Washington must have pictured her as Virginia knew her; Sally Cary of Ceely's on James River, Sally Cary of Williamsburg, Sally Cary Fairfax of Belvoir. He could not have visualized the widow of Bath whom he had never seen. Perhaps she came to him now as the slender girl of her portrait; in a gown with tight bodice and very full skirt, a gown untrimmed save for white frills at its low-cut square neck, and in its flowing, elbow-length sleeves. The girl in the portrait is standing, with her left arm uplifted, and her hand holding one full-blown rose.

It may have been so that Washington saw her, as he wrote the words: "Five and twenty years have nearly passed away. . . .

"During this period," the letter continues, "so many important events have occurred . . . as the compass of a letter would give you but an inadequate idea of.

"*None of which events, however, nor all of them together have been able to eradicate from my mind the recollection of those happy moments, the happiest in my life, which I have enjoyed in your company.*"

As you read, your mind inevitably underscores the words. You have asked yourself repeatedly, in the anxious crowded years of General Washington's life, and again in his years as president, whether he remembered, or whether his devotion to Sally Fairfax was a forgotten phase in the life of his heart. And five and twenty years later you are answered. The years have been packed with

events; yet "None of which events, nor all of them together" have dimmed the memory of "those happy moments, the happiest in my life, which I have enjoyed in
your company."

The letter goes on to say that, worn out by the toils
of his labors, he is again seated under his vine and fig-
tree. He knows that she will be interested in the addi-
tions he has made to Mount Vernon, to his offices and
gardens. He tells her about the new Federal City on the
Potomac, of the elegant buildings which are going up
there. He speaks of his anxiety for the Republic, of his
fear that it may be drawn into war: "If it can steer
clear of European politics, stand firm on its bottom and
be wise and temperate in its government, it bids fair
to be one of the greatest and happiest nations in the
world."

He tells her, too, of how often he gazes across the
fields to where her old home, Belvoir, stood before it was
destroyed by fire. And when he gazes, he says that he re-
flects upon its former inhabitants with whom "we lived
in such harmony and friendship."

You can see him on his white horse, looking across
the fields and back through the years; and remembering.
And to his memories you add something he once said:
that "love may and ought to be under the guidance of
reason."

Then his letter wonders that Sally Fairfax remains
in England, when all her nearest relatives are in Virginia.
It concludes by saying that Mrs. Washington is writing
to give her news of the changes in the neighborhood and
in their family.

And Washington himself (as he often did) drafted

the letter which Martha copied: the draft exists in his handwriting.

When Bryan Fairfax delivered these letters at Bath, there must have risen up before Sally Fairfax, as she read, a figure six feet three inches tall, muscular and slender, as yet unwearied with living. For it would be Colonel Washington who stood before the childless aging widow of Bath. General Washington she had never seen, nor the president. It was the young colonel that she had known.

In the last month of the last year of the eighteenth century in the young New World, Farmer Washington rode over his plantation on a certain Thursday morning.

It had been a busy and a happy year. Agriculture was as always his favorite amusement and he had just finished a long paper on the cultivation of Mount Vernon, and the rotation of its crops.

In the beginning of this year just ending, on his birthday, "at about candle-light" in the drawing room of Mount Vernon, Nelly Custis who was so dear to him, had been married to his nephew, Lawrence Lewis. And in November she was at Mount Vernon for the birth of her first child. Mrs. Summers, the midwife, had been sent for, and Washington's old friend, Dr. Craik. Nelly's baby was just two weeks old on that December morning when Washington rode over his plantation.

It was a cloudy morning. He had set down in his diary that the night before there had been a huge circle around the moon.

Soon after he rode out it had begun to snow, and

then to hail, and finally it had settled down to a cold steady rain.

When he came in it was after three o'clock, and since Mrs. Washington was waiting dinner for him, he did not change his dress; his greatcoat, he said, had kept him warm. But snow still clung to his hair.

The next day he was hoarse, his throat was sore, and it was snowing so hard that he gave up the idea of riding out. But he refused medicine. "Let it go as it came," he said.

He spent the evening with the newspapers, reading aloud anything that he thought entertaining or interesting.

And that night he entered in his diary what are probably his last written words:

"Dec. 13. Morning snowing and about three inches deep. Wind at north-east. Mercury at 30°. Continual snowing 'til one o'clock, and about four became perfectly clear. Wind in the same place, but not hard. Mercury 28° at night."

In the course of that night, between two and three in the morning, he waked Mrs. Washington and told her that he had an ague. He was breathing with effort and he could scarcely speak, but he would not let her get up to call a servant for fear she would catch cold.

In the morning he sent for his overseer and had the man bleed him before the doctors came. All day he suffered great pain; no remedies gave any relief.

"Doctor," he said, "I die hard, but I am not afraid to go. . . ."

And at dusk he said, "I feel myself going. I thank

you for your attention. You had better not take any more trouble about me, but let me go. . . ."

At ten o'clock that night George Washington died.

And when the last breath flutters, it is a brave great gentleman who is gone.

# CHAPTER FOURTEEN

# Bondage

WASHINGTON was gone. Without him independence for the United States might possibly not have been won. Under his wisdom a nation had been created, a standard raised, to which, as he used to say, the "wise and honest might repair." He had set an example of impartiality and integrity in high office. In promoting the James River and Potomac canals he had led the way to the development of the great West. Yet one problem which had long disturbed him was still unsolved. He was gone—but slavery remained.

And now that it is no more, now that it has receded into the mists of vanished things, the word itself —slavery—stirs in the mind of today certain pictures, become so legendary that they are accepted without conscious thought:

A dear old black mammy, very fat, wearing a starched white apron, and a bright bandanna head-handkerchief. Probably she is putting a child to sleep, crooning softly, "Swing low, sweet chariot." Or the swift image which the word "slavery" brings into focus may be some faithful old black Joe, mourning that "Massa's in de cold, cold ground."

Such pictures slide into view down the easy ways of tradition. Of course, you know that the source of Negro slaves was in African jungles; but illogically, in the instant of flashing reaction to the thought of bondage, those slaves of the long ago appear to be transported from the Dark Continent as thousands of white-aproned mammies and devoted black Joes. Unless the mind pauses to reason, it does not immediately visualize a cargo of jungle savages, from a land where slavery was a common thing; where men often sold, or pawned, their wives and children, where victorious tribes enslaved, or executed those they captured; and where, when a chief or the head of a family died, many of his wives and slaves were sacrificed.

You don't see these savages living in such terror of witchcraft that those suspected were sometimes roasted alive, slowly mutilated, or fastened to stakes when the water was low, and left there to be drowned with the flood tide.

You don't see a people dominated by fear of evil spirits which must be continually propitiated, a people among whom superstitious practices took the place of sanitation and medical care. You don't see fish laid in the sun to rot before being eaten, or people feeding upon the decayed carcasses of animals, and sometimes upon human flesh.

Yet it was from such as this that the affectionate mammies and the black Joes were evolved; it was from such material that the slaveowners made cooks and nursery maids, seamstresses, field laborers, bricklayers, carpenters, masons, gardeners, coachmen, and butlers.

American slavery was the most tremendous experiment the world has ever seen. Primitive savages in vast numbers were picked up, transported across the sea, and set down in a strange land, among an alien people who had over them a complete control. It was an amazing experiment. But no one thought of it as an experiment: the whole thing was unconscious. Slavery had its beginning in this country, because the tobacco, cotton, and rice plantations needed labor, and the African was better adapted to such work under a southern sun than was any other race. The demand for this labor was supplied by traders who found a fortune in buying slaves in Africa for the paltry price of watered rum or lengths of calico; and then selling them at fat profits to the plantations.

All this began in a period when men were less sensitive to human rights than they are now. If it is to be judged, it should be by the standards of the time; remembering that in those days witches were burned and drowned; gossiping women were punished in the ducking stool; hanging was the penalty for a long list of crimes, and severe flogging was considered necessary in the proper rearing of children.

But why, after all, judge slavery now that it is past and done with? It is enough to say that the slave traders of old England and of New England share the blame with the slaveowners.

It is as a vast experiment in the influence of two races, one upon the other, that slavery in America is a subject so fascinating that the impressions of those who saw the strange experiment in operation must always be of interest.

Some thirty-five years after that December day when George Washington lay down to die, an English novelist, Miss Harriet Martineau, made a visit to the

South. She came with so great a horror of human bondage that she had a nervous dread of the moment when
she would look upon a slave for the first time.

But when finally she becomes familiar with slavery,
you find that nothing has struck her more than the
patience of slaveowners. "In this virtue," she thinks,
"they probably surpass the whole Christian world; I
mean in their patience with their slaves . . . when I
consider how they loved to be called 'fiery Southerners,'
I could but marvel at their mild forbearance under the
hourly provocations to which they are subject in their
homes."

Miss Martineau goes one Sunday with her hostess to
dine on a neighboring plantation. The carriage is ordered
to come back for them at eight o'clock. To their concern it arrives at six; the slave-coachman saying that
his master has sent him to say that they must return
directly. But when they reach home, the "master" is
much surprised. The coachman, it appears, has invented
the message in order that he may have the evening to
himself. And Miss Martineau is astonished that her host
and hostess merely laugh.

"Patience," she explains, in that degree in which
she constantly sees it, "can be obtained only by long
habit. Persons from New England, France or England,
becoming slave-holders, are found to be the most severe
masters and mistresses, however good their tempers pre-
viously." They cannot "sit waiting half an hour for the
second course, or see everything done in the worst possible manner, their property wasted . . . their plans
frustrated . . . themselves deluded by artifices—they
cannot, like the native proprietor, endure all this unruffled."

Reading Miss Martineau, you remember Washington's struggle with slave labor. Since he was so much away from Mount Vernon, as general and as president, his correspondence with his overseers reveals this struggle. He writes that it is his foremost desire that the overseer be particularly attentive to the Negroes in sickness; they are never to work when unfit for it, and should then be taken care of. He has a doctor engaged to look after them by the year. If they are ill they must have wine when necessary.

Wine when necessary . . . Then what increase of sickness!

"I find by the reports," Washington writes, "that Sam is in a manner always returned sick; Doll at the Ferry and several of the spinners frequently so, and Ditcher Charles . . . what sort of lameness is Dick's, and what kind of sickness is Betty Davis's? And is there anything particular in the cases of Ruth, Hannah and Pegg that they have been returned sick for several weeks together?"

He goes on to say that he cannot conceive how it is possible that six thousand twelvepenny nails could have been used in building the cornhouse, and that he believes it would take a week for his carpenters all working together to build a chicken coop. In four years, even with the aid of fifty thousand dollars from the sale of land, his plantations have just managed to keep out of debt.

Six thousand twelvepenny nails to build a cornhouse . . . Yes, it was patience that most impressed Miss Harriet Martineau, visitor from England.

Twenty years after her stay in America, the Reverend Nehemiah Adams of Boston is forced to spend three months in the South on account of his health. He is a zealous abolitionist and confesses that he comes with feelings of dread and curiosity—with anticipation of the groans and the clanking chains which he has so often heard described.

It is in the harbor of a southern seaport town that he first sees slavery. He goes ashore and slaves are all about him. He is astonished. They are all in a good humor. The delivery of every trunk on shore, he says, is the occasion of some bit of repartee. "I began to like those slaves. I began to laugh with them. It was irresistible. Who could have convinced me an hour before, that slaves could have any other effect upon me than to make me feel sad?"

In the streets, the Reverend Nehemiah finds it difficult to pass the slaves without smiling: they have a singular effect upon his spirits; he says that he has never seen a happier, better looking, more courteous set of people.

He reminds himself of all that he has heard of slave auctions, of fugitives hiding in dismal swamps, and he realizes that he has known nothing of the everyday life of slavery.

On Sunday he is amazed at the dress of the slaves on the street: well-fitting broadcloth suits, polished boots, white Marseilles vests, brooches in their shirt bosoms, gold chains, elegant sticks; the women dressed with taste and refinement. On the way to church a little girl about eight years old trips along ahead of the Reverend Nehemiah. He admires the profuse flounces on her dress, her light-colored boots, her mohair mitts, her sunshade. He approves the hymnbook in her hand. Then, when the child happens to turn her head, he sees that she is black.

When he observes all this he says that he cannot help remembering the thousand paupers on Deer Island near Boston.

Ten years later, Frederick Olmsted, also from the North, travels in the South. In contrast to the British novelist, and the Reverend Nehemiah Adams, Mr. Olmsted is a practical man of affairs, observing Negro bondage from the economic angle. He calculates that the cost of getting anything done under slavery is double the cost with free labor; that it requires four times as many people and takes four times as long. He watches slaves at work and reports that they appear to him to go through the motions of labor without putting strength into them.

Mr. Olmsted visits a James River plantation. In the three hours that he spends with the owner, he says that not more than ten minutes pass without interruption by slaves, coming with childlike confidence and dependence, asking help or direction of some sort. The planter even has to leave the dinner table three times.

"You see," the planter explains to Mr. Olmsted, "the trouble and responsibility of properly taking care of your negroes. You see how constantly I am called upon . . . The slaves are careless and wasteful. To make anything of farming a man has got to live a hard life. . . ." But "they are interesting creatures, Sir, and with all their faults have many beautiful traits. I can't help being attached to them and I am sure they love us."

And Mr. Olmsted, in the course of his southern travels, makes the discovery that gangs of Irishmen are employed at the hardest labor, such as draining the land. "But why not slaves?" he asks. "Oh, it's dangerous work. A negro's life is too valuable to be risked. If a negro dies it's a considerable loss you know."

Mr. Olmsted notes how greatly slaves have to be humored to get them to work. He and the Reverend Mr. Adams both describe the method of tasking slaves; setting as a day's work an average stint, and paying the slave whatever he does above that amount. They also describe the custom of giving each slave a plot of ground, where he can raise pigs, poultry, and garden produce, which he may sell or use for himself. Not having to consider old age or sickness, his daily living provided, a slave's personal money may be spent upon the "foppish finery" which so impresses Mr. Olmsted in Richmond; or such money may be used by the slave to buy his own freedom. All this is very surprising to Nehemiah Adams and to Mr. Olmsted. Free Negroes themselves owning slaves, are astonishing to an abolitionist; and what is he to think of a Negro woman owning her husband, and when he displeases her, threatening to sell him downriver?

Looking through the eyes of these long-ago visitors to the South, it is plain that slavery was not a one-way matter. In a very real sense the slave owned the master, as in another sense the master owned the slave. Property is always possessive, especially when that property is alive—when it is human.

Practical Mr. Olmsted realizes that the slave may in a thousand ways retaliate upon an unfair master, or upon one he dislikes. In the most innocent manner in the world he may destroy tools, neglect cattle and horses and mules, sham sickness, or run away. These are his punishments for punishment. The master may, of course, sell him, but everybody well knows that he who sells must almost invariably sell at a sacrifice. The owner cannot simply discharge an unsatisfactory slave; he is held legally responsible for him; he must make the best of one who is troublesome; he can get rid of him only by selling him; or by taking the loss of freeing him.

But the Negro slave had a stronger hold upon his master than any power of retaliation. He was so touchingly responsive to affection, so engagingly playful and childlike, so impulsive, so without bitterness, that he created a new relationship between employer and employed. Only the utterly heartless could be indifferent.

When Miss Martineau asks herself what are the morals of the society which is subject to slavery, her answer is that the most obvious is Mercy. "Nowhere, perhaps, can more touching exercise of mercy be seen than here. I saw endless manifestations of mercy, as well as of its opposite. The thoughtfulness of masters and mistresses and their children, not only in the comforts, but the indulgence of their slaves, was a frequent subject of admiration with me."

Yet nothing could alter the fact that it was slavery: a thing in itself "diabolical," as the author of Virginia's Bill of Rights described it.

Not Miss Martineau, nor the Reverend Nehemiah Adams, nor Frederick Olmsted, for a moment condoned slavery as an institution; they honestly reported the life as they saw it, without changing their conviction that fundamentally it was wrong.

In the reaction of race upon race under the conditions of bondage there was often the cruelty which you would expect, and often—more often—that beauty of mutual loyalty and mercy and patience, that affectionate happy intimacy which so astounded travelers like Miss Martineau, Mr. Olmsted, and Nehemiah Adams, D.D., abolitionist from Boston.

The men of plantation Virginia, who had so large a part in the winning of American independence and in the creation of a United States, understood how serious the slavery question was. Washington wished from his soul that the legislatures of the various states could see the policy of its gradual abolition. Jefferson prophesied that nothing was more certainly written in the book of Fate than that this people would one day be free.

But how was it to be brought about with justice both to the owner and to the slave? What, for instance, was to become of the enormous numbers of Negroes who would be set adrift by freedom? Such Negroes as had already been freed by their masters, or who had bought their own freedom, did not have an easy time. They were not welcome in the free states.

Mr. Olmsted tells the story of a Negro who purchased his freedom and went to Philadelphia. A few weeks later he was back in Virginia. "Oh, I don't like dat Philadelphy," he explained. "Ain't no chance fo' colored folks dere. 'Spec' if I'd been a runaway de white folks dere would of took care o' me. But I couldn't git anythin' to do. So I jes' borrow ten dollar of my brudder, an' come back to ole Virginny."

The free Negro was a perplexing problem. People thought that colonization, perhaps in Africa, would be the only solution.

✦

For nearly two hundred years Africa flowed, a black river of life, westward across the sea, across that dreadful "Middle Passage," into the South. For nearly two hundred years slave ships from Guinea came to anchor in James River. Africa thus poured into British America; the great experiment constantly supplied with fresh material, with "New Negroes," as they were then called.

And as the bondage was a mutual thing, so the experiment was also.

In America the curse of witchcraft vanished: the sacrifice of wives and slaves on the death of their lords was no more; the power of vengeful gods who must ever be appeased faded; medical care and sanitation lowered the death rate; of the evils of Africa only slavery remained.

In his new world the African slave found a new language and a new religion. His emotional soul had a genius for worship, and into the Christian religion he poured all his heart, his history, his drama, his humor, his unique musical rhythms. He made of it a warmly passionate thing. The Negro spirituals are African psalms, set to African music:

Their thought is often very humble:

> Keep a inchin' along.
> Massa Jesus comin' bime-by
> Keep a inchin' along like a po' inch-worm.
> Massa Jesus comin' bime-by
> Massa Jesus comin' bime-by.

With the humility there is also the Negro's shrewd picturesque analysis of character:

Hypo-crite an' de concubine,
Livin' among de swine,
Dey run to God wid de lips an' tongue,
An' leave all de heart behind.

Sometimes these songs call upon those forces of nature, feared and adored on the great Dark Continent:

O hear dat lumberin' thunder,
A' roll from do' to do',
A' callin' de people home to God.
Dey'll git home bime-by.

O see dat forkéd lightin'
A' jump from cloud to cloud,
A' pickin' up God's chillen,
Dey'll git home bime-by.

They take the crucifixion and make it break your heart:

Were you dere when dey crucified my Lord?
   Were you dere?
O—sometimes it causes me to tremble, tremble! . . .
Were you dere when dey nailed him to a tree?
O—sometimes it causes me to tremble, tremble. . . .
Were you dere when dey pierced him in de side?
O—sometimes it causes me to tremble, tremble. . . .

In many of these songs you hear the cry of slavery:

Lord, have mercy, mercy! Lord, have mercy.
Lord, have mercy over me, over me!
An' befo' I'll be a slave, I'll be buried in my grave
An' go home to my father an' be free . . .
Lord, have mercy. . . .

There are songs, too, of triumph, when all God's chillen will shout all over God's Heaven; when all will have a robe, a crown, shoes, a harp, a song and wings; and thus will shout and walk and play and sing and fly all over God's Heaven.

And in none of their songs is there to be found ever one single word of bitterness.

Out of the great experiment there was given to America, not only these immortal spirituals, but there was given also a new laughter, the rhythm of new dancing, a new awareness of the invisible world, and a new intimacy with all living creatures; with Br'er Rabbit, and Sis' Goose, Sis' Cow, and Br'er Turkey Buzzard.

The great accidental experiment had brought the African Negro thus far. And as it was not a one-way bondage, so it was not a one-way experiment; for the genius that is Africa crossed in the slave ships and entered permanently into the life of America.

ONG THE ROAD TO APPOMATTOX

*All who lived in Virginia during the first sixty-five years of the nineteenth century were travelers upon a road whose destination was Appomattox. Those who died along the way were spared knowledge of the journey's end; but those who lived were to suffer defeat and surrender.*

*Robert E. Lee, Matthew Fontaine Maury, Edgar Allan Poe, and the black slave Jasper—each born in the first dozen years of the century—were of the company who followed that road. And among the travelers born later were Roger A. Pryor and his wife, Sara Agnes Rice; George E. Pickett; and nearly twenty-five years after that, little LaSalle Corbell.*

# CHAPTER FIFTEEN

# Robert and Edgar

ROBERT was always good."

So his father, Light-Horse Harry Lee, wrote from his wandering exile in the West Indies. It had been four years since he had seen Robert, and the child had then been not more than five years old. Yet, writing from those faraway islands under the wind, he took comfort in little Robert's goodness. There was poison in almost every other memory.

When he thought of his courtship of Robert's mother he remembered how he would gallop down the long driveway that led to Shirley. There was no more lovely place on James River than Shirley. There was dignity in the rhythm of its white columns, and in the repetition of its many-paned windows; in the tawny red of its mellowed brick there was a tender warmth, and the carved white pineapple on its roof was the symbol of its hospitality.

Ann Carter was like the house. Not every girl of twenty would have known how to appreciate, as she did, a man of Harry Lee's fame and achievement. Many girls would have thought only of the seventeen years difference in their ages. But Ann had valued his experience and delighted in his talk. She was proud that Lafayette and Washington were his friends, she gloried in his record in the Revolution, and in the fact that he had been three times governor of Virginia; loving him for these things as well as for the fact that he was dashing, handsome Light-Horse Harry.

But to think of Ann and of Shirley was to realize that she no longer owned any interest in the place. There was pain in the memory of that day when she had set out in a rickety carriage to drive across country to her old home. She had looked so ill. Three babies had come fast; already another was soon expected. And Harry Lee knew that he was ruined; bankrupt by ill-judged speculation in land. Therefore Ann must travel in a broken-down open carriage, exposed to the cold winds of late autumn. And how ill she was! Unfit for the shock of finding her father dead; and for discovering that he had left her only an income from a trust, carefully safeguarded that Light-Horse Harry might not touch it. Perhaps, but for this humiliation to her husband, Ann might have stayed on at Shirley until her baby was born.

But of what use to say perhaps? Nothing now could alter the fact that creditors had beat upon their door, and that Robert had been born to a mother so anxious, so grieving. And what could ever erase from Ann's heart the disgrace of a husband jailed for debt?

During the winter of Robert's birth—in the year 1807—Thomas Jefferson was president; under him, the Congress had abolished the importation of slaves, the law to go into effect on the first day of 1808, when the constitutional restriction expired.

But when the personal life is so bitter as Light-Horse Harry's had become, historical events could scarcely have counted. And the thoughts that followed him over the sparkling Caribbean, from enchanting island to enchanting island, must have been melancholy personal memories; memories of Shirley, of Stratford where Robert was born, then of prison, of release, and at last of the little brick house in Alexandria where, when he was freed from jail, he had moved Ann and their four children—with once more a baby expected.

In Alexandria they might have lived in peace on the small income that Ann had from her father—if only that dreadful thing had not happened in Baltimore.

Still, could he blame himself for that? He had not believed in going to war again with England; and it had seemed right to go to Baltimore so that he might help the editor whose paper was opposing the war. A man ought to stand by his convictions.

Now Henry Lee's mutilated face, his shattered nerves, would not let him forget the angry mob which had attacked the office of the paper.

Thus he sailed the Caribbean, seeking health and the peace he might never find. He wrote to Carter, his eldest son, warning him against speculation and debt. But for Robert he felt no anxiety: "Robert was always good."

A year later Light-Horse Harry Lee died, on his way home to be united once more to his family.

Robert was then eleven years old, Carter away at college, his brother Smith a midshipman in the navy, his sister Ann in delicate health, Mildred was only eight; and their mother had become an invalid. Many duties fell upon Robert. He became his mother's nurse and housekeeper; yet found time for school, for hunting,

for swimming with the boys in the river, and every year
for a gay visit to his relatives at Shirley.

Robert was happy and never knew that he was
good.

⚙

Meanwhile, in Richmond, Frances Allan was delighting to set on little Edgar Poe's dark curls a purple
cap with a gilt tassel, to put upon his feet pumps with
shiny buckles, and to dress him in voluminous trousers
of yellow silk. Then together they would drive about
Richmond paying calls.

*Sing for the ladies, Edgar. . . . Dance for the
ladies. . . . Recite one of your pretty pieces for the
ladies.*

Everyone agreed that Edgar was remarkable. Even
John Allan began to take pleasure in the social triumphs
of his little foster son; though he could not quite get
over the fact that the boy's parents had belonged to
the wicked profession of the stage. Allan, implacable
toward any fault in a woman, saw something certainly
ugly in the fact that Elizabeth Poe did not know what
had become of her husband. As star of a touring the-
atrical company she had arrived in Richmond with a
baby daughter and three-year-old Edgar; but without a
husband.

Edgar got the impression very early that there was
something disgraceful in his life, something unhappy
that made him different from other children. He knew
that his mother had died . . . died in the furnished
room back of Mrs. Phillips's millinery shop in that part
of the town known as the Bird-in-Hand, because of an
inn of that name; famous for its spitted mutton. And

he understood that as a homeless orphan he must be grateful for the good home Mr. Allan gave him.

Edgar was taught to call Mr. Allan "Pa" and Mrs. Allan "Ma," but little by little he came to know that he only called them by those names, that it wasn't real, because "Pa" wouldn't agree to adopt him legally. Not to be legally adopted must be a dreadful thing, since "Ma" was so unhappy about it. But "Pa" said, wasn't he providing a home, and didn't he plan to give the child as good an education as any boy in Richmond?

From his own mother Edgar had nothing but the miniature of herself which was all there was to leave him. The miniature fixed her image in his mind. "Ma" was beautiful, with dark hair piled on her head, and dresses that made her look as stately as a statue; but his mother, the girl that looked out of the miniature, had long dark curls falling to shoulders childishly frail, and she had enormous eyes, wide-apart eyes, very big eyes.

Of course, he couldn't actually remember her; he had been only three when she died, and childless Frances Allan had taken him home to be the son of her heart. He couldn't actually remember, yet neither could he forget. Nothing seemed real—not even his own mother.

Travelers in that long ago have described the Virginia where Robert and Edgar were growing up.

There was as yet no railroad. People journeyed on horseback, in private carriages, or by river boat and stagecoach. It took two days to make the hundred and twenty-six mile trip overland from Washington to

Richmond; and the stages were only covered wagons, open at the front, and drawn by four horses.

For much of the way the road passed through dense forests of oak and dogwood, pine and cedar. Often it was so narrow that the wheels actually grazed the trees; at other times it was as wide, they say, as the London Turnpike; but so bristling with the stumps of trees that it was wonderful to see the driver guide the coach between them. Every little while creeks and rivers crossed the way, the coach reeling down a slippery bank, splashing through water often alarmingly deep, and then struggling up the opposite bank.

As the stage lurched and jounced along it startled wild turkeys and sent them rushing into the deep woods. It excited squirrels which darted graceful and curious among the branches, and occasionally a pack of hogs would gallop snorting in panic across the road; hairy scrawny creatures with razor-backs, and sharp-nosed faces.

It was a lonely road. At intervals of a dozen miles or so there might be a tiny settlement with a tavern, or the tavern might be only a single house standing in the forest. You knew the tavern by placards advertising for runaway slaves and stolen horses, or giving notice of taxes to be paid.

Sometimes in the doorways of solitary log houses lonely white women stood to watch the stage pass. "Neat women of cheerful countenance." And you might hear a Negro voice singing:

> "De hen an' chickens went to roos'
> De hawk flew down an' bit de goose.
> He bit de ole hen in de back.

I do believe dat is a fac'. . . . .
Oh, Jinnie, git de hoe-cake done, my dear!
Oh, Honey, git de hoe-cake done!"

Occasionally the stages had to negotiate a passage around a great hogshead of tobacco, bound from plantation to warehouse. Iron hoops were clamped about the hogshead, pivots attached at the ends. And mules were harnessed to each hogshead, to drag the heavy load.

From the road you did not see the Virginia of the rivers, where plantation houses sat serene among gardens and lawns, shadowed by oaks and tulip poplars; such houses as Shirley where young Robert Lee spent so many happy days.

The taverns where travelers stopped served huge meals of fowls and turkeys, ham and partridge and eggs, with many kinds of hot bread. The landlords always came forward to hear what news the travelers brought, who they were, where they were going, and for what object.

The travelers, too, were curious, recording in their books whatever interested them. They were amazed by the heat of summer, fireflies were wonderful, and they were astonished by the violence of the thunderstorms which crashed and rolled across the heavens. The Richmond of Edgar Poe's childhood they thought a large, elegant city, its ladies handsome, its men affable, high-spirited and patriotic.

In the autumn of 1824 a serene old man visited the United States. Thirty-five years before, adventurous and ardent, he had fought beside Washington in the American Revolution. Now he had come back, and no man ever received so great and joyous a welcome in a foreign land. For General Lafayette was more even than the brave soldier who had made America's struggle his own; he was the very spirit of the New World. "I have always loved liberty," he said; "I have loved it with the enthusiasm of a religious man, with the passion of a lover, and with the conviction of a geometrician."

The United States went wild over this gallant white-haired figure out of its past, dressed still in the outmoded fashion of his youth, with cocked hat, knee breeches, swansdown waistcoat, and blue coat with gilt buttons.

In Alexandria, in tribute to the memory of his old friend, brilliant Light-Horse Harry, he paid a call upon the widow in the little brick house.

Of course, Robert shone in the glory of General Lafayette's visit. And upon Edgar, too, the great Lafayette left an impression. Perhaps in all his life Edgar never knew a prouder, happier day. Artillery thundered in salute and bands played as the steamer from Norfolk brought Lafayette up James River to Richmond. Four white horses drew the hero's carriage through streets packed with cheering crowds. And in the procession marched Edgar himself. The press of the day states that in the parade there was a "pretty looking company of small boys dressed in hunting shirts, and styling themselves the 'Morgan Legion.'" Of this "Legion," sixteen-year-old Edgar was the lieutenant, handsome and erect, fair-skinned and brown-haired, with grey eyes veiled by astonishingly long lashes.

In that same year John Allan inherited a fortune from a rich uncle, and the Allans moved into an imposing dwelling which Frances Allan filled with costly furnishings.

And Edgar was the son of the house. Yes, but was he really? The house was his home, that was true. He had been accustomed by the Allans to luxurious living. But how secure could he feel? Actually, he did not belong anywhere. "I am a Virginian," he would say; but even that was only partly true, for he had been born in Boston.

This was the year he fell in love with little Elmira Royster; and she had given him her promise. He would soon be gone to the university; but, of course, Elmira would write; they would have each other's letters. Frances Allan herself drove with Edgar to Charlottesville, entered him at the university, and left him there; for the first time in his life free from all restraint.

Thomas Jefferson was seventy-seven when the University Charter was granted. The years that remained to him were spent in bringing true this his dream of forty years. He himself laid out the beautiful campus and was the architect of all the buildings. He personally supervised every detail of their construction. He was the most widely cultivated man of his day in America, and the university course as he planned it added to the classics the study of modern languages and of all the sciences. He selected a group of able professors, and became himself the first head of the university. He was past eighty when it opened its doors to receive students.

Jefferson, passionately believing in democracy, considered that students should govern themselves, that professors should teach, but not discipline. The merchants of Charlottesville exploited for their own ends this new freedom for youth. They offered credit; whatever the young gentlemen wanted was theirs. In due time their fathers would receive the bills. An orgy of liberty reigned. They were all so young, bewildered in the too-strong light of unrestrained freedom.

In its first years, before this plan was wisely modified, the most valuable lesson Jefferson's university taught was that democracy cannot survive unless Washingtonian realism is fused with Jeffersonian idealism.

But Edgar, then only seventeen, did not theorize about democracy. He was wondering why Elmira did not answer his letters. He wrote again and again, imploring a word from her, but there was only silence.

So it was that, troubled about many things, Edgar began to gamble.

At West Point Cadet Robert E. Lee rose when reveille sounded at dawn. There was half an hour for dressing. The sunrise gun announced a before-breakfast study period. Then thirty minutes for breakfast. After that, morning dress parade, followed by study. Dinner at one. Study and recitation until four, and from four to sunset military exercises, ending in dress parade, roll call, and supper. Study until lights out at ten o'clock. No cards, no tobacco, no liquor, and disobedience sternly punished.

It was in July and the heat heavy in Charlottesville. Thomas Jefferson was now eighty-three. And in the shimmering heat he felt death lay hands upon him. Unworried about the hereafter, he made ready to go. He talked of the university, the hopes he had for it, and his confidence in its future. So the second and the third of July passed. From time to time he fell asleep, but when he roused his mind was alert. On the evening of July third he seemed to have drifted into a coma, but suddenly he spoke to the doctor sitting at his bedside:

"Ah, doctor, are you still there?"

His voice was faint, as though coming from far away. The doctor assured him of his presence. Then the voice questioned: "Is it the Fourth?"

These were the last earthly words of Thomas Jefferson, author of the Declaration of Independence.

Not so long ago he had written to John Adams: "The flames kindled on the 4th of July 1776 have spread over too much of the globe to be extinguished by the feeble engines of despotism."

Morning came, and at one o'clock on the afternoon of the great anniversary of the Declaration, Thomas Jefferson quietly ceased to live.

And in Massachusetts, on that same day, John Adams sat muttering unintelligibly in his chair, a palsied old man whose time could not be long. Through the open windows there came the noisy explosion of rockets and firecrackers.

Suddenly, then, the meaningless mumble of old John Adams cleared. "Thomas Jefferson," he said, "still lives." And with those words he died; not knowing that Jefferson had preceded him by an hour.

In Charlottesville Edgar Allan Poe heard the solemn tolling of the bell. And, later, at West Point the routine paused as the news was told.

Jefferson and Adams, signers of the Declaration of Independence, had died on the fourth of July.

Many wondered if there was some portentous, awful meaning in their passing together on that day.

## CHAPTER SIXTEEN

## "Fresh from His Sheep"

Young Matthew Maury rode over the mountains from Tennessee into Virginia. A neighbor had provided him with a horse, a grey mare named Fanny. At the end of the journey Fanny was to be sold and whatever price she brought sent back to her owner. In his pocket Maury had thirty dollars for Fanny's expenses and his along the way. He had earned the money doing some teaching at the local academy. Now he had Fanny and thirty dollars, and, best of all, he had his appointment as midshipman in the navy; he had Sam Houston to thank for that. Maury's father had contributed nothing. Sons were valuable in a pioneer farmer's family; an older son had gone into the navy, and had died of yellow fever aboard his ship as she was standing in to Norfolk. So, at the moment of Matthew Maury's riding away, his father had turned from him in mute sorrow.

But the life of the road blurs the edges of the past for those who travel, and Maury's bright blue eyes looked eagerly into the future.

When spring sunlight shimmers over a road, dreaming youth may summon the image of ambition to appear in the quivering light.

Whatever may have been Maury's vision on his ride over the mountains into Virginia he could not have foreseen the value of the work he was to do in the world.

He could not have dreamed that he was ever to be called the "Humboldt of America," the "Pathfinder of the Sea"—or that the great Humboldt himself was to say that Matthew Maury had founded a new science.

It was not possible for the young Maury to look into the future. Nearly half a century after he was dead, Julian Street, a writer from the northern states, traveling through Virginia, learned for the first time of Matthew Maury, and wrote that "there is no one living in the United States, or in any civilized country, whose daily life is not affected through the scientific researches and attainments of this man."

But achievements and honors could not have been revealed to Maury in the sunlight dancing on the road: it was enough for him to know that at last he had his appointment as midshipman in the navy.

Certain events in his life had combined to shape his destiny. There was the cobbler who made the family shoes. The cobbler had the habit, as he worked, of covering the soles of shoes with odd little y's and x's. When Maury came to know what they meant he found them to be a fascinating puzzle called algebra. The cobbler had introduced Maury to the mathematical universe.

Then when he was twelve years old he had been helped to an education by the accident of falling from a tree.

But for that his labor on the farm would have prevented his getting much more than the fundamentals of reading and writing and figuring; but the fall, which was from a great height, had so injured him that hard physical work was for a time impossible. So it happened that he was sent to the academy to get what learning it could furnish. By that time pioneer life had already shaped his body; not tall and slim, but stocky, with sturdy muscles.

And far back in his childhood, even before the family had migrated from Virginia to the Tennessee frontier, his brother John's going into the navy had established a connection for Matthew with the great wide world.

Now, as he journeyed, he resolved that he would make *everything bend to his profession*.

Meanwhile the grey mare, Fanny, was taking him over the mountains into Virginia where he had been born.

More than a hundred years ago his father's people had come to James River, Huguenots fleeing from persecution in France. And the Virginia of his mother's Cavalier forebears had welcomed the fugitives. His very name—Matthew Fontaine Maury—was woven into James River history. The Reverend Peter Fontaine had been chaplain on William Byrd's famous Boundary Line Commission. The Reverend Francis Fontaine had been professor at William and Mary. John Fontaine was one of those knights of the Golden Horseshoe who accompanied Governor Spotswood on his fabulous expedition into the mountains. Anne Fontaine had married Matthew Maury, and their son, James Maury, had moved to Albemarle County and established a school. Jefferson, Madison, and Monroe had been his pupils.

It was therefore to the home of his ancestors that young Matthew Fontaine Maury journeyed on his borrowed mare.

He found in Virginia living kin, as well as departed

ancestors, to welcome him; among them little Ann Herndon, young enough to look up to her new cousin, for she was only thirteen, and he a man of nineteen with an appointment as midshipman in the navy. Ann was a pretty thing; her eyes as blue as his own, her hair auburn, and her voice so musical that it echoed in his mind. Relatives were truly a delightful discovery. One of them bought Fanny, which made it possible to discharge the debt to Maury's frontier neighbor.

When Maury was assigned to the new frigate *Brandywine*, of course, the kin were delighted with his good fortune, for the *Brandywine* was to carry General Lafayette back to France. And the papers were saying that in "elegance and efficiency" the frigate had never been surpassed by any ship clearing from an American port.

In early September the *Brandywine* under full sail passed into Chesapeake Bay beneath a bright rainbow, linking the shores of Maryland and Virginia. A strong wind blew the ship swiftly between the Capes and out to sea, where contrary waves rocked and pitched her, from port to starboard and bow to stern. It was as though the sea were testing the green young midshipman, Matthew Maury; she would do her worst, and if he was undismayed, then he might claim the high title of sailor. And he remained undismayed.

General Lafayette took a fatherly interest in the midshipman aboard the *Brandywine*; he had many talks with the ruddy, brown-haired, blue-eyed youth who, while he walked the deck, studied problems in spherical trigonometry which he sketched in chalk where he could see them as he paced back and forth. Maury was conspicuous, too, as a man able to joke no matter how sea-sick he was, and he was very seasick. Lafayette, a poor sailor himself, naturally had a fellow feeling for similar sufferers.

As for Maury—to have sailed with Lafayette on the *Brandywine*, actually to have talked with him—no youth could ever forget that.

It was in June, some three weeks before Poe heard the tolling bell which marked the death of Thomas Jefferson, that Maury sailed again out of the harbor of Norfolk, this time aboard the frigate *Macedonian*, with orders to proceed to South America . . . bound once more for the future, with Rio de Janeiro the first port of call.

He says that when standing his watch he felt "God's voice in every wave that claps its hands, and in every breeze that blows." The ocean appeared to him as a "face upon which time writes nothing," and of the clouds moving across the sky, he said "they have com-mandments to fulfill." He saw the beauty of an ever-lasting wisdom in the universe of sky and sea, and longed to understand that wisdom.

Echoes of human life aboard drifted to where he stood. Often strains of music floated out over the waves; men off duty were making merry; one had a flute, an-other a fiddle. The rhythmic pounding of feet meant that in the fo'c'sle sailors danced. Occasionally there would come to him the sound of a lash and an agonized cry as some wretched fellow took punishment at the gangway; and sometimes death visited the ship, and then around the decks there went the shout: "All hands to bury the dead."

Sixty-two days out from the bay into which James River pours its tawny water, there was Rio, with the breath-taking beauty of its green hills rising from the blue harbor; with the tragedy of slave ships anchored there, and in the streets an emperor's gilded chariot drawn by six mules magnificent in gilt trappings. Then Rio slid into memory; the host of albatross which hover about Cape Horn joined the company of remembered things, and the west coast came into the focus of the present. The waves broke now upon that long, arid strip of land which is Peru, with the Andes towering, snow-crowned, above it.

Maury meditated on the astonishing difference between South America's east and the west coasts; he noted winds and currents, and meditated. When the frigate *Vincennes* arrived in the harbor of Callao bound for the Orient, he asked to be transferred; he must see more of the world's oceans, he must observe new currents and new winds.

He sailed to the Marquesas, to China, Manila, Java, Sumatra, down the coast of Africa, around the Cape of Good Hope. And slowly a dream was taking shape within him. He dreamed of a time when the mariner could accurately map his course. To that end he set himself to study the ocean.

When Maury finally returned to Virginia he had been gone four years. Blue-eyed Ann Herndon was no longer a child, and almost his first act ashore was to fall in love with her. Before he was again ordered to sea they were engaged. He had a little seal made which she was to use only on letters to him; it was engraved with the word "Mizpah"—"the Lord watch between me and thee, when we are absent one from another."

And then he sailed away, this time as master of the *Falmouth*; again to Rio, again around the Horn, and again to the west coast. Plotting the *Falmouth's* course, he more than ever realized the need for an accurate science of navigation.

This was a memorable year. Maury was absorbed by the great vision of a charted navigation; and from time to time there came to him a letter whose seal bore the word "Mizpah."

Then in the hot summertime of Virginia he went home and was married.

And Ann Herndon told him that when she first saw him, long ago when he was newly arrived from the wild frontier, he had seemed to her "like young David, fresh from his sheep."

# CHAPTER SEVENTEEN

# Knight of the Gentle Heart

Robert Lee's instinct was to send his roots deep into the soil he loved, there in peace to live and at length to die. Once he said that all he wanted in the world was a Virginia plantation, no end of cream, fresh butter, and fried chicken; not one fried chicken, or two —but unlimited fried chicken.

All day on his plantation he would be busy; roads and fences would have to be kept up, buildings would need repair, livestock would require continued care, and always there would be the cycle of sowing and reaping. For companionship he would need only Mary and the children. Could anything be more delightful, he thought, than romping with little children? They were never too young to be your friends. Then, as they grew older, it was important that his boys should be taught to ride properly, sitting the "dragoon" seat, and never rising in the saddle. Mary would see that all the children knew their Bible, and that the girls learned to sew. It would be his part to help with the other lessons.

But Lee did not own so much as an inch of land, and he had chosen the army as his profession.

Graduated with honor from West Point, he entered cheerfully upon a soldier's wandering life, and almost at once he was ordered to Cockspur Island, off the coast of Georgia. The wandering had already begun.

His next assignment stationed him at Fortress Monroe, at the mouth of James River. It was then that he married Mary Custis of Arlington, great-granddaughter of Martha Washington.

They had a merry wedding. The company laughed and danced, with no presentiment of Appomattox to dim the future. Lee, people said, was bound to rise in the army; his very looks, his handsome distinguished presence surely guaranteed him success. Something set him apart from other men. Everyone was aware of it— everyone but himself. As for Mary Custis, she was a sensitive, quickly responsive girl, with the gift of making people happy. And the many relics of George Washington which made Arlington so sacred to Lee seemed to grant benediction upon this marriage. In Mary's father—George Washington Parke Custis—there was a living link with Mount Vernon. And among the servants at Arlington was a woman who had been Martha Washington's maid. She had been in the room, standing near the door, on the night Washington died; and now she saw Mary Custis married to Robert Lee, whose father, Light-Horse Harry, had been Washington's friend.

At Fortress Monroe the young Lees were soon absorbed into the life of an army station. And, of course, they heard talk of Edgar Poe, since he had spent some time there before John Allan had arranged his discharge from the army and his admission to West Point. Nobody could understand why Poe had then disgraced himself by getting expelled from West Point. He'd made a good record in the army. Why get expelled from West Point?

But the real preoccupations of any army post naturally deal with promotions and transfers, flirtations and marriages, births, servants, and parties, and what is good for croup or teething.

Then suddenly news had come of a slave uprising; a bloody uprising in eastern Virginia.

People, terrified, remembered what had happened in Haiti; how the black emperor, Dessalines, had commanded his soldiers to seek out the whites; to seek in the cane-fields, under the thatch of roofs, among the branches of trees, even in the great ovens. The soldiers were to bring those they found to a place outside the town. Then, when Dessalines should give the signal by striking three times on his snuffbox, the massacre was to begin. All were to be butchered, with mercy for none. Dessalines had boasted that his horse would paw the ground in blood from one end of Haiti to the other. In revenge for the cruelty of French masters he would have his horse paw the ground in blood. There were refugees in Richmond who had fled from those atrocities.

Could such things happen in Virginia? But Virginia slavery had never been like that of the French islands. Dreadful things had taken place in the French islands.

Even while people argued, the insurrection had been put down, and Fortress Monroe slipped gradually back into its customary routine; this one had been transferred, another promoted; Mrs. Lee was expecting a baby and going home to Arlington for its birth.

There must have been talk also of England's freeing of slaves in her West Indian possessions, for it occurred at about this time. It had cost England twenty million dollars; for the slaveholders had been paid for the eight hundred thousand Negroes in bondage to them. There must have been discussion of this in Virginia, for there were many antislavery societies in the state and everyone was interested in the free colony of Liberia, whose capital—Monrovia—was named for James Monroe.

From Fortress Monroe, Lee was assigned to duty in Washington, and after that was sent to survey the boundary between Michigan and Ohio territories. Babies came to the Lees through the years, as regularly as the striking of a clock; more regularly unfortunately than army promotions. Lee was in the Engineer Corps where advancement was particularly slow. And Mrs. Lee had fallen into ill-health, spending much time at Arlington with her parents.

Without Mary and the children Lee was always lonely. "I am the father of children," he said, "so entwined around my heart that I feel them at every pulsation." On his long absences they were always in his thoughts.

In his every scheme of happiness he looked forward to retiring to a farm in some quiet corner among the hills of Virginia. He desired promotion only as a means of caring for his family; he seems never to have thought of it as recognition, or found in it a personal gratification. His tastes were utterly simple; a plantation, Mary and the children; nothing more was desired by this knight of the gentle heart.

Upon his return from the Great Lakes he was sent to the Mississippi in charge of important engineering works. His constructive mind enjoyed running dikes, building dams and piers. He was out with the laborers at sunrise, spending the whole day on the blazing river, and at night he worked under a hot lamp over plans and estimates until nearly midnight. He had a talent for handling labor, he understood economy, and he had a genius for engineering. He worked hard and lived hard.

But little of all this went into those letters home into which he poured the greatly simple life of his heart. To be alone among people he found very solitary, while in the woods he felt himself in sympathy with the trees and birds, taking delight, he said, in their company. And one day in St. Louis he happened to see a little girls' party: "Twenty-three of them," he wrote, "all dressed up in their white frocks and pantalets, their hair plaited and tied up with ribbons, running and chasing each other in all directions, the eldest not more than seven or eight . . . it was the prettiest sight I saw in the West, and perhaps in my life."

And when at last he was free to go home it was so joyful a thing to find himself once more on the soil of the ancient Dominion of Virginia that he nodded to the trees as he passed, chatted with the drivers and stableboys, shook hands with the landlords, and wanted to kiss every pretty girl he saw.

War with Mexico over the Texas boundary question sent Lee into active military service. In his first battle he won the title of major; his perilous crossing of the Pedregal, alone at night, brought him the brevet of lieutenant colonel, and soon after he won the brevet of colonel. During this war he was repeatedly cited for gallantry, intrepid coolness under heavy fire, daring and soundness of judgment. He constructed roads and bridges over which the army might pass; he brought forward guns and conducted columns under hot fire. General Scott called him the very best soldier he ever saw in the field.

Yet his heart was that of a man of peace. "You have no idea," he said, "how horrible a sight a field of battle is." And he wrote home describing how one day, near Jalapa, he had come upon a drummerboy with a shattered arm, who was unable to move because a dying soldier lay on the injured arm. A little girl, with tears pouring from big dark eyes, stood helpless over them. She was a barefoot creature, her slender brown arms crossed on her breast, her hair hanging to her waist in a long black braid, her tears streaming.

"The plaintive tone," Lee said, "of her 'Mille gracias, Señor,' as I had the dying man lifted off the boy, and both carried to the hospital, still lingers in my ear."

And, far away in Mexico, he had his little terrier, Spec, on his mind. "Can't you cure Spec?" he wrote his wife. "Cheer him up—take him to walk with you, and tell the children to cheer him up. . . . Tell him I wish he was here with me."

Mexico was followed by assignments which made it possible to have his family with him: he was put in charge of the modernization of Fort Hamilton and Fort Lafayette, and for a time he was superintendent of West Point.

Then, ordered once more to service in the field,

he slipped back into the old life of hard riding and hard fare, as though he had never known anything else. He went west, and to the Far South, riding many hundreds of miles on court-martial duty. He spent nineteen months at Camp Cooper on the Texas frontier, among Indians always eager to send an arrow into a white man.

In that country there was no timber for houses and he had to live in a tent. In a letter to his little daughter, Mildred (published for the first time in Freeman's great biography), Lee wrote that, like all good campaigners, he had brought some chickens with him. "I have only seven hens," he said, "and some days I get seven eggs . . . having no plank I have been obliged to make them a house of twigs. I planted four posts and bored holes in each, three feet from the ground, in which I inserted poles for the floor, and around which were woven branches. There are so many reptiles in this country that you cannot keep fowls on the ground. . . .

"This hen-house," he explained, "is shady, but furnishes little protection against rain. Soldier hens, however, must learn not to mind rain. . . . I have no cat, nor have I heard of one in this country. You will have to send me a kitten in your next letter. The Indians have none, as there are so many wolves prowling around that they frighten away all the mice. My rattle-snake, my only pet, is dead. He grew sick and would not eat his frogs . . . and died one night."

The death of his father-in-law brought Lee home from Texas on leave. It was a sad home-coming, for he found his wife sunk in chronic ill-health. The one happy event of that furlough was a trip to Shirley on the James, where he went for the wedding of his son,

Rooney. Shirley was for Lee a house of memories of his own childhood and youth, and of the tradition of his mother's girlhood, with Light-Horse Harry galloping down the long drive when he came courting. It was all as he remembered, with the James ever flowing past, oblivious of time.

When you see Lee there at Shirley you want to cry out—to warn him that time marches along a road which leads to Appomattox.

# CHAPTER EIGHTEEN

# Ravens

Edgar Poe dressed in black, his black frock coat buttoned up to his black stock, without a vestige of white anywhere, except for his abnormally pale face. His figure was held erect with an air of immaculate distinction; his step was light and quick.

The ancient peoples of Guatemala believed that each human being had his counterpart in an individual creature of the animal world: it might be any animal— a hummingbird or a jaguar or an armadillo. They thought that the life of some particular creature was identical with that of every human being; that it shared his joys and sorrows, lived as he lived, and died when he died.

The raven of Poe's creation seems in this mystic sense to be identified with him.

It was in December that he came home to Richmond from the university at Charlottesville, and Frances Allan was giving a Christmas party to celebrate his return. Would Elmira be there? But Elmira, they told him, was not in Richmond. She had gone away on a visit, and people said that she was to marry a certain Mr. Shelton, a prosperous middle-aged bachelor. But Poe had a thousand sweet proofs of Elmira's love, and she had given him her promise. Why should she marry anyone else? As John Allan's adopted son, there was nothing he could not give Elmira. But perhaps, since Mr. Allan had not legally adopted him, Elmira's father did not look upon him as the son of the house. Was he, after all, only a charity boy, saying "Pa" and "Ma" to his patrons? Was that why, now that he was come home, Elmira had been sent away? And why had she not answered his letters?

In "The Raven" that hour wrote itself in the lines:

Ah, distinctly I remember it was in the bleak December,
And each separate dying ember wrought its ghost upon the
    floor.
Eagerly I wished the morrow;—vainly had I sought to borrow
From my books surcease of sorrow—sorrow for the lost
    Lenore—

That was a troubled winter in John Allan's fine new house. Elmira remained away, and silent. Edgar could not return to the university unless Mr. Allan would pay off his angry creditors. This Mr. Allan refused to do. Poe confessed his ambition to be a writer; but that was nonsense to which Mr. Allan would not agree. And Frances Allan, so loved by her adopted son that it was his habit to speak of her as "dear Ma"— Frances Allan was ill and sad.

Perhaps gossip brought to Poe's ears a reason for her sadness. Perhaps he could accept no guidance from John Allan because he thought him a hypocrite. At any rate, a few weeks after that "bleak December" he and Mr. Allan quarreled, and Poe flung himself out of the house, into a future darkly uncertain.

Frances Allan, distracted with grief, tried to prevent Poe's leaving Richmond, but the small boat by which he journeyed to Norfolk slipped away unobserved from the tobacco-scented wharves at the foot of the hill. He had no definite plan. He was not yet twenty, and his mood of "strange, impending doom" came only in occasional nightmares; it had not yet fastened itself upon him. There was hope in his heart. The lovely James River houses stood in tranquil dignity upon the banks— Shirley and Westover, Carter's Grove, Claremont and Brandon, among their sheltering trees. Surely one day the quarrel with "Pa" would be made up, and he would go back home, to fall asleep at night to the sound of the old Jeems rushing over the falls at Richmond.

Meanwhile, under an assumed name, he enlisted as a private in the army, and was sent to Sullivan's Island off the coast of Georgia. He did not see Virginia again until the end of the year when he was ordered to Fortress Monroe. Then Frances Allan was dying, imploring to see Edgar once more. But Mr. Allan was convinced of Edgar's "black heart," of his "deep ingratitude"; considering him "alike destitute of honor and principle."

Frances Allan, growing ever weaker, begged that if she should die before Edgar came, they would not bury her until he arrived, for she would have her darling boy look once more upon her.

But while Poe was traveling by stagecoach from Norfolk to Richmond she died; forcing from her husband the promise not to abandon Edgar. She was buried the day before the stagecoach rattled into Richmond.

Then beside her grave Poe let his heart break.

Frances Allan was gone . . . and in Richmond he learned that Elmira was married.

And of the raven he wrote that it was

Caught from some unhappy master whom unmerciful Dis-
aster
Followed fast and followed faster till his songs one burden
bore—
Till the dirges of his Hope that melancholy burden bore
Of "Never—nevermore."

John Allan had promised not to abandon him, but
he would keep only the letter of that pledge. He arranged the discharge from the army which Poe wanted;
his record had been good and the discharge easily managed. Also Allan used his influence to get Poe admitted
to West Point. But it was not long before, restless and
unhappy, he deliberately got himself expelled, and went
to Baltimore to his aunt Maria Clemm, his father's sister,
a widow, earning as seamstress an uncertain living for
herself and an eleven-year-old daughter.

From time to time he sent appealing letters to
Mr. Allan. He could never accept the fact that Mr.
Allan was no longer "Pa" and Richmond no longer
home. "I am a Virginian," he would say, and then add,
"at least I call myself that."

Memory of the luxurious home in Richmond appears in "The Raven" in the "silken rustling" of the
curtains, in the "sculptured bust of Pallas" and in the
"cushioned velvet lining that the lamplight gloated
o'er." And Poe had described himself in that "stately
raven with mien of lord or lady," that "fowl with fiery
eyes"; garbed, like Poe himself, in the simple elegance
of black. And Poe's appeals by letter to Mr. Allan were
not unlike the tapping of the raven at the door.

Now and then Poe sold a tale or a poem, but not
sufficiently often and not for enough money to give
him any sense of security. Mr. Allan had written plainly

that he was to expect nothing either then or as a legacy. But Poe seemed unable to believe that he and Mr. Allan did not belong to each other. Even after John Allan married again and became a father, he still thought of him as "Pa."

"For God's sake," he wrote, "pity me and save me from destruction." That was his last letter to Mr. Allan. It was never answered, and when Mr. Allan died his will revealed illegitimate children for whom he made some small provision, but Edgar Poe was not mentioned.

Increasingly now he sought escape from a reality in which he felt he had no place, until he became a stranger in the actual world, living more and more in the abnormal world of his fancy, a place whose fantastic horror dwarfed the sordid facts of his actual existence. His stories and verses carry you into that alien world of his creation. And when not even the imagination provided release, there was drink and drugs. In a society which drank in genial good-fellowship, Poe drank, seeking only escape.

"I have absolutely no pleasure," he said, "in the stimulants in which I sometimes so madly indulge. It has not been in the pursuit of pleasure that I have periled life and reputation and reason. It has been in the desperate attempt to escape from torturing memories— memories of wrong and injustice and imputed dishonor —from a sense of insupportable loneliness and a dread of some strange impending doom."

In "The Raven" all this is to be found, and the end predicted:

"Prophet!" said I, "thing of evil!—prophet still, if bird or
devil! . . .

Is there—*is* there balm in Gilead?—tell me—tell me, I im-
plore!
   Quoth the Raven, 'Nevermore.' "

 .  .  .  .  .  .

And the lamplight o'er him streaming throws his shadow on
the floor;
And my soul from out that shadow that lies floating on the
floor
   Shall be lifted—Nevermore!

# CHAPTER NINETEEN

# Winds and Currents

Iₙ the year after Maury had married "charming Nannie, his first and only love," Poe came again to Richmond; that city haunted for him by memory of the dead mother who lived only in her miniature, of "Pa" Allan and "dear Ma," of himself as lieutenant of a company of boys escorting the great Lafayette, of Elmira Royster who had kissed and promised.

He returned to the familiar city as editor of the *Southern Literary Messenger;* his tale of the "Manuscript Found in a Bottle" had been winner in a prize contest, and through that he had made contacts which obtained for him the editorship. He brought with him to Richmond his child-wife, Virginia Clemm, daughter of his aunt Maria, his father's sister. Poe was then twenty-four and Virginia not yet fourteen; "Sis" was the little name by which he tenderly called her.

As editor Poe immediately made a reputation for savage book criticisms. Maury must have anxiously wondered what the *Messenger* would say of his book on navigation, his first book. Would Poe flay it?

But the review was favorable; "here," it announced, "is a work that strongly commands notice."

With Poe's editorship and the success of Maury's book, the married life of the Poes in Richmond and the Maurys in Fredericksburg started off with a cheerful flourish. Incomes were, to be sure, tiny, but hopes might well be vast.

Mrs. Clemm came over from Baltimore to keep house for Poe and the young little wife who was her daughter. When Poe was up late writing, Mrs. Clemm sat quietly beside him, every hour or so serving him a cup of hot coffee. She kept his clothes mended and brushed and cleaned. Virginia helped in household matters as a child might help. Poe adored her, and almost equally adored his mother-in-law, who so worshiped them both that they made up for her the universe.

The circulation of the *Messenger* multiplied with Poe as editor. On the surface the future promised happiness. But more and more Poe felt an alien in the normal world, belonging nowhere. Only he himself, Virginia, and Mrs. Clemm had reality; all else appeared to him a fantastic mirage, while in the strange imagined world of his creation he saw actuality. In its terror and its abnormality he felt at home.

It was a world where "black draperies shut out the moon, the lurid stars, and the peopleless streets—but the boding and the memory of Evil, they would not be so excluded." In the atmosphere was "a sense of suffocation . . . yet we laughed and were merry in our proper way —which was hysterical; and sang the songs of Anacreon —which are madness; and drank deeply, although the purple wine reminded us of blood." And then in that weird world "there came forth a dark and undefined shadow . . . but it was the shadow neither of men, nor of God, nor of any familiar thing."

Such was Poe's world, while for Maury flowers and babies bloomed, and ships roved the seas.

Then Poe ceased to edit the *Messenger*. Its owner appreciated his brilliant mind, and regretted!

If only Poe would keep away from liquor!

And Poe explained sadly: "I have not been driven to insanity by drink, it is insanity that has driven me to drink."

He lost his place on the *Messenger*, and the current of his fate carried him away from Richmond. Occasionally he found other editorial work, but he was never able to keep it. He had won literary reputation; he wrote and gave lectures; but these irregular earnings were not enough. From poverty he slipped into destitution. And Virginia was slowly dying of consumption.

The years passed, and at last Poe returned once more to Richmond; carrying in his heart the dark memory of Virginia's death. He could see her as she lay on the straw bed in the little cottage at Fordham. It was January and very cold. He had wrapped her in his overcoat and laid upon her bosom the big tortoise-shell cat. Virginia was cold and dying, with only the overcoat and cat to warm her. Poe and Mrs. Clemm held her hands and feet, that the warmth from their own bodies might pass into hers. And thus Virginia—Virginia who was always a child—had died.

After that Poe had been desperately ill. With his recovery he began slowly to write again and to lecture. In a strange, distracted way he became involved with one woman and another. In Richmond he again met Elmira, now a widow; they had discovered that, in the long ago, Elmira's father had intercepted their letters; the inexplicable silence was at last explained. So finally they came together. Elmira, the rich widow, and Poe,

broken by sorrow and drink and drugs; a threadbare
Raven now, in his rusty black, but still a Raven of
"stately mien"; a gentleman always, with the distinguished manner of the Virginian of his day.

From Richmond, Poe wrote Mrs. Clemm about
Elmira:

"My dear, dear Muddy: Elmira has just got home
from the country. I spent last evening with her. I think
she loves me more devotedly than any one I ever knew
and I cannot help loving her in return. . . . On Tuesday I start for Philadelphia. . . . If possible I will get
married before I start. . . ."

There was a postscript to say that the Richmond
papers were praising him to death—that he was received
everywhere with enthusiasm.

Poe's plan was to bring Mrs. Clemm to Richmond,
which he would make his future home. But on his journey north he got no farther than Baltimore. After four
days of delirium—of "constant talking—and vacant
converse with spectral and imaginary objects on the
wall . . . he became quiet and seemed to rest for a
short time"; then once more he spoke: "Lord help my
poor soul," he said, and with that he died.

He had been among those travelers whose feet were
set upon the way that was to lead to Appomattox. Now
he had fallen out of the procession.

And you wonder whether, in the mysterious depths
of his poet's soul, unknown even to himself, the "impending doom" which so tortured him was perhaps not
solely personal, but prophetic of that tragedy whose
climax was to be Appomattox.

When Matthew Maury was a child a fall from a tree had altered the current of his life. Now, after a visit to his parents in Tennessee, traveling to New York to join his ship, the stagecoach upset. Maury fractured a knee joint and a thigh bone. He was far from home and it was three months before he could travel.

Lying helpless, his mind went back to the day when, riding over the mountains into Virginia, he had resolved to make everything bend to his profession.

But suppose he should be lamed for life and unfit for active service, how was he to carry out that resolution? Well, if he couldn't follow his profession actively, then he must follow it in his mind. He would "cultivate," he said, "a few little patches of knowledge." Such a wilderness of subjects needed to be studied; should he choose ship building or ship sailing, winds or tides, storms or currents. Perhaps the destiny which had upset the coach would answer the question for him. After all, he insisted, "it is the talent of industry that makes a man. I don't think so much depends upon intellect as is generally supposed; but industry and steadiness of purpose, they are the things."

He wrote a series of articles on the reorganization of the navy; writing under the name of "Harry Bluff." One by one he discussed in detail the deficiencies of the service, and suggested remedies; documenting every point with facts and figures.

The articles were published in the *Messenger*. Harry Bluff became a sensation. Naval officers had the articles reprinted, and widely circulated, at their own personal expense.

And out of the words of the crippled Maury there eventually came into being a new navy.

The Harry Bluff articles brought him an assignment to the Department of Charts and Instruments at Washington. In the beginning it was a small routine position, but it decided what was to be the great work of Maury's life.

As master of the *Falmouth*, making accurate notes on his experiences around the Horn, he had dreamed of a science of navigation which would map the seas.

Suppose captains were provided with abstract logs on which to enter every day "the temperature of air and water, the direction and set of the currents, and the height of the barometer . . ." And suppose these captains "cast overboard at stated periods bottles tightly corked, containing on a slip of paper the latitude and longitude, and the day and month of the year." Suppose also that the bottles thus set afloat were picked up, "the latitude and longitude of the place where they were found noted in the captains' logs, with the day of month and year. Then—the logs returned to Washington, and a careful study made of their records—might it not be possible to map winds and currents along the ocean routes and to furnish navigators with reliable sailing directions?

It was a great dream—the dream of a new science of navigation.

Maury, now established in the Department of Charts and Instruments, began to study old logbooks found stored in Washington, at the same time he distributed to sea captains the abstract log which he had himself prepared.

Very soon he had more than a thousand captains recording their voyages. And from study of their logs he compiled Wind and Current Charts and Sailing Directions.

Mariners who used the Maury charts found that the dangers of the sea were lessened, and that they were able to reduce voyages by many days. Clipper ships cut the journey from New York around the Horn to California by as much as fifty days. A new route was plotted for the voyage between England and Australia, cutting nearly fifty days off the round trip.

The seaman's path, Maury said, "has been literally blazed through the winds—mile-posts have been set up on the waves, finger-boards planted, and time-tables furnished for the trackless waste."

All over the world mariners were now using the Maury charts, and from every part of the globe captains were constantly adding to the information upon which Maury based these charts. At the end of eight years he had collected records covering twenty-five million sailing days. The result was a lessening not only in time and in peril, but a saving of millions of dollars a year to all nations which used the Maury sailing directions.

Meanwhile visions were crowding his mind; he saw not only the charting of the ocean, but the establishment of a Naval Academy, the digging of a canal across the Isthmus of Panama, and the formation of a Weather Bureau which would aid farmers as the mapping of winds and currents was guiding the navigators of the sea.

In his spare hours at home he was writing; dictating to one of his daughters, with such gift of concentration that nothing disturbed him. He had no room set apart for his work, but in the midst of the family he would pace up and down dictating, wearing a blue Japanese dressing gown that someone had given him.

And often one of the younger of his children trotted behind him, using the sash of the kimono for reins, and shouting "Gee! . . . Whoa! . . . Back, sir . . . Gee!"

Under such conditions he wrote his *Physical Geography of the Sea,* a book which Humboldt declared had "created a new science."

And all that the man wrote breathed religion and poetry, as well as science.

In Europe Maury was known always as "The Great Lieutenant." In recognition of his service to the world, France, Holland, Austria, Sweden, and Prussia had gold medals struck in his honor. The Emperor of Russia made him "Knight of the Order of St. Ann"; the King of Belgium made him "Knight of the Order of St. Leopold"; France named him "Commander of the Legion of Honor"; the kings of Denmark and Portugal awarded honors to this "Pathfinder of the Seas" who, when he came riding over the mountains home to Virginia, had seemed to his little cousin Ann Herndon "like young David, fresh from his sheep."

And through Matthew Maury the United States government invited the nations of the world to confer on establishing a uniform system of observations at sea.

The conference met in Brussels. "Rarely before," Maury exclaimed, "has there been such a sublime spectacle" . . . the nations uniting to co-operate "in carrying out one system of philosophical research with regard to the sea. Though they may be enemies in all else, here, in the increase of knowledge for the good of all, they are to be friends."

# CHAPTER TWENTY

## "God-Made"

THE slave, John Jasper, was his mother's twenty-fourth child. He was born, it is said, in the year that Light-Horse Harry was attacked and stabbed by the Baltimore mob. At about that same time a very old lady had died in England in the city of Bath. She was Sally Fairfax, and she left a packet of letters written to her long ago by George Washington.

Jasper was born on the Peachy plantation in Fluvanna County, but soon after his birth he and his mother were transferred to the Peachy town house in Williamsburg, where his mother was put in charge of the spinning and weaving of clothing for the slaves.

As soon as Jasper was old enough he became oxcart boy, his duty being to stand authoritatively before the oxen while their driver loaded or unloaded the cart. But he was soon promoted to houseboy, and later the Peachys hired him out in Richmond. He must have seen the great reception to General Lafayette, when Edgar Poe marched as lieutenant of a legion of "pretty boys."

The next excitement in Richmond was the hanging of three Spanish pirates. Jasper undoubtedly saw them driven through the city, each pirate in a hooded purple robe, with the hangman's rope about his neck; and each seated upon his own coffin in the wagon which carried them to the waiting gallows.

Then when Jasper was fifteen he saw his first railroad train. In those days the Peachy family hired him out as a "stemmer" in Samuel Hargrove's tobacco factory. Nobody in the factory could strip the leaves from their stems faster than Jasper. In the years that he worked for Mr. Hargrove he grew tall and strong; his arms were immensely long and his skin black. In his young strength he loved pleasure; he was interested in women, enjoyed drink, and was fond of his pipe. So things were with him when, as he put it, he knew conviction of sin.

It happened on a fourth of July when he was walking across Capitol Square. He remembered that the square was full of people celebrating, and that all at once he, Jasper, the big jolly "stemmer" in Marse Sam Hargrove's factory, was convicted of sin. His sins seemed to weigh him down, numbing his spirit.

His conversion came six weeks later, on a morning in the factory. The joy of it broke from him in a cry. He often said that his first shout to the glory of the Redeemer could have been heard "clean across Jeems River."

A fellow slave taught Jasper to read, and he learned "a crumb here and a crumb there" until he could read the Bible. He had given up all that he considered sin. Now he devoted his spare time to preaching. The Bible was actual and vivid to him, and he made it live for his audiences. While he talked he acted out the story he told; sometimes he walked up and down clapping his hands, sometimes he broke into song. His words moved men, whatever their race, and whether they were sophisticated or primitive. His eloquence was irresistible. He called himself a "God-made preacher," and in that belief his face was luminous.

Jasper was Africa transplanted to Virginia, and he took from the white civilization the best it had then to give him. To that he added the dramatic eloquence and the profound faith of his own race. And he became great, because he valued greatness; and sincere because he admired sincerity; he became an aristocrat because he respected aristocracy, and holy because he reverenced holiness.

Thus, beside James River, he lived through the years of his bondage; lived to see Appomattox and what came after. . . .

Fortunately a Richmond clergyman—William E. Hatcher—wrote down some of Jasper's sermons, as he heard them, and published them in his *Life of John Jasper*.

When Jasper spoke, Hatcher says, his own people laughed and wept and shouted. "You couldn't hold still when Jasper sang."

"Some folks thought he was conceited. But he was too full o' de fear o' God to think he was some great somebody . . . But he mus' a' known God made him mo' of a man dan de gen'ral run. So he had good respec' fer hisself, an' felt dat a man like he was had got to behave hisself 'cordin' to what he was; but dat's different from bein' one o' dese giddy little fops always showin' hisself off an' braggin'. . . ."

"De ground got holy," Jasper's people said, "when he walked on it, he was so stately an' grave."

As for his stories, everybody delighted in his stories:

"Eve," he explained, "was over dar in de Gyarden o' Eden . . . she was by herself . . . don't know whar Adam was, but he'd better been tendin' to his fambly, 'stid o' gaddin' . . . Eve was saunterin' around de gyarden when de ole sarpint come gallevantin' down de road, all dyked up to kill. And what did he do, but go struttin' up to Eve, scrapin' an' bowin' like a fool dead in love!

"Dat was a awful moment in de history o' dis po' world. . . ."

Then, in familiar dialogue Jasper told the story.

Of Pharaoh and the children of Israel he said:

"It kinder 'muses me to observe God's keen way o' worryin' Pharaoh into lettin' His people go.

"De Lord decided to torment Pharaoh wid reptiles and insects.

"One day when Pharaoh come home from ridin', he find de palace hall full o' frogs scamperin' an' hoppin' aroun'. . . . He run in de parlor to git 'way from dem frogs; but dar dey was, on de fine chairs, on de lounges, in de piano . . . Jes' den de dinner bell ring, and in he go to git his dinner. Ha! Ha! Ha! It's frogs, frogs, frogs all around . . . squirmin' on de plates, squattin' up on de meat, playin' over de bread, an' little frogs swimmin' in de glasses o' water. When he try to stick up a pickle, Pharaoh's fork got stuck in a frog.

"De Queen, she cried an' told Pharaoh she gwine quit de palace befo' sundown if he didn't clear dem frogs out o' de house.

"Den de nex' mornin' Pharaoh wake up an' he was itchin' from head to foot; he fairly scratch de skin off his body, an' as I live he finds hisself covered over wid vermin.

" 'Bout dat time de Queen she spring up scratchin';
an', forgittin' her Queenship, she is dashin' round de
room shakin' her wrappers . . . Den dar was a yell
from de nursery an' de little Pharaohs come scratchin'
an' hollerin'. . . .

"Pharaoh was rich, but riches don't kill fleas, an'
soldiers can't conquer an army o' lice. . . ."

# CHAPTER TWENTY-ONE

# Miss LaSalle Corbell and Young Mrs. Pryor

Wʜᴇɴ LaSalle Corbell was a little girl, perhaps four or five years old, she went on a visit near Old Point Comfort, at the mouth of James River. She had been sent from home in the hope of escaping whooping cough.

Sallie, as she was familiarly called, was having a beautiful time on this visit. She was a gay little thing; she could dance and sing, and found herself very popular. Then she came down with whooping cough. And strangely—she could not understand why—she was popular no longer. Mothers cried out when they saw her: "Run away, little girl. My children can't play with you now."

Sallie was miserably lonely and very puzzled at the ostracism of whooping cough.

One day walking forlornly on the beach she saw a young man sitting on the sand under an umbrella. She had observed this young man before; he was often on the beach; reading, or watching the waves roll in and break. And, like herself, he was alone.

Now, suddenly, an idea occurred to her.

She crept under his umbrella; giving him quite a start, for he had not seen her coming.

"Have you got whooping cough?" she inquired earnestly.

Whooping cough? . . . Why in the world should she think he had whooping cough? The young man was amused. Sallie explained. She had seen him alone, not dancing with the others; and so she thought he must have whooping cough. She herself had whooping cough; that was why she was so lonely.

But no, it was not whooping cough that he had; he was troubled in his heart, he told her, because some-one he loved very much had died; and that, he ex-plained, was worse than whooping cough.

Sallie was sympathetic. She offered at once to be his little girl. She would comfort him and when she grew up to be a lady she would marry him.

Years later, she herself told the story of this meet-ing, in a book which she called *What Happened to Me.*

The young man under the umbrella was George E. Pickett, of the United States Army. He was born in Richmond in that year when Edgar Poe was falling in love with Elmira Royster and Robert E. Lee had just entered West Point as a cadet. Pickett, too, had gone to West Point, though ever so much later. And, like Lee, Pickett also had been in the Mexican War. As a young lieutenant he had scaled the parapet of the famous castle of Chapultepec, and under enemy fire had planted there the flag of his country.

This hero of Chapultepec was diverted by the child who had established herself under his umbrella, calmly adopting him and arranging for him his future.

Now, to Sallie whooping cough no longer mattered, for she had her Soldier to play with. They were every day together. Sometimes Pickett brought his guitar to the beach and sang to her. At other times he amused her by making little boats of bark and sailing them on pools left by the tide. He showed her how to dam up the water in larger pools, and how to build forts and garrisons in the sand. And he taught her to print the words "Sallie" and "Soldier."

Three years later Sallie and her Soldier met again. Now he was Captain Pickett, and had come to Fortress Monroe to take passage on the United States transport *St. Louis;* his destination, Puget Sound on the Pacific coast.

Sallie watched the ship sail out of the mouth of James River, taking her Soldier so far away. And a great grief filled her child-heart.

When it was decided that Sallie was old enough to go away to boarding school, her father took her to the seminary at Lynchburg, and they traveled by train. At Richmond a tall handsome man in the uniform of a colonel came on board. Even had Sallie's heart not been susceptible to all uniforms, because of her absent Soldier, she would have noted this man; for none who ever saw him could forget the noble beauty of his presence.

Sallie remembered so well that in her memoirs she recalled the man, and what he said that autumn day on the train. For he was Colonel Robert E. Lee, a man never to be forgotten.

Lee stopped to greet Sallie's father, who then turned over a seat, making room for the colonel to sit down.

He was a gallant gentleman, making himself charming to Sallie, teasing her for one of her curls; those brown curls which were just the shade of her Soldier's hair; his hair, too, wavy, and long in the fashion of the day.

But playful as he was with Sallie, Lee was serious enough in his talk with her father. He was home on furlough from Texas, he said, and had been summoned from Arlington in an emergency; ordered to Harpers Ferry, in command of troops to quell John Brown's raid on the arsenal and the town.

But all was now quiet, the colonel said: the hostages had been rescued and the insurgents turned over to the civil authorities, but before this was accomplished, several citizens had been killed by the raiders; one of them a free Negro, who had no part in the uprising.

The colonel thought the whole thing but the scheme of a madman; it was not John Brown's first exhibition of violence.

"But I am glad we did not have to kill him," the colonel said, "for I believe he is an honest old man . . . a madman, but honest and conscientious."

And Sallie's father said that he had asked his Negro foreman whether he thought John Brown ought to be hanged if the authorities convicted him. The foreman, shaking his head, had replied very slowly: "I know dat po' Marse John done brok' de law killin' all dem mens; but den . . . even ef he did . . . don't you think, suh, dat hangin' him would be a lil' *abrupt?*"

In Lynchburg, where Sallie was left to be educated, James River, the familiar river of her life, flows past the town on its way to Richmond, and to

Old Point Comfort where she had first met her own Soldier. And in Lynchburg she was no more than twenty miles from Appomattox Court House; a placid little place where nothing epochal had ever occurred.

But there was no reason for Sallie, dreaming of her Soldier, to think of Appomattox.

Young Mrs. Pryor wrote a letter to her friend, Mrs. Cochran:

"Dear Mrs. Cochran: May I have your receipt for brandy peaches? You know Roger is speaking all over the country, trying to win votes for a seat in Congress. I'm not sure he will be elected, but I *am* sure he will like some brandy peaches! If he is successful they will enhance the glory of victory—if he is defeated, they will help to console him."

Mrs. Pryor's hair had been still in braids, long brown braids burnished with gold, like the yellow lights which shone in her hazel eyes, when she had first met this Roger of whom she wrote, and he himself had been not quite sixteen.

From the moment when she had seen him run up her aunt's stairs, two steps at a time, she had blessed the fact that she had just been given a new bonnet of rose-colored silk, and a party dress—her first party dress; blue silk laced from throat to hem with narrow black velvet ribbon.

His first gifts to her had been a set of Shakespeare, Macaulay's *Essays*, Hazlitt's *Age of Elizabeth*, and volumes of Shelley and Keats. Whenever he could get away from the university, he had come and read them aloud to her. Thus had she been wooed. And when her lover was twenty-one they had been married; a cautious neighbor remonstrating: "Ah, why do you attach yourself to a comet?"

But in the brilliance of her Comet, Mrs. Pryor never needed any other light; willing always to pay the price.

As a young editor he had refused to go back upon his published opinions; his answer to the newspaper owner's reminder to think twice before giving up a large salary had been: "Damn your money!"

It was an age when to shirk a duel brought disgrace upon public men. The mere thought of a duel made Mrs. Pryor's lips turn blue and her hand tremble. For in campaigning against the Know-Nothing party her Comet had fought two duels.

"Oh, it was a dreadful time!" she often said. "The whole country was in an uproar. The Constitution was burned before a crowd in Massachusetts. And a man calling himself the Angel Gabriel went about rousing people against foreigners and Roman Catholics."

The Know-Nothing party, she explained, was a secret society. "I know nothing" was one of its passwords. Its object was to exclude from holding public office all Catholics and foreigners.

And it was in testimonial of his part in defeating the Know-Nothings that Virginia had presented Roger Pryor with a silver service.

Such things were dear to Mrs. Pryor's heart. To be a wife was to her a profession in which to glory.

An old *Virginia State Bulletin* gives a description of this comet who was her husband. "In his person," the writer says, he was "striking and graceful, of a

fascinating manner and irresistibly charming in speech
. . . There was the fire of genius in his eye and in his
well-tuned voice."

Men were known to ride sixty miles to hear him
speak. And the story was told of a man who exclaimed
that he had made this long journey, and stood for three
hours under a hot sun, just for the pleasure of hearing
Roger Pryor speak, even though his speech happened to
be abuse of the man's own political party.

Now, while he was campaigning for that seat in
Congress, young Mrs. Pryor wrote to her friend asking
her recipe for brandy peaches.

Into the Washington life that followed his victory,
Mrs. Pryor threw herself completely, her heart full of
patriotic pride in the capital of her country. She even
enjoyed listening to wearying speeches in the House and
the Senate. "None of it was very clear," she admitted,
"but surely everything was coming out right; everybody was working for the good of his country; we
belonged to it and were part of it; this thought glorified
all around us."

The Thirty-sixth Congress was long in session; the
country still seething over the trial and execution of
John Brown; and the men who, Mrs. Pryor so confi-
dently believed, were to "make all come right"—those
men were denouncing and insulting each other on the
floor of the House and the Senate. And the fateful words
"irrepressible conflict" were beginning to be heard.

Then upon a certain December day official Washington presented itself at a fashionable wedding. There,
in an armchair at one end of the room, was President
Buchanan. He looked aged, Mrs. Pryor thought, as he

turned to speak to her: "Do you suppose the house is on fire?" he asked. "I hear an unusual commotion in the hall."

"I will inquire the cause, Mr. President," she said.

When she came back, she stooped over his chair to say gently: "It appears, Mr. President, that South Carolina has seceded from the Union."

# CHAPTER TWENTY-TWO

# Irrepressible Conflict

Iᴛ appears, Mr. President, that South Carolina has seceded from the Union."

And the president whispered, like a man stunned: "Madam, might I beg you to have my carriage called."

It was December, and by the first of February Mississippi, Florida, Alabama, Georgia, Louisiana, and Texas had one by one followed South Carolina out of the Union.

What would Virginia's decision be?

A strong Union had been the dearest wish of George Washington. Virginia now urged a "Peace Convention," which might by some compromise save the Union. But the Convention failed in its purpose.

In Boston Edward Everett exclaimed: "The idea of a Civil War, accompanied as it would be, by a servile insurrection, is too monstrous to be entertained for a moment. If our sister States must leave us, in the name of Heaven, let them go in peace."

But that was not to be.

Lincoln, the new president, sent out a call for troops to subjugate the seceded states.

Now that the seceded states were to be coerced, Virginia felt that the great principle of consent of the governed was violated. In accepting the Constitution she had reserved the right to rescind, if that should ever seem necessary. Now, in bitter sorrow she repealed her ratification.

Colonel Robert E. Lee had been summoned from Texas to Washington, to report to General Scott, commander in chief of the United States Army. Lee had been all his life an army man. General Scott was aging. Lee, it was taken for granted, would succeed him. The highest honor for which a soldier might hope would then have been his.

But Lee could not accept command of the army that was now to be brought into the field.

"Though I was opposed to secession," he said, "I could take no part in an invasion of the Southern States. . . . If I owned the four million slaves in the South, I would sacrifice them all to the Union," but how could "I draw my sword upon Virginia, my native State?" He felt that he had no choice: he must resign his commission in the United States Army; resign from that service to which, as he put it, he had devoted the best years of his life and all the ability he possessed.

On the same day that Lee sent from Arlington his resignation from the United States Army, Matthew Maury in Washington resigned his commission in the navy. All that he as an individual could do to prevent the war, he had done. He had written personal appeals to the governors of Pennsylvania, New Jersey, Maryland, and Delaware, begging them to throw their influence against the "fratricidal strife"; urging for the

South equal rights in the Union; for he, like all Southerners, had long felt a discrimination against the South
in the matter of tariff and in the spending of public
funds.

But when Virginia seceded Maury resigned from
that position which gave him opportunity to carry on
the geographic work which was the passion of his life;
he resigned and went to Richmond to offer his services
to his state.

When this became known in Europe the Grand
Admiral of Russia, Duke Constantine, brother to the
czar, wrote inviting Maury to come to Russia, where
he promised that every advantage would be given, that
he might continue those scientific researches in which
he had "unveiled the great laws which rule the winds
and currents."

Maury's answer was that he had offered his sword
to Virginia; to defend those principles of self-govern-
ment for which Washington had fought.

Like Robert E. Lee, Matthew Maury renounced
personal prosperity and ambition.

From far away on the Pacific coast George E.
Pickett wrote to Miss LaSalle Corbell:

"You know, my little lady, some of those cross-
stitched mottoes . . . such as 'He who provides not for
his own household is worse than an infidel,' made a
lasting impression upon me; and while I love my neighbor, i.e. my country, I love my household, i.e. my State
*more;* and I could not be an infidel and lift my sword
against my own kith and kin, even though I do believe,
my most wise little counselor and confidante, that the

measure of American greatness can be achieved only under one flag. . . ."

So the sons of Virginia laid their all at her feet; to fight—not for slavery, for it is said that scarcely one in thirty of the soldiers of Virginia had ever owned a slave, or ever expected to—but to fight, as they believed, for the sacred principle of government by the consent of the governed.

And the men who made this supreme sacrifice— this vain sacrifice—could not know that the gallantry of their renunciation, of their heroic courage, was to place them among the immortals; a shining company riding forever in the sky of history; led by a sublime figure mounted on an immortal horse whose name is "Traveller."

When you see them on high, it is no longer to the tune of "Dixie" that they ride; it is to the triumphal music of the Valkyrie.

But it was the spirited earthly "Dixie" that young Mrs. Pryor heard when she watched the first troops march out of Petersburg:

> From Dixieland we'll rout the band,
> That comes to conquer Dixie,
> To arms! To arms! and rout the foe from Dixie,
> Away, away, away down South in Dixie.

So the regiments marched with flags waving, bands playing:

> Hooray! Hooray!
> For Southern rights, hooray!
>
> .   .   .   .   .   .
>
> Away, away, away down South in Dixie.

And none counted the odds against them. The available military strength of the North outnumbered that of the South three to one; in wealth it was nearly doubled; in the North were most of the railroads, most of the factories, and the shipyards; the North had a navy with power to keep her harbors open and to close all southern ports.

But men marching to the stirring tune of "Dixie" did not count the odds. They did not know that they marched along a road which was to lead to Appomattox.

Watching them as they step so bravely forth you long to warn them; for you can know what was hidden from them. Yet perhaps they would not have heeded your warning.

It is not known why little Miss LaSalle Corbell was not at school in Lynchburg on the eighth day of March in the year 1862. Perhaps it was the spring vacation. Or perhaps, since it was Saturday, she had come home for a week end.

However that may be, the young lady, on that balmy day, was sitting on her horse on the riverbank opposite Newport News.

Hundreds of people crowded the bank, and the eyes of all were fixed upon the new ironclad ship, the *Virginia*.

The *Virginia* was the old *Merrimac*, a 3,500-ton frigate, burned and sunk when the United States Navy abandoned the yard at Norfolk.

And while Matthew Maury was mining James River, and experimenting with torpedoes, the *Merrimac* had been raised, rebuilt as an ironclad, and named the *Virginia*.

It was because such a ship was something new in the world that people gathered in great numbers to see her make her trial shakedown. The waiting crowds did not know that this was to be anything more than a tryout; for the *Virginia's* engines had scarcely been tested since their long submersion; not one of her guns had been fired; her crew were as yet untried. In fact, workmen had been busy aboard her up to the moment when she left her dock.

It was a strange craft which the crowd saw steaming slowly down Elizabeth River and out into Hampton Roads. An iron ram was bolted to her prow, and her gun deck was covered with a sloping wooden casement to which were attached plates of iron.

Would her armor really safeguard her against gun-fire? Or was she just a huge metal coffin in which all aboard her would be buried? Of course, she was not designed to fight heavy seas; her purpose was to protect the harbor of Norfolk. And few had faith that she could do even that. As for use in the river, drawing twenty-two feet of water, she could not be of service much above its mouth. The most that you could say was that she was a hope. . . .

Sallie Corbell, sitting lightly on her horse, her field glasses focused upon the *Virginia*, heard people about her thus questioning.

Yet because the *Virginia* was a hope, however uncertain, the crowd cheered as she slowly steamed out of Elizabeth River, and into Hampton Roads.

Breathless they watched her round Craney Island. Straight ahead, about four miles distant slightly to the right, the Federal fleet was anchored off Fortress Monroe; and to the left, at about the same distance, lying in the mouth of James River, were two United States men-of-war—the *Congress* and the *Cumberland*. Toward these ships the *Virginia* headed.

It was washday on the *Congress* and the *Cumberland,* for you could see clothing hung to dry in the rigging. Dazzling sunlight glinted on the unruffled water of the flood tide. The air was soft, and warm, as though it were May instead of early March. The boats of the two men-of-war were attached to their swinging booms; and in the boats men lay idly, unsuspicious of trouble; while slowly the *Virginia* approached across the smooth shining water.

As she drew nearer, the men in the boats sat up, and at the portholes faces appeared, staring at the apparition that was the *Virginia.*

Then Sallie, seated on her horse, saw suddenly a "flash of fire, pale against the white day, a puff of smoke, drifting, wreathing . . . floating off into space."

So she described it later, and with that apparently innocent puff of smoke there came to her a deep roar, as of a dreadful thunder.

Guns from the *Congress* and from the *Cumberland* hurled broadsides against the *Virginia;* and she answered in kind.

The crowds sent up shouts of triumph; seeing that the *Virginia* proceeded steadily ahead, unharmed; forging ahead toward the *Cumberland,* firing as she went; plowing ahead—straight into the wooden side of the *Cumberland.*

Then, reversing her engines, the *Virginia* slowly backed away; the batteries from Newport News, the guns of the *Congress* and the *Cumberland* simultaneously pouring fire upon her. Yet all that they could do availed them nothing; every volley glanced off from her sloping metal sides.

But the *Cumberland*—Sallie saw that the *Cumberland* reeled; and then with a great terrible shudder, began to sink; sinking with her guns roaring; going down with all aboard her . . . sinking . . . until at last there was nothing visible above the yellow waters but the Union flag fluttering for a final moment before it also vanished.

"For days we had seen her," Sallie afterward said, "threatening us . . . but it was pitiful to watch her go down."

The *Cumberland* was gone, and laboriously the *Virginia* was manipulating her rusty engines to turn back and attack the *Congress* which, in trying to escape, had run aground.

Three Federal frigates appeared, coming from Old Point Comfort—the *Minnesota,* the *St. Lawrence,* and the *Roanoke,* hurrying to the rescue of the *Congress* which was now in flames; the flames "like banners flapping in the rigging."

Her defense was gallant but at last she hoisted the white flag of surrender.

The *Virginia* then sent out a launch to take off men from the burning ship; and two Confederate gunboats went also to her aid, under heavy fire from the frigates and the shore batteries.

At midnight the magazine aboard the *Congress*

exploded; and briefly, before her end, the *Congress* stood forth, a ship of fire in the darkness.

Sallie Corbell was up early on the following morning. Her uncle was just putting off in his boat, and she ran to ask if she might not go with him.

Of course, she might *not* go.

Her uncle, refusing, stepped aboard, and Sallie stepped after him. The boat was off before he turned and saw her.

"You little daredevil, you! I've a good mind to drown you."

But a laugh went with those ferocious words.

And so it came about that Sallie saw the first battle between two such ironclad ships ever to be fought in the world. For a second armored craft had arrived during the night. It was Ericsson's invention; the *Monitor*, come down from New York.

There had been rumor of the strangeness of the *Monitor*, but no one had expected it to be half so queer as it actually was. "It's just a tin can on a shingle," somebody said; for its circular revolving turret rose from a flat, water-level deck; that was all there was except a low square pilothouse. The whole thing was not a quarter the size of the *Virginia;* but more easily handled, and with the advantage of drawing only twelve feet.

In the battle of the previous day the *Virginia's* smokestack had been perforated, and her prow had been broken off in ramming the *Cumberland;* so that it was like a dilapidated fighting cock that she returned to the fray.

Now, for four hours on that Sunday morning in

Hampton Roads, the pygmy *Monitor* and the *Virginia* bombarded each other. Once, when the *Virginia* ran aground, the *Monitor* circled round and round her, seeking in vain some vulnerable point.

Finally the *Monitor* turned in the direction of Fortress Monroe to replenish her ammunition, and the *Virginia*, unable to pursue her into low water, steamed back to her base while the tide was yet high enough to let her pass.

The two ships never again met in battle; but the contest which Sallie Corbell that day watched from her uncle's boat changed forever the naval warfare of the world.

The London *Times* exclaimed that on the day before the *Monitor* met the *Virginia* England had possessed one hundred and forty-nine first-class warships, but of that number on the day after that battle in Hampton Roads one hundred and forty-seven were no longer of the first class; since only two of the fleet could do battle against ironclads.

Young Mrs. Pryor and Sallie Corbell were both in Richmond at the time of the battle of Seven Pines. Sallie's Soldier and Mrs. Pryor's Comet, now both become generals, had fought at Williamsburg, and side by side they headed their brigades in this battle of Seven Pines, which, in the irony of war, took its name from a clump of pines standing green and fragrant in a serene landscape converted by war into a scene of horror.

Throughout the days of fighting the thunder of

guns shook the heart of Richmond, while on the field marked by seven pines McClellan's army of a hundred thousand met the Confederate force of sixty-three thousand.

Then the wounded and the dead poured into Richmond. Hospitals overflowed into private homes, and black streamed from doors where the dead lay.

Sallie thought she had never seen roses so lovely as in that June when the battle of Seven Pines was fought; that June when ambulances left a trail of blood in the streets through which they passed; when in the deadwagons stiffened bodies were heaped one upon another; when those of the wounded who were able to walk marched weary and sick into the city. But the roses seemed never to have bloomed so bright in the gardens, while from the open windows there came often a scream of mortal agony.

Anesthetics—morphine and chloroform, opium—were contraband of war. The South had only such merciful relief as could now and then be smuggled through Federal lines.

Could it be that Richmond had ever been gay, that once from its open windows there had floated light laughter and song? Only the mockingbirds singing in the gardens and on the chimneytops seemed to remember song:

> Listen to the mockingbird,
> Listen to the mockingbird.
> The mockingbird is singing all the day.

The *Virginia* and the *Monitor*, the sinking *Cumberland*, and the burning *Congress* had been great spectacles of warfare: their death and agony had not been present to the eyes of those who looked on. But the battle of Seven Pines flooded Richmond with all the hideous anguish which is war.

General Pickett hoped that Sallie, home for her summer vacation, had gone on a visit to a school friend in the mountains: he would, he said, have her "beautiful tender eyes spared the horrors" which he knew the battle "must have poured into sad Richmond."

Mrs. Pryor, like other women of Richmond became, overnight, a nurse. And through the crowded hospitals there often passed the powerful black figure of the slave Jasper. Soldiers who were sufficiently well to listen loved to hear his picturesque version of the Bible stories; his deep tender voice lifted in song took them back to the plantation homes so dear to them, and his reverent faith brought them peace.

Sallie Corbell seems never for a moment to have been absent from the mind of General George E. Pickett. On the night that he led his brigade across the Chickahominy, the night before the battle of Gaines's Mill, he sent a letter to her to say that he was refreshing his soul by writing her; the little boarding-school girl, of whom he spoke as his "promised wife."

Gaines's Mill—the name is placidly suggestive of fruition, of sowing and harvesting, of farmers bringing their grain to be converted into flour and meal. And now the pastoral name—Gaines's Mill—was to belong to a great battle. There, on a level field of oats at the foot of a wooded cliff, the Confederates attacked McClellan's army which defended the cliff with tiers of artillery and infantry. Charging at the head of his brigade, Pickett was shot from his horse and a ball penetrated his shoulder.

But he led on, cheering though his arm hung helpless, while his horse followed as if its master still guided the reins.

When the doctor came up he ordered Pickett from the field; insisting that the ball should be immediately extracted.

"No, doctor, take the bullet out here; quick! I must go back. See, my men need me."

The doctor obeyed, and Pickett went back into the battle until, weakened from loss of blood, he had to be sent home to Richmond; leaving his brigade to continue with Lee's army in pursuit of McClellan's retreating forces.

It was September before Pickett was able to return to the army; the September of Lincoln's Proclamation of Emancipation.

In that month, too, Sallie went back to school; but in a year she was to be graduated, and then—so they planned in Pickett's weeks of illness—then they were to be married; just as she had arranged when as a little girl she had crawled under the umbrella of a lonely soldier on the sands of Old Point Comfort to inquire gravely whether he had whooping cough.

But before that marriage took place they were now and then to see each other, there were to be other battles, and there was to be Gettysburg. . . .

The romance of Sallie Corbell and Pickett, some twenty years her senior, is one of the rare love stories of the world. From the beginning he filled all her life.

To know the man—George E. Pickett—was to love him. As a boy he won the affection of Abraham Lincoln; and as a lieutenant in Mexico he was loved by Grant, Longstreet, and all who fought beside him. On the Pacific coast he had made true friends among the British officers, while the Indians felt that he belonged to them.

Looking into Sallie's glowing eyes one day, the dashing cavalry officer, Jeb Stuart—he who was called the "eyes of the army"—said of her Soldier: "Pickett can do anything. When I see him dance, I think he ought to be a dancing master; when I see him ride, I think he ought to be a cavalry leader. When he whistles, I think he ought to be a bird. When he sings, it seems to me that he ought to be an opera star. And when I see him lead a charge, I feel that he ought to spend his life on the battle-field."

Wherever he happened to be, Pickett sent back letters to the brown-eyed girl with chestnut curls lying upon her shoulders like the curls of a child; letters which, long after it was all over, she shared with the world.

He calls her all manner of endearing names—"my prettice," "my precious," "my darling," "my strayed angel of the skies." And always he signs the letters "Your Soldier"; for from the long-ago beginning that has been her name for him.

He cries out to her to come to him: "Come into the valley of the shadow of uncertainty and make certain the comfort that if I should fall I shall fall as your husband."

As he is setting forth to intercept a cavalry raid, reported to be coming down the south side of James

River, he writes that he is sending her a "little box of *dulces*" and a note "filled with adoration."

And from camp with Lee's army, marching north into Pennsylvania, he reminds her of their last farewell; how, when he heard the gate click, shutting him outside, he could not leave with that sound in his ears. That was why he had gone back into the house to say good-bye once more. He tells her that when finally he went away he did not hear the unbearable click, for he had been careful not to close the gate.

And on that fatal march north he writes again: "I never could quite enjoy being a Conquering Hero . . . No, my Sallie, there is something radically wrong about my Hurrah-ism. I can fight for a cause I know to be just, can risk my own life and the lives of those in my keeping . . . but when we've conquered, when we've downed the enemy . . . I don't want to hurrah. I want to go off all by myself . . . to lie down in the grass . . . far from all human sound, and rest my soul . . . and get back something—something I never knew I possessed 'till I had lost it—'till it was gone—gone."

Pickett tells Sallie how, on the way to Gettysburg, the army sang and told stories, always in a spirit of gay banter, inspired with absolute faith and confidence in success. "And now," Pickett said, "I'll tell you a great secret . . . So listen and cross your heart you won't tell . . . I love you—love you—love you, and, oh, little one, I want to see you so. That is the secret."

Then—in his letters—the final day of Gettysburg came to Sallie; the day of Pickett's charge.

He speaks of his men, exhausted by their long march in "dust and heat beyond compare." He describes the difficulties between the Confederate line and that of the Yankees; "steep hills, tiers of artillery, fences, infantry . . . batteries," and the charge which must be made over "nearly a mile of open ground . . . under the rain of their shrapnel."

The letter is penciled at intervals on scraps of paper.

"Our line of battle faces Cemetery Ridge. Our detachments have been thrown forward to support our artillery which stretches over a mile along the crests of Oak Ridge and Seminary Ridge. The men are lying in the rear, my darling, and the hot July sun pours in scorching rays almost vertically down upon them. The suffering and waiting are almost unbearable."

Reading this letter Sallie, far away on James River, is as surely present at Gettysburg as when she looked upon the battle between the *Virginia* and the *Monitor*.

"Suffering and waiting almost unbearable" . . . And then—"at one o'clock, the awful silence was broken by a cannon-shot, and then another . . . more than a hundred guns shook the hills—the whole world a blazing volcano . . . Then the forming of the attacking columns. My brave Virginians are to attack in front. Oh, God in mercy help me as He never helped before. . . ."

It was nearly three o'clock when Pickett closed the letter, begging Sallie to remember always that he was hers, now and forever.

Fifteen minutes later, mounted on his black war horse he shouted the order: "Forward!" . . .

When it was over, when the Confederate defeat at Gettysburg had passed into history, he writes on July fourth, on the sixth, and on the eighth:

"The moans of my wounded boys, the sight of the dead upturned faces, flood my soul with grief . . . My

brave boys, full of hope and confident of victory . . .
though officers and men alike knew the odds against
them . . . Over on Cemetery Ridge the Federals be-
held a scene never before witnessed on this continent—
an army forming in line of battle in full view under
their very eyes—charging across a space nearly a mile
in length . . . moving with the steadiness of a dress
parade. . . . They moved across that field of death as
a battalion marches forward in line of battle upon drill
. . . two lines of the enemy's infantry were driven
back; two lines of guns were taken—and no support
came. . . .

"Dear old Lewis Armistead, God bless him, was
mortally wounded at the head of his command, after
placing the flag of Virginia within the enemy's lines.
Seven of my colonels—were killed. Nine of my lieutenant colonels . . . wounded; three killed . . . The
loss of my company officers was in proportion . . . my
division is almost extinguished. . . ."

He writes how the soldiers' reverent love for General Lee never faltered in this hour of overwhelming
tragedy. "We'll move on anywhere you say, Marse
Robert, even to hell."

And Pickett overheard a rough fellow say, as he
wiped away the tears with the back of his hand: "Dag'-
gone him, dag'gone him, dag'gone his old soul, I'm
blamed ef I wouldn't be dag'gone willin' to go right
through it all and be killed again with them others, to
hear Marse Robert, dag'gone him, say over again as how
he grieved bout'n we-alls losses and honored us for we-
alls bravery! Darned ef I wouldn't!"

Two months later Sallie Corbell was getting together a Confederate bride's trousseau. She had dresses of home-woven fabrics dyed with homemade dyes. Buttons were carved from peach stones. Trimmings were made from various sorts of seeds, and laces were hand-knit of thread spun from flax. She had a poke-shaped hat of grey straw, braided by the family servants. Another hat was fashioned from the lacelike tissue lining of gourds. Milkweed balls supplied its decoration, and picked cotton shaped into balls and tinted any color you liked furnished bunches of grapes or pink roses which were very becoming. Her party dresses were made from the court robes of her great-grandmother, and friends presented a wedding gown of white satin, which became, in a manner, a community wedding gown, used by succeeding brides.

So at last LaSalle Corbell was married to Major General George E. Pickett; the tall soldier with the memory of Gettysburg in his eyes.

And in their honor guns were fired, bugles blew, and bells chimed; while for a moment war paused, for these two who had loved so long, so deeply, and so romantically.

❀

"I have a queer feeling in my stomach, mamma . . . No, it doesn't ache . . . but it feels like a nutmeg grater."

It was one of Mrs. Pryor's little brood, her son Theodorick Bland, who was speaking. "A queer feeling . . . like a nutmeg grater."

His mother well understood what was the trouble; for famine had come to Petersburg. Once there had been flocks of pigeons, but they were gone now. Constant cannonading had driven the fish from the river. The very rats and mice had disappeared. Venturing one day under shell fire to the market, Mrs. Pryor found on sale only some jugs and cakes of sorghum molasses, and a single frozen cabbage.

The long siege of Petersburg had begun.

General Grant's army had come down into tide-water Virginia. In trying to hold him back from Richmond, General Lee had fought his last great successful battle—the battle of Cold Harbor.

On the eve of that battle Pickett, lying alone in his tent, had serenaded his absent Sallie with the familiar songs they loved: "Last Night the Nightingale Woke Me," "Her Bright Smile Haunts Me Still," and "The Harp That Once through Tara's Halls." And then his mind had strayed back to his life as a soldier on the Pacific coast; and he found himself singing a song learned from a British captain aboard one of her Majesty's ships stationed there. The captain had told him that both the words and the air had been composed by the unhappy queen, Anne Boleyn.

Now, lying in his tent on the night before the battle of Cold Harbor, he found himself singing that mournful song:

"Oh, Death, rock me asleep!
Bring me to quiet rest.

. . . . . . .

Toll on the passing bell, ring out my doleful knell.
Let thy sound my death tell. . . ."

On the morrow there had been the battle of Cold Harbor, on that field just north of the Chickahominy where, two years before, the battle of Gaines's Mill had been fought.

Now it was General Grant who made the assault, and the fire of Lee's army had stretched seven thousand Union soldiers wounded, dying, and dead upon the field.

Pickett had written his wife of how he sang Anne Boleyn's song; and later he wrote her of the victorious battle. But—"Oh," he cried, "this is all a weary long mistake. May the merciful and true God wield power to end it ere another day passes!"

And after the familiar signature, "Your Soldier," he had written, "I love you—love you—love you."

These fragments from Pickett's letters are from the collected letters, published years later by LaSalle Corbell Pickett, under the title: *The Heart of a Soldier.*

The Cold Harbor victory had delayed only briefly the inevitable siege which had now begun; it had but put off for a little the doom of Richmond and of Petersburg. For within a fortnight Grant had transported his great army across the James, uniting with the forces under General Butler. And at Petersburg the combined armies confronted what remained of Lee's Army of Northern Virginia.

The siege was on and the famine begun.

Soldiers were hungry, so weak that the slightest wound was pretty certain to mean death. Horses were dying of starvation. And Mrs. Pryor's little son was saying that his stomach felt like a nutmeg grater.

Federal guns swept the city, their shells screaming, ricocheting, bursting. People made dugouts where they might take refuge in times of the heaviest bombardment.

And two months after the battle of Cold Harbor, there was brought to Pickett in camp news of the birth of his son.

All along the Confederate lines soldiers built bonfires to honor the "little General"; and in the Union lines, too, at General Grant's suggestion, Pickett's old friends lighted fires for his son; and a note of congratulation, signed "Grant, Ingalls, Suckley," was passed over from the Union lines to the Confederates.

"Grant knows all about *me*," General Lee said one day to General Pryor. Actually he had sent a message to say that he knew what General Lee had for breakfast every morning. And Lee's reply had been that surely that could not be possible; for if he did know he would certainly send him something better. "Yes, Grant knows all about me," Lee said. "And I know too little about Grant. Now, General Pryor, you were a schoolboy here, and have hunted in all the bypaths around Petersburg. Knowing the country better than any of us, you are the best man for this important duty."

The idea was that General Pryor should head a small squad of men and scout the country, to learn of Grant's operations. It was dangerous business. And at the end of November General Wilcox came to tell Mrs. Pryor that her husband had been taken.

"You have to know it," he said, and she saw that his face quivered. "You have to know it. The general won't return. The Yankees caught him this morning."

And through the window she saw her husband's horse, standing riderless.

General Wilcox tried to console her with hope that he might soon be exchanged.

But when he had gone she could feel no hope, but sat huddled over the fire, sick with fear.

Then—as she often told the story—the click of an officer's spurs aroused her. An officer came to say that General Lee sent her his "affectionate sympathy."

And outside in the yard she saw a grey figure mounted upon a grey horse—General Lee on his horse Traveller; waiting until his message had been delivered, when, not intruding upon her grief, he rode slowly away back toward the lines.

And only the enemy could tell Mrs. Pryor her husband's fate. She could only hope, and somehow provide food for her children.

She got out an old trunk filled with all that remained of her Washington life; that faraway life of four years ago when she had been named one of the Capital's four greatest beauties.

She ripped her finery to pieces, made it over into hat trimmings, cuffs and collars—furbelows which she sent into Richmond and sold.

And while she worked her heart was with her captive husband; going back over the battles in which he had had a part—Williamsburg, Seven Pines, Gaines's Mill, Mechanicsville, Seven Days, Frazier's Farm, the second Manassas, Antietam, the battle of the Deserted House in the Blackwater country. In memory he stood before her while she sewed; tall, erect, slender, tossing back his thick black mane of hair.

Now . . . where was he?

The first information was printed in the New York *Herald*, which stated that a rebel officer, waving a paper for exchange, had appeared in front of the Union lines. He had been taken, and proved to be the "famous Roger A. Pryor." Later, a "personal" inserted in a northern paper told Mrs. Pryor that her husband was imprisoned in Fort Lafayette. After some weeks elapsed she began to get letters sent to her through the lines.

In the long months of the siege of Petersburg, General Lee often passed Mrs. Pryor's door, and she thought how he had aged under the agony of the hopeless desperate responsibility he carried. Jeb Stuart, who, Lee said, had never brought him a false piece of news—Jeb Stuart was dead. Stonewall Jackson, whom Lee called his "right arm," was dead; they and many others on whom he had relied were gone. She knew that he took upon himself a responsibility almost beyond endurance. She knew that when there had been defeat, he had assumed the blame. After Gettysburg he had said: "All this has been my fault. It is I that have lost and you must help me out of it the best way you can."

As he rode past her door she knew that he was breaking his heart. He had but forty-five thousand men; men crazed with hunger. Grant had a hundred and sixty thousand, well-fed and fit.

Day after day Mrs. Pryor watched Lee riding by mounted on Traveller, the horse that was dear to all the South because of faithful service to his master.

Then, on a morning in March, Traveller stopped before her door and General Lee came into the room where she sat sewing.

He stooped and took her little girl up in his arms.

Mrs. Pryor, raising her hazel eyes, saw that he had news which he would break to her; yet because of the light in his face she was not alarmed.

He spoke of her husband. "You let the Yankees catch him," he said. "Now he is coming back to be with you again, on parole until he is exchanged. You must take better care of him in the future."

After a few minutes' talk Lee walked to her window, and stood there looking out.

"Is it worth my while, general," Mrs. Pryor asked, "to put the plowshare into those fields?"

"Plant your seeds, madam," he said. And then he added: "the doing it will be some reward."

She thought then that he must have hope . . . a little hope . . . perhaps.

But in just twenty days the long road was to arrive at Appomattox.

# CHAPTER TWENTY-THREE

# He Smote His Hands Together

O<small>N</small> the morning of Sunday, the ninth of April, General Lee dressed himself in his best. In the field he ordinarily wore a plain grey uniform, high cavalry boots, and a wide-brimmed grey hat, low on his forehead; only the stars on his collar marked his rank. But on the morning of April ninth he put on dress uniform, a red silk sash, gold spurs, and a sword in a handsomely decorated scabbard.

He did not trouble about breakfast.

There was a little corn meal; and a small tin can in which each man in the order of military precedence boiled his share of the meal; eating this gruel as soon as it was cool enough, and then passing the can to the next in line. But no one remembered seeing General Lee eat anything. While others were cooking their gruel over a small fire of twigs, the general was dressing himself in his best.

It had been long since the army had seen him in anything but his simple field kit. And now on this desperate morning he amazed them by the elegant dress which so became his distinguished person.

"I have probably to be General Grant's prisoner and thought I must make my best appearance," he explained quietly.

When you see him standing there it seems incredible that such as he should speak of being any man's prisoner.

Two years before, Viscount Wolseley had visited Lee in camp at the front; and was so deeply impressed that he said afterward: "I have met many of the great men of my time, but Lee alone impressed me with the feeling that I was in the presence of a man who was cast in a grander mould, and made of different and finer metal than all other men. He is stamped upon my memory as a being apart and superior to all others . . . I have met but two men who realize my ideas of what a true hero should be: my friend, Charles Gordon was one, General Lee was the other."

Gordon of Khartoum and Lee of Virginia were thus linked in Wolseley's mind.

Sitting in a tent at the Confederate front, Wolseley had had a long talk with Robert E. Lee.

Lee had explained that he hated slavery, but that he thought it wicked to give freedom suddenly to some millions of people, incapable yet of using it with profit to themselves or to the country. But it was not, he said, for this that he fought; he fought, he believed, for those same rights which had led George Washington into revolution.

Now, on that Sunday morning in April, in the green gay spring, with peach and cherry and apple trees in bloom, dogwood white in the woods and everywhere frogs piping, Robert E. Lee stood among his officers, saying that probably, before the day was done, he would be General Grant's prisoner.

In his conduct of the war Lee had never been free to act entirely as he thought best. For the past year he had wished to lead his army to the base of the Blue Ridge, where he might have found food for the men and for their horses; at the same time drawing General Grant into the interior, away from James River, by which food and recruits were continually supplied to his great army.

But Petersburg was the key to the defenses of Richmond, and Richmond was the capital of the Confederacy. It was decided that the capital must not fall.

So Lee had remained entrenched about Petersburg, his men on less than half rations, then on less than one-third rations; a little meal each day, and every few days a small portion of bacon. They were ragged—these hungry men—and thousands of them were barefoot; their horses were starving; and for all this Lee's heart was breaking, though no disaster had yet daunted his spirit.

In February President Lincoln had come down to Hampton Roads to confer with the Confederacy, but nothing had come of their discussions.

And in March it was conceded that the one hope was to withdraw Lee's army and unite it with Johnston's forces which were to come up from North Carolina. But if this were to be done, it must be done quickly, for already Sheridan was marching through Virginia, and might at any moment cut off communications to the south. The sole hope lay in speed.

The Confederates must strike Sheridan before Grant could join him.

Speed . . . only speed could save them. And already the heavy spring rains were making of every road a slough of despond.

It was just a few days after Lee had stood at Mrs.
Pryor's window, looking out over the fields, saying,
"Plant your seed . . . The doing it will be some re-
ward," that he had ordered Pickett to march at once to
Five Forks, some twelve miles away, to prevent capture
of the Southside Railroad.

At the same time the army must be immediately
withdrawn. But before that was accomplished Grant
had made another assault. Lee held his position throughout the day; and then, in the protecting blackness of
night, with no beat of drum, or bugle call, Lee began
the retreat, his heart heavy with the news just come,
that at Five Forks Pickett's forces had been crushed.
And General Hill had been killed.

So, in rain and darkness, what was left of the Army
of Northern Virginia moved out of the lines about
Richmond and Petersburg, with orders to destroy all
bridges after passing over them.

The plan to join Johnston was desperate; but not
altogether without hope.

The retreating forces—from Richmond and Petersburg, and what remained of Pickett's division—were to
proceed to Amelia Court House, some days' march inland. Lee had commanded that rations and ammunition
should meet them there. From Amelia—with all possible
haste—they were to hurry south to Danville, to unite
with Johnston.

This was the plan with which Lee began the retreat.

And on that retreat a young Englishman marched
with Lee's army. When it was all over, he told what he
saw. He saw mules and horses give up the struggle. He
saw their abandoned wagons burned that they might

not be taken by the pursuing Federals. He saw famished soldiers drop from exhaustion; their rifles falling from hands too weak to carry them longer. Men, mules, and horses were laid down side by side to die. Their dead bodies cluttered the roads, and from the blazing wagons ammunition, set off by the flames, burst with deafening, terrifying roar, and great pillars of smoke rose through the grey rain. And behind was the oncoming Union Army, well-fed and fit.

But at Amelia Court House there would be rations. Thirty thousand Confederates, faint with hunger, marched, thinking of the food that would be waiting at Amelia.

All this was written upon General Lee's mind to be forever remembered.

The army reached Amelia in the early morning. But in Amelia it was found that no rations had arrived. Supplies of ammunition were waiting, but there was no food.

Lee sent out wagons to scour the countryside, begging meat, meal, corn. Time—precious time—must be lost while he awaited their return; and from all directions the Federals were advancing upon them.

Yet there remained spirit in Lee's weary, hungering, disappointed army, spirit to cheer their commander; spirit even for the banter and laughter so dear to the gallant Army of Northern Virginia.

They waited for the wagons another day; again it was raining. In Richmond, Union forces had taken possession of the city which was in flames. The wagons which had gone out with Lee's appeal for food were coming back, most of them empty; for the farms, too, were destitute. And, below Amelia, Federal troops blocked the way south. There now remained but one direction in which he might move; he might advance along the road which, passing through Appomattox, led to Lynchburg. He would telegraph to Lynchburg to have rations sent to meet them; and he would march the army; he would march it throughout the night; for messengers had brought news that on his very heels were the Federal armies of the James and the Potomac. Without respite, his own weary men must march, march, march, through the deep mud of the rain-soaked roads. March—they stumbled now, rather than marched.

Yet, on the next day, as so often on that long retreat, they rallied against Federals blocking the way. So the Army of Northern Virginia fought as it retreated.

❖

It was after dark on the fifth day of the retreat that a courier came with a letter from General Grant to General Lee.

General Grant expressed himself as sure that the results of the past week must convince General Lee of the hopelessness of further resistance. "I feel that it is so," Grant wrote, "and regard it as my duty to shift from myself the responsibility of further effusion of blood, by asking of you the surrender of that portion of the C.S. Army, known as the Army of Northern Virginia."

Lee replied at once that, while he could not agree on the hopelessness of resistance, he shared Grant's desire to avoid bloodshed, and he therefore asked the terms of surrender which Grant would offer.

And in the morning Lee moved his army forward,

toward Appomattox where he hoped to find that rations had arrived from Lynchburg. If he could get food, he might even yet march his men by another route south to join General Johnston.

It was Saturday, a bright sunlit day; so quiet a day that almost it seemed as though they had outstripped the Federals in that race for Appomattox.

At dusk there came to Lee, on the march, a letter from General Grant, giving the terms of surrender; they were simple, requiring merely that the "officers and men who were surrendered should be disqualified to bear arms until properly exchanged."

Lee made immediate reply; he did not think that the emergency demanded surrender, but he would be pleased to meet General Grant for discussion on the following morning at ten o'clock "on the old stage road to Richmond, between the picket lines of the two armies."

That night Lee's army camped in the woods about two miles from Appomattox and twelve miles south of James River. With the fall of night they saw themselves surrounded by a ring of glittering campfires. The Federal forces lay now across their line of advance. If they were cavalry it might be possible to cut a passage for the army. But if they were infantry, then Lee feared he must surrender.

With this knowledge he rose early and dressed himself carefully in his best.

Yet he still hoped it might be cavalry that blocked the way. Fog lay upon the scene, veiling the truth.

A general sent out to investigate was attacked by cavalry and a strong force of infantry. "I have fought my corps to a frazzle," he reported, "I can do nothing more unless I am supported."

"Then," said General Lee, knowing support impossible, "then there is nothing for me to do but to go and see General Grant, and I would rather die a thousand deaths."

"Oh, general," an officer exclaimed, "what will history say of the surrender of the army in the field?"

"They will say hard things of us. They will not understand how we were overwhelmed by numbers. But that is not the question, colonel: the question is, is it right to surrender this army. If it is right, then I will take all the responsibility."

He might have sent officers to discuss the business of surrender. Grant, in order that Lee might be spared the humiliation, had suggested it. But Lee did not shirk.

And out of the far past, like an echo in the halls of memory, there come to you the words of Light-Horse Harry: "Robert was always good."

Thus Lee, taking an escort of two members of his staff and their orderlies, rode to meet General Grant.

In the parlor of the house chosen for the conference he waited.

And in half an hour General Grant arrived. There came with him some dozen Federal officials. The expectant hush of the moment was broken by their arrival, by their jangling spurs and clanking swords. Removing a pair of yellow gloves, Grant came directly forward and shook hands with Lee, who was standing at the end of the room opposite the door.

They had not met since the Mexican War, and the conversation began with some talk of that campaign.

It was Lee who first spoke of the momentous matter which had now brought them together.

Grant again stated the terms as Lee had understood them; and at Lee's suggestion they were put into writing. Grant lit a pipe, and while he wrote, puffs of smoke drifted upward in the room.

When the document was put into Lee's hands, he took out his spectacles and wiped them carefully with his handkerchief; and then slowly read Grant's conditions of surrender: ". . . officers to give their individual parole not to take up arms against the Government of the United States . . . arms, artillery and public property to be stacked and turned over to the officer appointed. This will not embrace the side-arms of the officers; nor their private horses or baggage. This done . . . officers are then to be allowed to return to their homes not to be disturbed by the United States authority so long as they observe their paroles."

"That will have a very happy effect," Lee said.

Grant asked for suggestions. Had Lee any suggestions?

Yes, there was just one. In the Confederate Army, he said, the cavalrymen provided their own horses. They would want them to plow ground for planting corn.

General Grant agreed; he would give orders that those who owned horses or mules might take them home.

Marshall was then directed to write out Lee's acceptance of the terms.

And Lee spoke of the Federal prisoners he was holding—a thousand or more such prisoners whom he was unable to feed properly, and he explained that he was expecting several trainloads of rations from Lynchburg; he would like to have them for his men when they arrived. He did not know then that his trains had been captured by Sheridan.

As to the prisoners, Grant said he would, of course, be glad to receive them in the Federal lines; and he would send over to Lee twenty-five thousand rations.

"That will be a great relief."

Then Lee signed the acceptance which Marshall had written out.

So ended the long road to Appomattox.

And Marshall, grandson of the great chief justice and aide-de-camp to General Lee, in describing the scene of surrender, would have you know that he "cannot give any idea of the kindness and the generosity and magnanimity of Grant and the officers with him."

Among the Federal officers who waited outside the house there was General George A. Forsyth. He saw Lee as he came from the interview. He watched him cross the porch to the head of the steps. He saw him pause there, and the look in Lee's eyes impressed General Forsyth. "His eyes," he says, were "fixed in the direction of the little valley . . . in which his army lay."

Standing at the head of the steps, Lee "slowly drew on his gauntlets, smiting his gloved hands into each other several times . . . evidently utterly oblivious of his surroundings. Then, apparently recalling his thoughts, he glanced deliberately right and left, and not seeing his horse, he called in a hoarse, half-choked voice: 'Orderly! Orderly!'"

And Forsyth describes how, when the soldier brought the horse, Lee went down the steps and stood at Traveller's head while he was being bridled. "He reached up," Forsyth says, "and drew the horse's forelock out from under the brow-band, parted and smoothed it, and then gently patted the grey charger's forehead in an absent-minded way, as one who loves horses, but whose thoughts are far away."

Then, still like a man in a dream, he mounted, and as he settled into the saddle, Forsyth heard break from him "unguardedly . . . a long, low, deep sigh, almost like a groan in its intensity."

And at once, through a countryside fair with blossoming fruit trees, Lee rode away . . . back to his army.

When they saw him coming, they began to cheer; then seeing the look on his face, they cried out to know if they were surrendered.

Lee halted. "We have fought the war together," he said, "and I have done the best I could for you. You will be paroled and go to your homes until exchanged."

Tears filled his eyes.

"General, we'll fight 'em yet!"

"General, say the word, and we'll go in and fight 'em yet."

And they stretched out their hands to him, hoping to touch him, or failing that, to touch Traveller; to pat the horse which was inseparable in their minds from his master.

Then Lee turned aside from the road into an apple orchard; there walking back and forth in the warm bright sunshine, he fought the despair that welled up within him.

It was sunset before he rode on toward his headquarters, under the great white oak.

And one who saw him has described how General

Lee rode between "two solid walls of men . . . formed along the whole distance . . . awaiting his coming . . . As soon as he entered the avenue of these old soldiers . . . who had stood at their duty . . . in so many battles, wild heartfelt cheers arose which so touched General Lee that tears filled his eyes and trickled down his cheeks."

When the men saw his tears, their "cheers changed to choking sobs . . . each group began in the same way with cheers, and ended in the same way with sobs, all along the route to his headquarters.

And they were thus moved, not by the surrender of their lost hopes, but by love for the general who broke his heart for them.

# OUT OF DEFEAT

# CHAPTER TWENTY-FOUR

## Victorious Lives

H E shall be hanged! Damn him!"

So Stanton, secretary of war, had vowed when friends of General Roger A. Pryor appealed to him for the general's release from prison. Even General Grant refused to consider Pryor's release; for he was held as hostage for the safety of a Union officer.

"He shall be hanged!" That was what young Mrs. Pryor had feared, as she sat sewing through the last months of the long siege of Petersburg, converting the frocks of her happy past into furbelows by whose sale she hoped to give bread to her hungry children.

To be hanged—was that to be the end of her Comet?

She did not know that in Washington good friends were working for his release; that, Grant and Stanton having refused it, they had gone to President Lincoln himself. As Lincoln listened to their plea, he remembered how at Manassas, when General Pryor had captured a camp of Federal wounded, he had at once paroled them and their surgeons and their ambulances.

She did not know that therefore the president had given the order for her husband's "parole until exchanged."

Then General Lee had come to break the good news gently.

She did not hear the whole story until her Comet returned, pale and thin after his imprisonment. Stanton, he told her, was so incensed at his release that he gave orders to seize him; but even while search was being made for him, he was at the White House with President Lincoln. During their conversation, Lincoln spoke freely of his grief at the failure of the Hampton Roads conference. He explained how he had gone down to Hampton Roads, where on board a ship lying in the harbor he met representatives from the President of the Confederacy, in a vain attempt to negotiate a peace.

In his talk with Lincoln it was obvious to General Pryor that the president hoped the southern people might renew the negotiations.

But Destiny was not to be turned aside from the road to Appomattox. And there followed the final battle at Petersburg.

Mrs. Pryor then abandoned her home outside the city and took her children into the town. The battle had been lost, and General Lee led the Army of Northern Virginia in retreat.

Jefferson Davis had fled, and Richmond was burning.

George Pickett's young wife watched the wind carry the flames from building to building. She saw the fire devour warehouses and shops, public buildings, and mansions which had known Washington and Jefferson, Patrick Henry, John Marshall, Poe, and the notorious Aaron Burr. Above the great roar of the flames, and the crash of falling buildings, there were cries of terror and of agony. Drunken, looting mobs added horror.

On the following day Federal troops took possession of the city, raising once more the stars and stripes above the Capitol.

Deserted by the servants, little Mrs. Pickett was alone with her baby. With the child in her arms, she answered a knock at the door.

She saw standing before her a man, whom she later described as tall, gaunt, sad-faced, and dressed in ill-fitting clothes. When he spoke his accent told her that he was from the North.

"Is this George Pickett's place?" he asked.

"This is General Pickett's home, sir, but he is not here."

"I know that, ma'm. I know where George Pickett is, but I just wanted to see the place."

In her story of *What Happened to Me*, Mrs. Pickett related that conversation as she remembered it.

The stranger, she says, explained that down in old Quincy, Illinois, he had often and often heard George Pickett describe his Richmond home, and heard him whistle the songs of Virginia. So the stranger had come because he wanted to see the place; though he knew that Pickett was not at home.

"I am Abraham Lincoln," he added.

"The President!"

"No—no—just Abraham Lincoln, George Pickett's old friend."

"I am George Pickett's wife, and this is his baby."

And when the baby stretched out his hands, Lincoln took him in his arms, with a tenderness which Mrs. Pickett never forgot. Always she would remember, too, his deep kind voice, and his eyes; his "intensely human eyes," and his sadness.

Lincoln was unexpectedly again in Virginia, coming by river steamer to City Point; for the purpose of an interview with Grant. Federal victory was near, and Lincoln's mind full of the future. "Let them down easy," he said. He would not hear of persecution when the war was over. He would have no part in vindictiveness or hate. He believed that slavery was the sin not of the South alone, but of the nation. He had wanted to bring the war to an end by offering four hundred million dollars to the South in payment for their slaves; provided that they accept the Union and abolition. When his Cabinet refused, he had said sorrowfully: "You are all opposed to me."

On the eve of victory he was insisting that there should be no hatred, no persecution.

It was not until he had left her that Sallie Pickett heard her husband's death cried by newsboys in the streets: "Pickett killed at Five Forks! His whole division captured." But she did not believe that her Soldier was dead. She refused escape from the frenzied city; he had said that she must remain where she was until he came back to her. She would remain. "He is not dead," she insisted.

Then, one morning, she heard the voice for which she waited: "Whoa, Lucy," the voice said. "Whoa, little girl." It was the voice of her Soldier, stopping his chestnut mare at the door. George Pickett had come home from Appomattox.

And Traveller had brought General Lee through the stricken city, to the house on Franklin Street where his crippled wife waited.

Heavy rain was falling. Mud had spattered the

horse and his rider. Yet, defeated, surrendered, sorrow-ful, the noble dignity which set Robert E. Lee apart from all others remained.

In the streets through which Lee rode, the slave, Jasper, was working. Negro mobs, believing that their new liberty freed them from any need to earn a living, crowded the city. But Jasper had at once gone to work; until he could do something better, he would clear bricks from the streets.

At Appomattox, on the day following the sur-render, Grant and Lee had met between the lines of their armies. Their conference was without witnesses, but when Lee returned to his headquarters he told Marshall, his aide-de-camp, that Grant had asked him to go to Mr. Lincoln. "I want you to meet him," Grant had said. "Whatever you and he agree upon will be satis-factory to the reasonable people of North and South."

But Lee reasoned that, as he was only a soldier, he could not meet Mr. Lincoln, or undertake to make peace terms; that was the prerogative of Jefferson Davis, President of the Confederacy.

Grant understood; then he himself would go to Lincoln.

News of Lee's surrender reached Abraham Lincoln in Washington, on his return from City Point. He had thought that he could never again be glad. Now the load was lifted, and he was happy. It might be given to him to prevent hatred and persecution. The very city bloomed as if to celebrate his joy, the gardens fragrant with lilac blossoms.

Then General Grant arrived in Washington and was invited to be present at the Cabinet meeting which met on the morning of April fourteenth; there he heard Lincoln urge liberal terms of peace, declaring that he would have no part in revenge.

And in the evening Lincoln went to the theater, his face serenely joyful that there was to be peace.

Three days later news came to James River that Abraham Lincoln had been shot at the theater, and that he was dead.

"My God!" George Pickett cried. "My God! The South has lost her best friend and protection in this her direst hour of need!"

It was just seven days before his death that Lincoln had left City Point. The Confederate prisoners there had cheered him on his return from visiting Richmond. The last journey of his life had been that trip to James River; and he had come with "malice toward none," with "charity toward all." He had walked in the streets of stricken Richmond, and had visited Petersburg during the siege. On his way back to Washington his eyes had rested upon the tender green and the magic whiteness of dogwood along the riverbanks.

"I want you to meet Mr. Lincoln," Grant had said to Lee on the day after the surrender at Appomattox. "Whatever you and he agree upon will be satisfactory to the reasonable people of North and South."

The bullet fired in Washington had made that impossible.

Lincoln had profoundly desired that the surrendered southern states should be treated as though they had never left the Union. Yet in the tragedy of his death the flames of hate roared high. That violent minority of agitators, who bring upon the world wars in which they themselves so rarely fight, now shouted for vengeance.

George Pickett's friends in Grant's army warned him of danger; so urgently that they at last convinced him that he must take his wife and child and go to some place of safety, until the hot passion for revenge should have died down. The warning reached him at his father-in-law's plantation, near the mouth of James River. He must at once go into exile, his advisers insisted, and he must depart with all possible secrecy.

Pickett went alone. His wife was to take the boat to Baltimore, to remain there with relatives until she heard from him. She was to travel as "Mrs. Corbell and infant." Pickett would telegraph, using his middle name, Edwards. If his message read: "Still danger of contagion," she was to remain in Baltimore; but if it read: "Edwards is better," she was to take the next train to that city from which the telegram had been sent.

Sallie Pickett was not yet eighteen. She had once made a visit to North Carolina; otherwise she knew nothing beyond James River Virginia, and she had never in her life been alone. Now her father put her on the Baltimore boat and she traveled north; Mrs. Corbell and baby.

In Baltimore she waited, and when the telegram came announcing that Edwards was better, she went by train to New York, sitting up all night in the day coach. From New York she traveled by boat to Albany; a small frightened creature, knowing herself to be an absurd figure in the grey, home-plaited poke bonnet, her wartime gown of homespun, and a full black silk wrap with tiers of ruffles. Fashions had changed, and the women about her were wearing close-fitting short cloth jackets. She describes how terribly conspicuous she felt. Her baby was cutting its first teeth and wailing miserably. Certain female fellow travelers of the reformer species explained the wailing on the ground that she was not its mother. She must be reported as an evil character escaping with a kidnaped baby; obviously too young to be its mother.

What was she to do? She was so scared that in answering the questions put to her she only increased the impression of guilt.

Then a kind woman—for she met much kindness on that forlorn journey—came to her rescue.

"Do you nurse your baby?" the woman asked gently.

"Yes."

"Then that will help to prove that it is your own."

Sallie Pickett flushed; she had never nursed the child in public, but she now opened her gown and took him to her breast.

Pickett's telegram had been sent from Montreal. His wife set forth knowing only the name of the city to which she was to go. When the train pulled into the station other passengers left with the secure air of knowing how to find the hotels or homes where they would be welcome. She sat waiting.

Three men passed through the car. She scarcely

dared raise her eyes to look at them. Then a voice said: "Don't you know your own husband, little one?"

It was her Soldier; with his long hair shorn, his whiskers gone, no longer wearing the grey Confederate uniform, but dressed in brown Scotch tweed. And the two men with him addressed him as "Mr. Edwards," and herself as "Mrs. Edwards."

❋

To the end, on the very eve of Appomattox, southern soldiers had sung:

> "The race is not to them, that's got
> The longest legs to run,
> Nor the battle to the people
> That shoots the biggest gun."

Yet those who marched to those words had at last been compelled to surrender.

When the news came to Petersburg, young Mrs. Pryor's first thought was that it had all been for nothing—all the suffering, the bloodshed, the death. Her mind went back to that night when, stooping over President Buchanan's chair, she had said: "It appears, Mr. President, that South Carolina has seceded from the Union."

Now, she thought to herself, now all is over; that war "which has changed our lives—giving us mutilation and wounds for strength and health; obscurity and degradation for honor and distinction . . . pain and death for happiness and life."

The Virginia through which the soldiers traveled to their homes, after stacking their arms at Appomattox, was a land stripped bare, a battleground where railroads and bridges had been destroyed, homes and barns burned, farmyards raided; a land whose money was now so much worthless paper.

Virginia was prostrate.

And yet . . . nothing, after all, could crush spirits believing that "the race is not to them that's got the longest legs."

After the surrender, Mrs. Pryor returned to the home outside Petersburg from which she had fled on the morning of Grant's final assault. General Pryor had gone to Richmond looking for employment, and she took the children back without waiting for his return. She never forgot the devastation she found: "Grass and flowers were gone, the carcasses of six dead cows lay in the yard . . . The evening air was heavy with the odor of decaying flesh. As the front door opened millions of flies swarmed forth . . . Within, pieces of fat pork lay on the floors, molasses trickled from the library shelves . . . nothing was left in the house except one chair out of which the bottom had been cut, and one bed-stead fastened together with bayonets. Picture frames were piled against the wall. Every one was empty. One family portrait of an old lady was hanging on the wall, with a sabre cut across her face."

Mrs. Pryor's old servant, Aunt Jinny, appeared and helped put the children to bed, on quilts laid down upon the floor. She described how the house had been sacked, how the cellar had been dug up, seeking treasure; the outhouses, she said, were even now full of strange Negroes, come from nobody knew where. But there was at least food for that night. The compassionate wife of a Federal officer had sent a basket of provisions.

Then, while her children slept, Mrs. Pryor watched beside her window, afraid to lie down to sleep. Heavy rain fell, and then the moon slowly straggled out. Its light revealed the uncovered arm of a dead soldier buried just outside the window where Mrs. Pryor watched.

In the weeks that followed, a plague of fever swept Virginia, and in that wretched house to which Mrs. Pryor had returned all fell ill. General Pryor came home from Richmond where he had found no work, and nursed them back to life, with the help of old black Jinny.

They survived; but how was he, a Rebel who had lost all, to earn a livelihood for a wife and seven young children?

A Federal officer advised that he go to New York.

"He won't consent to go there," Mrs. Pryor said.

"Then send him for the sea trip. Perhaps the trip will shake off his chills."

He went, Mrs. Pryor pawning her watch to pay his way. But he insisted that it was to be for a week only.

In these pages, Mrs. Pryor's story is told as heard from her lips, and as given in her *Reminiscences*.

In the weeks following the surrender Lee's soldiers turned to him asking what they should do.

"Go home," he said, "all you boys who fought with

me. Go home and help to build up the shattered fortunes of our old State . . . make her great again . . . all must get to work, and if they cannot do what they prefer, they must do what they can."

For himself, he would set Southerners an example of loyalty to the Union. He refused the invitation of an English nobleman who offered him for life a "mansion and an estate commensurate with his individual merits and the greatness of an historic family."

He was deeply appreciative. But he refused: "I cannot desert my native State in the hour of her adversity. I must abide her fortunes and share her fate."

Many offers came to him, but he declined them all. "I am looking," he said, "for some little quiet home in the woods, where I can procure shelter and my daily bread. . . ."

It was at the end of the summer following the surrender that an offer was made to Lee which he did accept. He was elected president of Washington College at Lexington. In the final year of the war, Hunter's soldiers had sacked Lexington; the college library had been broken up, and the buildings so wrecked that they were almost uninhabitable. Only four professors remained, and about forty students.

Still Lee accepted the position. He said that he had led the young men of the South in battle; he had seen many of them die; now he was comforted that his remaining years might be given to training other young men "to do their duty in life."

He was fitted for the task by his experience as superintendent of West Point.

But the vengeful minority grudged him even so poor a position as president of a college in ruins.

"Satan," they said, "wouldn't have him to open the

door for fresh arrivals." They thought the President of the United States should forbid his holding such an office.

This time the agitators failed, and Lee, mounting Traveller, rode to Lexington.

The town of Lexington is on the western side of the Blue Ridge, with all about a lovely world of mountains. It stands on the bank of North River, and North River flows southward into the James.

And Cornelia MacDonald of Lexington was standing at her window on the day when General Lee rode into the town, come to take over the presidency of Washington College. "I saw him," she says, "riding on his old war horse, Traveller . . . erect and straight, looking like the great old soldier that he was . . . his bright dark eyes and kind smile lighting up a face that was noble as well as handsome. . . .

"Slowly he passed, raising his brown slouch hat to those on the pavements who recognized him, and not appearing conscious that he more than anybody else was the object of attention. He wore his military coat divested of all marks of rank; even the military buttons had been removed. He doubtless would have laid it aside altogether, but it was the only one he had, and he was too poor to buy another."

So opened the final chapter of General Lee's life, and at the same time there had begun the terrible period of reconstruction in the South; the era of the carpetbaggers, like a horde of vermin infesting the conquered states; betraying the last wishes of Abraham Lincoln.

The South, Lee feared, "has yet to suffer many evils

and it will require time, patience and fortitude to heal her affliction." Silence and patience, he thought her only course. But he believed that one day reason and charity would prevail.

His own consolation he found in his work for the poor wrecked little college which bore the name of the man whom he had worshiped all his life—Washington. He set to work to repair the buildings, to plant the grounds in trees and shrubs and roses. The number of students were increased, new professors were added and new courses of study.

Lee would not consciously dwell upon the past, nor fear the future; he believed that human virtue should equal human calamity; he spoke little of the war and always reluctantly: his genius for delight in simple things, his gentle humor shone upon the daily life of the college, and of his home, as light plays upon the surface of a river; while, beneath, the deep water flows unseen.

You feel that only with Traveller did he permit himself really to remember. He and Traveller had been through it together; together they had known the brilliant victories, together they had known defeat. Now, still together, they went out into the lovely hills about Lexington. "Traveller and I," he said, "whenever practicable wander into the mountains, and enjoy sweet confidence."

An artist once wrote him, asking for a description of Traveller. His reply was that if he were an artist he would picture him as of fine proportions, a muscular figure with a broad forehead, delicate ears, and a quick eye. And if he were a poet, Lee said, he would sing of Traveller's endurance of toil, of hunger, thirst, heat and cold, and of the dangers and sufferings through which he had passed.

But, being neither artist nor poet, Lee adds that he can only say that Traveller is a Confederate grey, and that he carried him through the Seven Days' battle around Richmond, the Second Manassas, Sharpsburg, Fredericksburg; through to the end at Appomattox, and that in all that time the saddle was scarcely off his back.

And you must know, Lee concludes, "the comfort he is to me in my present retirement."

Once, when absent from home, Lee wrote: "How is Traveller? Tell him I miss him dreadfully, and have repented of our separation but once—and that is the whole time since we parted."

When Lee came in from his long rides through the mountains, he would call for that daughter to whom long ago he had written from Texas about his soldier hens and his pet rattlesnake: "Where is my little Miss Mildred? She is my light-bearer! The house is never dark when she is in it."

One day, riding through the mountain forest, he met a solitary old Confederate soldier, also riding through the forest. When the man recognized Lee he stopped:

"General Lee, I am powerful glad to see you, and I feel like cheering you."

Then the old soldier waved his hat high: "Hurrah for General Lee!" he shouted. And when the general had said good-bye and ridden away, the cheers followed him until he was out of hearing. "Hurrah for General Lee! . . . Hurrah! . . ."

Lee himself described the incident to his family,

and his son, Robert, relates it in the *Recollections and Letters* of his father.

When his son, Fitzhugh, was married, Lee was persuaded to go to Petersburg to the wedding. He went reluctantly, for he had melancholy recollections of the place, but his presence at the marriage was so much desired that he could not refuse. And all along the way people crowded to see him, and in Petersburg the streets were thronged.

After he went home to Lexington he wrote Fitzhugh how happy the experience had been. "When our armies were in front of Petersburg," he explained, "I suffered so much in body and mind on account of the good townspeople, especially on that gloomy night when I was forced to abandon them, that I have always reverted to them in sadness and sorrow. My old feelings returned to me as I passed well-remembered spots and recalled the ravages of the hostile shells. But when I saw the cheerfulness with which the people were working to restore their condition and witnessed the comforts with which they were surrounded, a load of sorrow which had been pressing upon me for years was lifted from my heart."

Reading this, you understand something of his thoughts on those solitary rides with Traveller; something of what flowed beneath the playful gallant serenity with which he met each day of life.

When he returned from a journey he would say, yes, he had had a pleasant time, but "they make too much fuss over the old Rebel." And everywhere he urged: "Work for Virginia . . . build her up . . . make her great again."

He was ever thinking what he himself might do to build up Virginia. In childhood he had learned to assume responsibility. His whole life had tended to develop in him resourcefulness. In the army he had belonged to the Engineer Corps: that training had made him practical, exact. As construction engineer he had shown a great gift for handling laborers. War had proved him one of the world's greatest generals. And whatever life had taught him he longed to contribute to the service of defeated Virginia.

Now, as head of the college at Lexington, all that he had learned he would make of practical value to youth.

But he would do more. In the Valley of Virginia there was rich farm land, mineral springs, iron, and natural wonders to attract the traveler. The Valley needed a railroad. To reach Lexington at that time you had to journey fifty miles by canal, or by stage twenty-three miles over a rough mountain road. There must be a railroad through the Valley, linking the southwest with the northeast. It would certainly bring prosperity.

Lee went to Baltimore to help raise money to build it. And in the following year he was made president of this road which was one day to be; though he himself was not even to see its first rail laid.

Matthew Maury was on his way home from England, and in the dazzling harbor of St. Thomas, where the sun shines bright upon houses yellow and blue, red and white, among foliage brightly green, all rising from an azure bay, he heard of the collapse of the Confederacy, and the death of Abraham Lincoln.

Maury had now to decide what he must do. In England he had represented the Confederate Navy. It had been necessary to leave his family in Richmond, taking with him only his youngest son. The separation had been long and anxious, and he was eager to be at home. But he realized the danger of arrest, and that might not yet be; he knew that he must live for a time in exile.

He wrote, surrendering his sword; making it clear that he considered himself bound by whatever terms had been granted to General Lee and other Confederate officers.

Then, by degrees, a grandiose scheme shaped itself in his mind. Maximilian was emperor of Mexico. Maury went to Mexico and was at once appointed director of the Imperial Observatory; he then submitted to the emperor his scheme for a Virginia colony in Mexico. Maximilian was enthusiastic, and Maury wrote eagerly to Virginia. He recalled the Huguenots—his own ancestors—fleeing from persecution, and establishing themselves upon James River. Of the Southern people, he said, "Never since the Edict of Nantes has such a class of people been willing to expatriate themselves."

Maximilian drew up a decree offering title to lands, free from taxation for a year. Seeds, tools, machinery, domestic animals were to be admitted duty free. The immigrants might become naturalized; they were promised liberty of religion; they might bring in Negro servants under terms of indenture. But there was to be no slavery, Mexico having freed all slaves more than a generation before. And immigrants who had lost everything were to be given their passage by sea.

Maury felt himself the savior of his people.

The new settlement was to be called "Carlotta Colony" after the empress. It was to be located at Córdoba; one of the loveliest spots in Mexico. On one side rose snow-capped Orizaba, and on the other side you looked away to the Gulf. Coffee grew wild; the most luscious pineapples cost a cent apiece; fig trees, oranges, and bananas flourished; tobacco and temperate fruits could be cultivated; the air was fragrant with gardenias and orange blossoms.

Maury was enchanted. He wrote to his wife, his "dear, sweet friend and partner." She must take the children and go to London until he was ready for her in Mexico. He wrote also to General Lee. What would Lee think?

But Lee did not approve the great scheme.

"I have a great admiration for Mexico," he explained, "but I shall be very sorry if your presence is lost to Virginia . . . the thought of abandoning the country and all that is left in it is abhorrent to my feelings, and I prefer to struggle for its restoration, and share its fate, rather than to give up all as lost."

Early in the New Year Matthew Maury left Mexico to meet his family in England. He knew the Mexico scheme was opposed by most of his Virginia friends, as well as by the authorities in the United States, but he did not realize that the government was insisting on the withdrawal of French troops from Mexico. Within a month after Maury's departure Maximilian wrote that he could no longer back the new colony. In fact, Maximilian himself was now powerless, and abandoned to his fast-approaching doom.

Maury could no longer go on with the colonization, nor was it yet safe to return to Virginia. He must wait. Meanwhile, in London, he opened a school of instruction in the science of electric torpedoes.

Then at last a general pardon was proclaimed in the United States and Matthew Maury came home. He spent the first winter in Richmond, writing a survey of the material resources of Virginia, and in the spring he went to Lexington as professor of physics at the Virginia Military Institute. Only a fence, in which there was a gate, separated Maury from the grounds of Washington College and from the home of his old friend, Robert E. Lee.

Long ago, a penniless boy riding over the mountains from Tennessee into Virginia, Maury had vowed to make everything bend to his profession. But he had sacrificed his profession to his state; now he came home to make his profession serve Virginia in that struggle which Lee called "making her great again."

In whatever time might be spared from his work as professor of physics, Maury traveled up and down the country, making speeches on agriculture, urging a system of forecasting weather, which would do for the farmer what his wind and current charts were doing for the navigator. At intervals, as new editions were called for, he revised his great physical geography of the sea; and he wrote a general geography for use in schools.

So the years passed, and Lee wrote to his son, Fitzhugh, that Traveller's trot was harder to him than it used to be. And then so great a weariness came upon him that he was no longer able to ride.

In March of the year following Maury's coming to Lexington, the doctors sent Lee south for his health. Everywhere an ovation greeted him. Had you not known the facts you would have thought him a conquering hero, and not a general who had surrendered his army.

On the way home Lee made his last journey to James River, visiting once more the old home at Shirley. In September, 1870, he was in Lexington for the opening of college, and early in October—exactly five years and six months after Appomattox—he was gone; sinking without complaint or repining, gently, serenely into death.

At the end it was clear that his mind had wandered back to those days of which he had been so reluctant to speak; for he was heard distinctly to command: "Tell Hill he must come up" . . . Hill, who was killed during the week that preceded Appomattox.

Then after a pause came the last words: "Strike the tent."

After that there was nothing more.

Two years later Matthew Maury, returning from a lecture trip, said to his wife, "My dear, I am come home to die." But he lingered yet four months, well enough now and then, to dictate the final revision of his famous *Geography*.

When he was gone he left the world richer in knowledge than he had found it. He was a man of dreams, and he seldom failed to dream true. The Carlotta colony in Mexico had not succeeded: he had once had an impracticable scheme for eliminating slavery in the United States, which had come to nothing. But the first transatlantic cable was laid upon a course charted by him. The Naval Academy of which he had dreamed came into being, as did the railroad across the continent, and the canal spanning the Isthmus of Panama, all of which he had foretold; the Weather Bureau which he worked to establish is a reality; and he himself saw the charting of the seas which his studies had made possible.

Of all the honors which came to him that which would perhaps touch him most deeply, could he know it, is that every chart sent out by the Hydrographic Office in Washington is headed by the words: "Founded upon the researches made in the early part of the nineteenth century by Matthew Fontaine Maury, while serving as a lieutenant in the United States Navy."

That, you feel, would mean more than all else; just as General Lee would find profound and humble gratification in the fact that after his death Washington College was called "Washington and Lee"; uniting his name with that of the man he most revered.

In New York Roger Pryor, late of the Confederate Army, had been writing for a paper and at the same time studying law; hoping eventually to be able to bring his family from Virginia.

"You know," one of Mrs. Pryor's little sons confided to her not long after they had finally moved to the North, "You know, mamma, I'm going to change Rebel's name. I'm going to call him Prince."

Rebel was the child's dog; so named not with any political significance, but by reason of the dog's temperament.

"I'll call him Rebel at home, but Prince in the street, because when I call him Rebel in the street the boys stone him."

That was a way out for the dog, but for the family there could not be one name for the public and another for the home. For them there was no escaping the fact that they were considered Rebels, and that they had come to live in an enemy city.

Yet since they had come in that spirit of reconciliation which General Lee preached, that spirit which Abraham Lincoln had urged, they made friends, and in those first years much kindness brightened the bitter struggle against poverty.

General Grant came to the modest hospitality which Confederate General Pryor was able to offer.

Mrs. Pryor one day showed Grant the met-bullets which had been picked up outside her door in Petersburg.

"Those are Minie-balls," Grant commented. They were shot from rifles of equal calibre, and met precisely equidistant to a hair . . . I have seen one other. It came from Vicksburg. Where was this found? At Petersburg, possibly?"

"Yes," she said, "but not when you were shelling the city. It was picked up after the last fight."

"Now, Mrs. Pryor," Grant smiled, "don't you go about telling people that I shelled Petersburg."

Although Jasper, immediately after the Richmond fire, had gone to work clearing the streets he had not forgotten that he was, as he put it, a "God-made preacher." And on one of the small green islands of the

James, opposite Richmond, he organized a church of nine members; in a little shanty formerly used as a government stable.

There he preached, baptizing his converts in the waters of the James. At the end of a year his church membership was so large that it was moved into Richmond, taking over a carpenter's shop in that part of the city known as "Africa." Later he had a real church building, seating nine hundred. It was named the Sixth Mt. Zion Baptist Church, but everybody thought of it simply as Jasper's Church.

Jasper's fame was now spreading over the country, and even to Europe. Many came in curiosity to hear the black preacher; all went away impressed by the greatness of the man; by his perfect faith, his humor, his gift of mimicry, his dramatic eloquence.

His own people revered and loved him. Nobody, they thought, was so kind as Jasper, or so honest; a man who paid his debts and lived frugally; who was never "a money grabber," and always generous to the poor.

But among the Negroes a postslavery generation was growing up. There were now new clergymen, ambitious to forget ancestral bondage. They resented Jasper's racial identification with his past.

They detested that famous sermon "De Sun do Move," which he had preached some two hundred and fifty times. His interpretation of Bible stories mortified those made supersensitive by the tradition of slavery. And they felt humiliated by his "Dialogue with Death."

Failing to appreciate the greatness of the man, they protested that he was "no more fit for the pulpit than a whippoorwill."

But to the end Jasper never lost his hold over his

congregation. "I often wondered," one of them said, "how he could be so umble-like when so many cacklin' fools was bodderin' him."

In his latter days, Hatcher says, Jasper often spoke of his own death.

"Chillen," he would repeat, "my work on de earth is done. I doan' ax death no mo' odds dan a horse-fly. . . . Comparatively speakin' my time in dis world is skin-deep." And, "in Heaven first of all I'll go down an' see de River o' Life. I loves here to go down an' see de ole muddy Jeems—mighty red an' muddy, goin' along slow an' gran' an' quiet; like 'twas tendin' to business. But de Jeems ain't nothin' to de river which flows by de Throne . . . Yas, in Heaven I'll go first to see de River o' Life. . . ."

When this man died, it was said in Richmond that it was "as the fall of a tower."

Mrs. Pryor no longer spoke of her husband as "General"; for he had been elected a judge of the Supreme Court in what had been an enemy city when he had first settled there with his wife and seven young children.

Now Mrs. Pryor called him "Judge," but in her heart he never ceased to be her Comet.

He had remained slender, tall, erect, his black hair was scarcely grey, and he still wore it long; still had the habit of tossing his head, like a spirited horse; just as he was described in Mrs. Chestnut's *Diary from Dixie*. In that momentous week of the firing on Fort Sumter, Mrs. Chestnut had written: "Pryor of Virginia spoke

from the piazza of the Charleston hotel. I asked what
he said. An irreverent woman replied: 'Oh they all say
the same thing, but he made great play with that long
hair of his, which he is always tossing aside.' "

In this manner Mrs. Pryor saw him moving through
the years of their life together; dauntless, reckless, in-
vincible. She herself was of a completely opposite temperament: tranquil, though with a high spirit of her
own and a flashing humor; devoted to flowers and music
and children, a woman's woman.

In the last years of their life they sat much together
in the bay window, looking quietly down the street, re-
living their eventful lives.

And from time to time, as the Judge recalled her
courage and endurance in danger and hardships, he
would exclaim, half to himself: "Wonderful old lady!"

Even when she had been taken from him, after
their sixty-three years of marriage, he continued
through what remained to him of life to exclaim softly:
"Wonderful old lady!"

As soon as treason charges against the leaders of
the Confederacy had been dropped, Pickett returned to
Turkey Island in James River, where he built a cottage
to take the place of the home burned during the war
by order of General Butler. And two years after the
death of Matthew Maury, George Pickett, lying mortally ill, called his Sallie to his arms. And so he died.

Mrs. Pickett lived through the first thirty years of
the twentieth century; lived a widow without her Soldier for nearly as long as Mrs. Pryor had been married

to her Comet. The "young Pickett," whose birth General Grant had celebrated with bonfires in the Federal lines, grew up to be, like his father, a soldier in the United States Army; fighting for his country in the Spanish-American War. Mrs. Pickett lived to see him die, and to see her two grandsons also enter the army, and to see them both go into the World War.

General Lee had urged upon the South: "Make your children Americans." And it had come about, as he hoped, that the old wounds were healed.

Their story is told. One out of bondage, the others out of defeat, they had come victorious; into a victory which is above material success.

After the death of General Lee there were found in his old army satchel various papers which had remained undisturbed since his return from Appomattox. Among them was the parole which he received from General Grant at the surrender. And there were other papers on which Lee had written, evidently for his own comfort and strength, those thoughts which he would keep near him.

Upon one of the papers he had put these words: "There is a true glory and a true honor: the glory of duty done—the honor of integrity of principle."

# CHAPTER TWENTY-FIVE

## "Make Her Great Again"

THEY are a people who never know that they are beaten.

At Jamestown, when the specter of fever and Indian massacre haunted the early colonists, they were yet of such buoyant spirit, so fond of all manner of festivity, that actually—under the very shadow of the tomahawk—a certain revenue was raised by a tax levied on the finery in which they appeared at church.

And many years later Mrs. Pryor told of meeting a friend in the streets of Petersburg soon after the long siege had been lifted and the ports opened again to trade. The friend explained that, with the last five dollars she possessed, she was going to buy citron and raisins and currants, sugar, butter and eggs, brandy and spice.

"Mercy!" Mrs. Pryor exclaimed. "Are you planning to open a grocery store?"

"A grocery? No, I'm going to make a fruit cake!"

Two years later, when General Lee, on the occasion of his son's marriage, had made his first visit to Petersburg after the surrender, the load of sorrow, he said, was lifted from his heart when he saw the "cheerfulness with which the people were working to restore their condition."

That spirit of resilience was to make Virginia great again.

In a white parsonage scarcely more than a cabin, on the narrow peninsula which separates the James and York rivers, Walter Reed was born, ten years before the War Between the States. Armies and conflict were familiar to his boyhood, growing up as he did in that region which was so often the battleground. But somehow, in spite of war and in spite of defeat, the son of that poor little parsonage contrived to achieve an education. When he was only seventeen he graduated in medicine from the University of Virginia. Then he took a second medical degree in New York at the Bellevue Medical College. His first practical experience was on Blackwells Island. Before he was twenty-one he had been made a district physician in New York. He was twenty-four when he entered the army as assistant surgeon. After that he saw duty in Dakota, Nebraska, and Arizona, as well as in various of the eastern and southern states. In the frontier army posts of those days he was often the only physician in the region. Preceding even the horse-and-buggy doctor, he was the doctor-on-horseback; carrying in his saddlebags what medicines and instruments happened to be available. These conditions developed in him ingenuity and self-reliance.

After eighteen years of this pioneer experience he went to Baltimore, to work in the laboratories of Johns Hopkins; from Johns Hopkins, raised now to the position of surgeon, and the rank of major, he was made professor of bacteriology at the Army Medical School in Washington. Then, during the Spanish-American War, when the army camps were swept by typhoid, Reed was chosen head of a board to study the causes and the spread of the disease. The investigations laid bare all the evil secrets of typhoid.

But the most dramatic story of Walter Reed's life was set in the Island of Cuba.

It was June of the year 1900 when he was sent to Havana as president of a board which was to devote itself especially to a study of that mysterious scourge called Yellow Jack. Dr. Carlos Finlay of Havana was convinced that the disease was conveyed through the mosquito; but his theory had not been proved, and many scientists jeered at the mere idea.

Walter Reed came to the conclusion that only through experiments upon human beings would it be possible to test the theory. Under his direction began those perilous experiments for which men heroically offered themselves. Soldiers and physicians, Cuban as well as North American, volunteered, allowing themselves to be infected by mosquitoes which had bitten yellow fever patients. These men suffered—some of them died. But they proved the guilt of the mosquito *Aedes Aegypti* as a transmitter of the disease. Dr. Carlos Finlay had been right.

The result was momentous. Often the United States, from New York to Texas, had been devastated by yellow fever. It was yellow fever that defeated the French attempt to dig a Panama Canal, and the plague of this strange disease had held back progress in many other parts of the world. Certain cities were shunned as pestholes of infection. And now, at last, mankind understood how to protect itself. In Panama, the long-dreamed-of canal was accomplished, and tropical regions whose very name had meant death became happy and prosperous.

In the science of navigation, Matthew Maury had

made Virginia great; in medical science through Walter Reed she performed a priceless service to man. A hospital in Washington bears Reed's name, and the simple parsonage beside York River is preserved as a memorial to him.

When Maggie Walker was a little girl in Richmond, Jasper was preacher in the Sixth Mt. Zion Baptist Church. Maggie went to the Lancaster School where her teachers were southern white women, with great interest in the colored children under their charge. After school hours Maggie helped her mother, who took in washing for a livelihood. And when she had graduated from high school, Maggie went back as teacher to the old Lancaster School. In Baltimore an ex-slave-woman had founded a society whose object was to provide for Negroes in sickness and death. Branches of this organization were formed in the James River towns, and early in the century Maggie Walker became a member. Out of this grew her idea to found a penny bank. She called it the St. Luke Penny Savings Bank. Its aim was to encourage thrift; even children, who sold papers and ran errands, must be taught to save. Maggie Walker's bank also made loans for home building. With the bank's help many Richmond Negroes built and owned their own homes. Maggie Walker was the first woman in the United States to become the founder and president of a bank.

Eventually the institution became a Consolidated Banking and Trust Company, with a hundred thousand dollar building of its own. And one of Virginia's governors said that if all the money spent by the state on Negro education in fifty years had done no more than educate Maggie Walker the state would have been fully repaid.

Bill Robinson doesn't remember how he came to be called Bojangles; it began when he was a child in Richmond; everybody called him Bojangles.

In those days he did not know that he was to become a professional dancer. His job was exercising horses, but sometimes, he says, he danced in beer gardens, and people gave him pennies.

Today, this Richmond Negro has become the world's greatest tap dancer.

And if you haven't seen Bill Robinson dance, you've never seen tap dancing!

His feet have created a new art, an art so gay, so careless, that it appears magic, as though it happened without the conscious knowledge of the dancer.

His famous "stair-dance," he says, came to him in a dream. He dreamed that he was to be made a lord by the King of England, and that when he went to receive this honor, the king was awaiting him at the head of a flight of stairs. "I didn't like the idea of just walking up steps before the king," he explains, "so I thought I'd dance up, and the next morning when I woke up I knew I had a good idea."

It has been John Rolfe's fate to be famed as the husband of Pocahontas, but he was much more than that: he was the first of America's great business leaders —the father of the tobacco industry.

Two hundred years after John Rolfe, carrying on the tradition of industrial vision, Cyrus Hall McCormick, invented the harvester which he named for his native state, calling it the "Virginia Reaper."

Such pioneers would rejoice in the material prosperity which Virginia has achieved since Appomattox. It is said that she has fewer tenant-farmers, or "share-croppers," than any of the southern states. To agriculture and fisheries she has added modern industries—the manufacture of cigarettes, of nitrate, and of rayon. Norfolk has a great Navy Yard, and has become also the important port that Matthew Maury predicted it would be. The oldest and best equipped Shipbuilding and Dry Dock Company in the country is at Newport News. It was founded by Collis P. Huntington, not himself a Virginian, but an empire builder whose wide vision included Virginia. "We shall build good ships here," he said. "We shall build them at a profit if we can, at a loss if we must, but always good ships."

And this shipyard which, after millions had been poured into it, did build good ships at a profit, has indirectly influenced the art and culture of the whole country, for Archer Huntington, who inherited the business from its founder, has used those profits to establish libraries and museums of art.

The tradition of exploration in Virginia began with those Venturers who first came over from England. Later Spotswood and his Knights of the Golden Horseshoe went to see what lay behind the mountains, and William Byrd left his home on James River to explore wilderness Virginia; George Rogers Clark conquered for Virginia the vast territory, now the central states, which were her gift to the Union; and Lewis and Clark explored the Far West. The mother of the Wright brothers was a Virginian, so that it is fitting to find a great experimental aviation field on James River.

And today there is another exploring Byrd; this one flying the Atlantic, soaring over the North and South poles, and heading expeditions for scientific study of the antarctic—Admiral Richard Evelyn Byrd.

It was from Jamestown that the first written works in the British New World were sent back for publication in England. And after those early chroniclers, Robert Beverley and William Stith were Virginia's historians, while William Byrd's manuscripts give a vivid, lively picture of the first years of the eighteenth century. And since Appomattox new writers have come to make her great in Letters. Mary Johnston's historical novels brought the seventeenth century to life. Thomas Nelson Page painted an idealized portrait of the War period. Douglas Southall Freeman's biography of Robert E. Lee is a magnificent achievement. James Branch Cabell created the land of Poictesme as the setting for his unique art. Ellen Glasgow, the first novelist to write realistically of the South, heads the list of America's writers of fiction. Emily Clark, in her *Innocence Abroad* quotes Miss Glasgow as saying: "Because I am a Virginian in every drop of my blood and pulse of my heart, I may speak the truth as I understand it . . . at least the faults of Virginia are my own faults, just as I hope the peculiar virtues of Virginia are my own also."

In the year after Appomattox Edward Valentine came home. He had been studying sculpture in the ateliers of Europe. Now he returned to the old house in

Richmond with the huge knocker on its door. He had come home in time to sketch and model Matthew Maury and General Lee from life.

The drawing of Maury pictures him seated, listening to the waves, while the noble sculptured figure of Lee in the chapel at Lexington lies in majestic slumber at peace.

It was seventeen years after Appomattox that the musician and composer, John Powell, was born in Richmond; born to interpret in music the James River country, as Ellen Glasgow interprets it in fiction.

General Lee had urged the mothers of the South to make their children Americans; and as Americans they went out to battle in the Spanish-American War, while in the World War soldiers were trained at Camp Lee near Petersburg, and from the port of Norfolk in great numbers they were shipped overseas to France.

But when Lee spoke of greatness there was in his mind, too, the Virginia statesmen. He would have that high tradition carried forward.

There must be in America a never-failing supply of men who believe in representative government, and Virginia must continue to provide her quota of such men. Woodrow Wilson has been added to the number of presidents from Virginia; and James River has given such statesmen as Carter Glass and Harry Flood Byrd. Carter Glass has declared as his creed, "personal honesty and national honesty . . . there are things more precious in the world than gold . . . a principle of government is a principle of government irrespective of time."

# CHAPTER TWENTY-SIX

# A Dream

Nobody ever thought of the restoration of colonial Williamsburg until Dr. Goodwin came to be rector at Bruton Parish Church. It was his vision that it must be done; "dedicated," he said, "to the hope and purpose that the future may learn from the past."

That was his dream.

And if a dream is to come true it must be desired with a profound intensity. For dreams do not come true of themselves; virtue, as the Bible puts it, goes out from those who work miracles.

And it was a miracle that a dream should result in the restoration of colonial Williamsburg.

Williamsburg's glory had passed when, more than a hundred and fifty years ago, the capital of Virginia was removed to Richmond; though the final act of the drama of the Revolution was played upon that narrow tongue of land between the James and York rivers. The British, American, and French armies in succession were quartered in Williamsburg. Before he entrenched himself at Yorktown, Cornwallis had occupied the house of the president of William and Mary College. And during the Yorktown siege the governor's house at Williamsburg was the hospital for American soldiers and the college building a hospital for the French. In the War Between the States Williamsburg again saw battle.

With the years various buildings were destroyed, by flames and by vandalism. And nobody had any money to restore the ancient glory of the town.

Then, early in the present century, Dr. W. A. R. Goodwin came as rector to Bruton Parish Church. Patriotic groups, small in numbers and poor, were doing all they could to preserve what remained of Jamestown, and of the old tombstones in Bruton churchyard; even the children helped, getting up lawn parties where they sold ice cream and cake and lemonade.

But that colonial Williamsburg would ever be restored—no one dreamed of such a thing until Dr. Goodwin came with his vision.

When you ask how the idea came to him he tells you that it seems always to have been in his mind. He was sixteen when he first bought a book with his own money. He earned it working in the cornfields, and the title of the book was *Buried Cities Recovered*. The cities described were of the Near East, not of Virginia. But the purchase shows that from the beginning he was fascinated by the restoration of lost cities.

The World War shattered Williamsburg's drowsy tranquillity. A munitions town grew up near by; and all that is hideous in galvanized shanties and filling stations startled the decaying loveliness of the old city.

But no matter! Those who really dream are of dauntless determination.

In February, 1924, Dr. Goodwin came to New York to make a speech. The occasion was a dinner arranged with the object of building a hall on the campus of William and Mary College, in memory of those fifty students who had met at Raleigh Tavern, in the great year of the Declaration of Independence; and there founded the Society of Phi Beta Kappa.

Originally it had been intended that the president of William and Mary was to make the speech, but he was unable to come and sent Dr. Goodwin in his place. He chose as his topic William and Mary College—after Harvard the oldest in the United States; William and Mary and its historical environment; that was his subject. And he spoke from his heart, with the fervor which makes dreams come true.

He had no idea that Mr. John D. Rockefeller, Jr., was in his audience.

A year later, Mr. Rockefeller visited Williamsburg, and as he walked the streets with Dr. Goodwin the town was peopled for him with the illustrious dead, come alive through Dr. Goodwin's enthusiasm. And who can walk with Washington and Jefferson, Marshall and Henry, and the young Lafayette, and remain unmoved?

Shortly after that, Mr. Rockefeller decided that he would finance the restoration of colonial Williamsburg.

But before that happened, Dr. Goodwin had managed to restore Bruton Parish Church, then with the aid of Chapter III of the Colonial Dames of America, he was engaged in the restoration of Wythe House, when a certain Mr. Perry, of a Boston firm of architects, chanced to visit Williamsburg. He met Dr. Goodwin and freely gave his professional advice.

In the period before the idea of a general restoration was known, Mr. Perry and Dr. Goodwin worked together in the deepest secrecy. Measurements of the streets were made at night, and photographs were taken from the air. Mr. Perry himself did not know of Mr. Rockefeller's interest.

Then Dr. Goodwin began to buy one piece of property after another. Williamsburg was amazed. Why was he doing it, and where on earth was he getting the money?

Quietly, little by little, nearly the whole area that had been the colonial town was purchased; some of it bought outright; some of it on condition that those who wanted to live out their lives in their ancestral homes might continue to occupy their purchased and restored homes; provided they permitted whatever restoration was thought necessary. For Dr. Goodwin's dream was a re-creation of eighteenth-century Williamsburg; buildings, gardens, and streets, all must appear as in that vanished day. Every detail must be authentic.

Finally it became known that Mr. Rockefeller was to restore Williamsburg. But before plans were drawn, a department of research was organized. In Williamsburg they tell you that the whole restoration has cost more than fifteen million dollars, and that a hundred thousand was spent in preliminary research. However accurate those figures may be, certainly vast sums have been expended, and trained investigators have explored historical records in this country, France, and England. They consulted old documents; wills, land grants, insurance policies, inventories, contemporary newspapers; histories, volumes of reminiscence, and old books of travel. Extensive architectural investigations were made. Bit by bit they accumulated the information needed; not only for the restoration of existing buildings, but for the erection of others long ago destroyed by fire.

The library of William and Mary College provided a drawing made as early as 1702 by the Swiss traveler Michel; giving details of construction, as well as a picture of the first college building. And in the same library was a map of Williamsburg made in 1782 by a Frenchman quartered there during the Revolution, on which is shown, drawn to scale, every building then in existence. In the Huntington library in California, the investigators discovered a floor plan of the Wren Building which was the main building of the college. This drawing was made by Thomas Jefferson.

The plan and the front façade of the building were known, but there was no clue to its appearance from the rear, until a crude sketch of it was found in a young girl's notebook, dated 1856. She had made the sketch chiefly, it seems, with the object of locating the rooms of some of her friends among the students; for written above several of the windows are the young gentlemen's names.

The Governor's Palace also had been burned, and a modern high school stood in its place. But the Reverend Hugh Jones, writing early in the eighteenth century, left a description of it; and of this, too, Thomas Jefferson made a floor plan, eventually found in the archives of the Massachusetts Historical Society.

And in the Bodleian Library at Oxford Miss Mary Goodwin discovered a copperplate engraving showing all the William and Mary buildings, the Capitol and the palace, as they were at the time when Hugh Jones was writing.

Possessed of all this information, the work of restoration and reconstruction began; the firm of Perry, Shaw and Hepburn being chosen as architects.

In excavating, often the actual foundations were discovered intact. There were found also fragments of stone, marble moldings, flagging, pictorial tile, carvings, and pottery; and these were faithfully copied in this re-creation of Williamsburg. It was necessary also to manufacture brick, matching exactly the colonial variety, and to mix paint in the tints used at that time. It was an enormous undertaking.

"None but those who believe in ghosts should come to Williamsburg," Dr. Goodwin often says. When you visit Williamsburg you begin, little by little, to see its ghosts. The scene familiar to those who lived in colonial days has been re-created for them. It is not strange that they should return, as birds come to the little houses which have been thoughtfully—expectantly—provided for them.

As you pass along Duke of Gloucester Street you remember—and, remembering, see a lanky uncouth man with strange bright eyes, about the color of which no one could agree. The lanky man is leading his horse, walking slowly, in conversation with his friend, Paul Carrington. It is Patrick Henry, who that day, in the House of Burgesses, has shouted: "If this be treason—make the most of it."

Or you may come across Richard Bland on his way to the Capitol; his old head a library of Virginia history.

In the prison you are sure that you hear the jailer's step creaking on the narrow stairs as he makes a tour of inspection; perhaps on the eve of their hanging he has come to see that the condemned followers of the pirate Blackbeard are safe, and that none will cheat the gallows by escape.

In the Apollo Room of Raleigh Tavern the high-bred ghost of Sally Cary—she who married George Fairfax—may greet you; and because she is herself of so sophisticated and timeless a beauty, her eighteenth-century gown appears to you as fancy dress worn for some costume party.

But perhaps the apparitions that appear for you will be of a later date. It may be that you will meet the spinster, Miss Gibbie; and that she will explain, as she was fond of doing, that the poet Milton was responsible for her remaining unmarried. He made the Devil so fascinating, in his "Paradise Lost," she will say, that no man she ever met could compare with him.

Or, it is the slave, Jasper, who will be your Williamsburg ghost; Jasper in the days when he had just been promoted from oxboy to houseman in the Peachy establishment.

Or, you may see Lafayette, as the young marquis come from France to fight in the American Revolution.

And it will be a pity if, with a heart full of memories you do not everywhere—in the streets and the Capitol, in Raleigh Tavern and the palace—feel the dear great presence of George Washington.

❁

Turning from this talk of ghosts, Dr. Goodwin becomes profoundly serious. "The restoration," he says, "is done—the physical, material restoration. But that is only the beginning. It is for you—all of you who come here—to bring about a spiritual restoration."

# CHAPTER TWENTY-SEVEN

# Lady at the Palace

Aᴿᴱ you working today?"

The question was put to one of the official hostesses of restored Williamsburg.

"Working? Oh no," she smiled. "Today I'm a lady at the palace."

She looked the part. Her hair was like snow, frozen into shining ripples. Her eighteenth-century gown was a vivid fuchsia, its long skirt widely distended with hoops, their width giving to her silhouette the effect of a lady on a valentine. Her bodice was a long, pointed basque, low and square-cut in front, with filmy white ruffles marking the square, and wider ruffles falling in cascades from the elbows. Her skin was fair; her eyes shone like windows behind which a light burns; she had dignity, and in the carriage of her head there was a happy confidence.

"Today I'm a lady at the palace."

The phrase expresses the way the women of Williamsburg feel about their work as official hostesses.

Every morning at ten o'clock the buildings are open to the public, but for an hour before that the hostesses, each in eighteenth-century dress, may be seen going from their homes to whatever happens to be their post for the day. It may be Raleigh Tavern, the Capitol,

Travis House, or the palace; for they are shifted daily, serving the various buildings in rotation.

You see them passing along the streets under the trees, seeming to float over the sidewalk as though they were brilliant birds, with fuchsia, blue, green, or red plumage, gliding over the surface of still water. Or perhaps they arrive for the day's work in the ornate post chaise which in pleasant weather drives down Duke of Gloucester Street, a blue-liveried coachman in the box, and a footman standing in his place at the rear. Or you see them maneuver their vast skirts in and out of modern motorcars.

In these Williamsburg hostesses there is created a band whose voices will carry tradition down through the years. So that through a living, human chain those things which are dramatic, or picturesque, or profoundly significant, will be related by word of mouth to the living, human chain of visitors who come from every state in the Union; for this is not a local shrine, it belongs to the nation.

The palace seems more identified with Lord Botetourt than with any of the governors who occupied it; perhaps because its furnishings are based upon the accurate inventory made at the time of his death.

Hoping to conciliate Virginia, George III sent a governor instead of merely a lieutenant governor. And that governor was the Right Honorable Baron de Botetourt.

He arrived in the year 1768, in the month of October, when the sun is golden and the foliage flaming.

He had sailed in state across the sea, and up the broad river, traveling aboard a man-of-war, a ship of the Royal Navy, carrying more than seventy guns.

It was not, however, his exalted state, but his sincere kind heart that won the Virginians' love and trust, in spite of the conflict between the House of Burgesses and the government of Great Britain.

Lively little Miss Anne Blair's quaint long-ago letter to her sister shows us Lord Botetourt on a certain August night in Williamsburg a hundred and sixty-eight years ago.

"Mrs. Dawson's family," she wrote, "stayed the Evening with us, and the Coach was at the door to carry them Home by ten o'clock; but everyone appearing in great spirits, it was proposed to set on the Steps and Sing a few Songs which was no sooner said than done: While thus we were employed, a Candle . . . was observed to be coming up street; (except Polly Clayton censuring their ill Taste for having a Candle such a fine Night) no one took any Notice of it—till we saw, whoever it was stop to listen to our enchanting Notes. Each warbler was immediately silenced. Whereupon the Invader to our Melody, called out in a most rapturous Voice, Charming! Charming! proceed for God's Sake, or I go Home directly—no sooner were those Words uttered, than all as with one Consent sprung from their Seats and the Air echoed with, 'pray, Walk in my Lord': No—indeed he would not, he would set on the Steps too; so after a few ha, ha's, and being told what all knew—that it was a delightful Evening, at his desire we strewed the way over with Flowers, etc. till a full half Hour was elapsed when all retired to their respective Homes."

Reading that letter, you fall in love with his Lordship, wandering in the night along the Williamsburg streets, his lantern in his hand, stopping to listen to young people singing and then crying out: "Charming! Charming! Proceed for God's Sake, or I go Home directly."

And in the manner of his death Lord Botetourt takes his place among those who add to the code by which they have lived, a fitting code by which they die.

Lying upon his deathbed in the palace, his good Lordship remembered that once Nicholas, treasurer of the colony, had said that it appeared to him that no man living had so much to lose by death as had Lord Botetourt; possessing, as he did, in such rich measure the blessings of life. For he loved people and was in turn loved. He had honor and distinction. He was of importance in the difficult time in which he lived. Had it been possible to avert war between the American colonies and Great Britain, Lord Botetourt was the man to have done it. And in addition to all that, every good material thing was his.

Such a man, Nicholas had said, must more than other men be reluctant to die.

And dying, Lord Botetourt remembered, and summoned Nicholas.

"I have sent for you," he explained, "merely to let you see that I resign those good things of which you formerly spoke, with as much composure as I enjoyed them."

So died Lord Botetourt in the palace, upon an October morning just two years after his arrival.

The entrance hall of the palace is tiled in squares of black and of white marble, and opening from the hall is a little room where coffee things are set out on a small table beside the hearth; a book of the period lies open on a yellow brocaded settee; while on another table knights and pawns and castles, kings and queens, await the player's next move, an old watch beside the chessboard to mark the time.

Farther along the hall is the state dining room where the table is laid as though the colonial governor that day expected guests. And in one corner of the room stands a high old-fashioned secretary, placed there because it was Lord Botetourt's habit to keep his papers in a secretary in the dining room.

The hall leads to a lovely glittering ballroom. Portraits of George III and his queen, of Charles II and Queen Catherine hang there. A spinnet stands open and music waits upon a rack. All is ready. At any minute the ball might begin.

Beyond the ballroom is a supper room, its windows overlooking the palace gardens. A great chandelier, once the property of the fabulously rich East India Company, hangs above the table. The walls of the room are decorated with eighteenth-century Chinese paper, brilliant with bright-plumaged birds. And then the hostess conducts you back through the ballroom, up a wide imposing stairway to the upper rooms; to the state bedchamber with its canopied four-poster, and its dressing room equipped with the simple toilet conveniences of the time. Another bedroom is paneled in celestial blue, and there is an upstairs sitting room, the walls hung with gold-embossed leather, because the inventory so describes them. Among the furnishings of this room is a glass-doored bookcase filled with books, and a reading chair with a candle beside it. Between windows looking out upon the green, there are long wall mirrors, because an old order was found requisitioning such mirrors to be placed there. Lord Botetourt's personal suite opens out of the room: bedroom, dressing room, and study.

And in the bedroom you remember how the dying Lord Botetourt said to Nicholas: "I have sent for you merely to let you see that I resign those good things of which you spoke, with as much composure as I enjoyed them. . . ."

If the day is cool, logs blaze in a huge kitchen fireplace, equipped with spits and cranes, a roaster, a toast rack, and capacious iron pots. The kitchen is supplied with every device used in the culinary art of the period. There are heart-shaped waffle irons, irons for the baking of cylindrical wafers, long-handled basters, enormous fluted pans for angel cakes, molds for puddings, in the shape of sheaves of wheat and bunches of grapes, a churn, and a cider press.

"Today," Lord Botetourt once wrote, "I entertained fifty-two at dinner."

And surely, after dinner, his guests must have strolled in the palace gardens.

The gardens fill an extensive square, enclosed in front by the palace buildings, on two sides by high brick walls, and in the rear by a tall white paling fence into which are set large ornamental wrought-iron gates. The broad gravel walk leading from the palace to these gates passes between grass plots and hedge-bordered flower beds. A procession of twelve tall cedars, clipped into cylindrical shape, marches toward the gates. At the end of the garden is the icehouse; a tapering grassy mound, in shape like a Maya pyramid, with a flight of steps leading up to a belvedere at the summit.

On either side of the enclosed garden are long vine-covered arbors, and an opening in one of the side walls wanders into an enchanting garden of box.

And the gardens, like the palace, the hostess tells you, have been built upon their original foundations, and their re-creation, too, is based upon contemporary letters and documents. So that you may feel that they are today much as when Lord Botetourt and his guests looked out upon them from the palace windows, or sauntered along their pleasant paths.

As the years pass and the buildings mellow, the present, too, will become tradition.

"I remember," the hostess of today says, "I remember when the restoration began."

Another generation will explain that it was from their mothers that they heard how it all came about. They will tell of the pains that were taken that every detail should be authentic.

One may say that she had from her great-grandmother the story of the hostess who, when a visitor compared Williamsburg to England, remarked: "When we want to see England, we go to England. When we want to see Virginia we visit Virginia."

And still another of those, as yet unborn, hostesses may quote how Mr. Rockefeller used to say that he had come to feel that "of even greater value than the preservation of the beauty and charm of the old buildings

. . . is the lesson they teach of the patriotism, high purpose and unselfish devotion of our forefathers to the common good."

So today will become woven into the pattern of yesterday, the words of today being added to those of the past.

In your memory of the palace, there is perhaps standing at its gate a white-haired hostess, in a wide, hooped gown of peacock blue. The October sun is in her eyes, and she has put up one hand to shade them. The pose suggests that she is watching for someone.

It is as though she were watching for Lord Botetourt to arrive in his gorgeous coach drawn by the six white horses.

Perhaps—in the year two thousand—another hostess in eighteenth-century gown may similarly stand at the palace gate in the October sun as though she, too, watched, hoping to see a figure out of the past; a slight figure in black clerical habit, moving with quick eager step across the palace green; the figure of Dr. Goodwin, his eyes radiant with the dream of a restoration dedicated to "interpret the past to the present and to the future."

## Memory of Time

HISTORY is the memory of time; the life of the
dead, and the happiness of the living. Captain John
Smith said that. He said it so long ago that the bells of
St. Sepulchre's Church in London, where he is buried,
are no longer rung, the ancient tower where they hang
not being strong enough to bear the vibration of their
ringing.

And when he was at home in London John Smith could hear the bells; for he lived in a house on Snow Hill, under the shadow of the church tower. In that house, when his hour came, he died; and was buried in St. Sepulchre on the south side of the choir, beneath a slab on which are cut the three Turks' heads of that coat of arms said to have been granted him by Prince Sigismund.

All this was very long ago, yet John Smith's words rang in my mind.

I had come to Westover on the James by way of the river, in a tiny launch where I had sat trailing my hand through its muddy waters.

Now, walking under the trees at Westover, and looking back over the James River story, I was agreeing that history is the memory of time.

Overhead the sky was profoundly blue, the clouds white and plump, like the breasts of gulls; and the trees of Westover flamed with the glory of that distant autumn when Pocahontas had danced before John Smith, singing: "Love you not me? Love you not me?"

And from the trees drifted scarlet and yellow leaves.

Reflecting, I walked under the trees which surround the gracious mansion of Westover. And the story of the river passed in procession through my mind while I walked.

As a small child I went on a visit to my grandparents (the Roger A. Pryors of this story), who had gone north to live in New York. My grandmother took me to see a circus parade, thinking it would be a thrilling experience for a plantation child.

Elephants had swung through the streets; there had

been camels and bareback riders, and a lion in his cage. But my grandmother said that I ignored these marvels; my great thrill was the emotion of the crowd. "Boys runnin'!" I shouted over and over; their excitement more to me than the actual parade. In vain my grandmother had pointed out the elephants and camels. I was intoxicated by the excitement of the crowd, not by the parade.

And under the trees at Westover it was the human emotions of the James River story that possessed me. After all, it is the hearts of men and women that shape events; and not the events that shape the people. Emotions are the shimmering medium in which history happens; the light and shadow of the epic of living; the very breath of its life.

It was thus that the story moved through my mind; beginning with Captain John Smith. And he was but recently dead, when eight generations ago my ancestors came to James River: William Randolph to Turkey Island, where he had built a home for his wife, Mary Isham of Bermuda Hundred; and on Turkey Island they had produced seven sons and two daughters; from whom came the families of Lees and Randolphs and Blands. Theodorick Bland had settled at Westover; one of his sons marrying Elizabeth Randolph of Turkey Island; their son being the Richard Bland of the first Continental Congress; he who was called the Antiquary, by reason of being the greatest authority of his day on Virginia history.

So it happened that eight generations ago these ancestors began to live as characters in the story of James River.

As I walked beside the river, dreaming that story, I saw a Negro coming across the lawn, the dry leaves rustling beneath his feet. It was, he explained, his task to show visitors about Westover.

Of course, we fell into familiar talk. To entertain him, I described how I had recently flown over James River, low above the treetops of Westover. From that we went on to talk of Westover itself; of the first William Byrd who had bought it from the sons of Theodorick Bland after his death; they being already established on other James River plantations. Then we talked of the second William Byrd, the explorer and author, who early in the eighteenth century had built the present house. But my new friend, the guide, whose name was Jack Porter, was convinced that some of the boxwood must have been planted by the first Theodorick Bland; because, Jack reasoned, the place had been his home for years, the boxwood was very old, and therefore must have been planted by Theodorick Bland.

And that reminded me that I wanted, before we left, to see his tomb—the tomb of my immigrant ancestor.

"It's in the little graveyard," Jack said, "where Evelyn Byrd is buried; though her father, Colonel William Byrd is buried in the garden." Jack would show me the garden and the tomb.

Then he inquired from what part of Virginia I had come. And when I told him, there was mutual rejoicing because we had been born and raised in adjoining counties. Jack had often visited at the Bruce estate, the plantation next to my father's. In fact, the present mistress of Westover was a Bruce.

"Oh, I knowed your father, knowed his place

well!" Jack said. We recalled to each other how white were the gates in the fences separating the fields, and how red the roads. We remembered the steepness of the gravel drive leading up to beautiful Staunton Hill where the Charlotte County Bruces lived; where Jack stayed when he came on a visit with the Halifax County Bruces.

And beneath our talk there flowed, unspoken, a stream of memory.

All at once the plantation of my childhood appeared before me: as it was in the tender spring; in the sudden summer heat; in the sparkle of autumn; and in the shiver of winter in a great drafty house heated only by wood fires.

In the dark of the moon the plantation was a world blackly mysterious. It shimmered when the moon was full. The trees cast shadows of unbelievable loveliness. A tiny screech owl spoke. Magic was a reality, and the glow of a will-o'-the-wisp traveling low over the ground was an unearthly thing. Sometimes majestic awful storms thundered and crackled, profoundly stirring a child to strange ecstasy. Skies cleared, and among flowers brilliant in a sedate garden mockingbirds sang, and in the late afternoon wood thrushes called and were answered. Tobacco marched in long green rows through the fields. A river flowed like hammered copper in the sun. And far off a voice was singing: "I looked over Jordan, an' what did I see?"

Such a plantation was part also of Jack's stream of memory.

"Ah," he exclaimed as we talked, "now I *is* at home!"

And I, too, felt at home; with the old ancestor

lying there in the graveyard, with the fact that the characters of the James River story had known Westover; and because my roots and Jack's were sunk in the soil of adjoining counties.

Jack explained that he had been born "sence surrender," but he'd known plenty of people who remembered the War Between the States; remembered it and talked about it.

In fact, he said, he was now reading a life of General Lee. It was significant that it was a biography of Lee that this Negro was reading, and not a life of Grant or Lincoln. Yes, he was reading, he said, a life of General Lee. "And you know what General Lee used to say?" Jack asked.

"No, what did he used to say?"

"He used to say that when it came to luxuries he craved two things—a pair of shiny boots and a well-groomed horse."

This was the Lee who now stood out in Jack's mind; while for me, among many imperishable pictures, there was the story, heard long ago, of General Lee refusing to exploit the worship which the South laid at his feet. People said that among the offers made him in those despairing days after the surrender was one from an insurance company which would pay him a huge salary—as much as fifty thousand dollars, they said— if Lee would accept the presidency of the company. He explained that he knew nothing of the insurance business.

"But, general, you will not be expected to do any work; what we wish is the use of your name."

"Don't you think," he smiled, "that if my name

is worth fifty thousand dollars a year, I ought to be very careful about taking care of it?"

While we talked Jack and I had been walking about the lawn at Westover, and had then come into the garden, with its late-blooming roses, its ancient boxwood, and the tomb of William Byrd, whose long epitaph Jack proudly rattled off by heart. From the garden we started across a field to the little graveyard where the romantic, lovelorn Evelyn Byrd, the lovely ghost of Westover, is buried; the graveyard where I would find also the tomb of Theodorick Bland. But, seeing that a car had driven up to the house, Jack stopped. "There's some people," he said, "come to see Westover. Now I can't go with you to the graveyard. I've got to take 'em round." Then looking appraisingly at the lustrous, high-powered motor, he added: "Looks like Yankees."

I went on alone, while he turned back.

"Yankees," I reflected, "come to visit Virginia."

It has been said that the South lost everything in that war to which it had given all. Lost! . . . Yes, certainly it had lost, but it had never really been defeated! For here were people coming every year from distant parts to Virginia; coming because something was there created which endures; something needed in the modern world.

Arrived at the tiny graveyard, with only a flock of cawing crows for company, I stood beside the Theodorick Bland tomb, on which, cut into the stone, were his arms, impaled with those of Anne Bennett, his wife, and beneath them in Latin, the motto of the Bland crest, whose translation is: *Hope, and live as brave men.*

In the light breeze yellow leaves, and crimson, fluttered; drifting, as the memories of three hundred years drifted on the wind of thought; memories of gallant deeds, of courageous endurance; of words, tender, noble, laughing, bold and strong, words of faith, and of a "true glory and a true honor."

To such remembered words, that motto cut into the stone of a tomb nearly three centuries old now added itself.

The low light of late afternoon lay bright upon the surface of James River; and in the light—as if guiding the way to that Venture which is the future—quivered the words of the motto: *Hope, and live as brave men.*

# Acknowledgments

For the opportunity to fly over tidewater Virginia I am indebted to Captain E. V. Rickenbacker, of the Eastern Air Lines; to Beverly Griffith for planning the route of the flight; and to the pilot, Captain Richard Earle Fell.

For his kindness in putting at my disposal all the resources of the Williamsburg Restoration I am most grateful to B. W. Norton; to the co-operation of Helen Bullock of the Restoration Department of Research; and to the courtesy of Mr. Thomas C. Miller of the National Park Service.

For valuable suggestions regarding source material it is a pleasure to thank the Reverend W. A. R. Goodwin, Rector Emeritus of Bruton Parish Church; C. L. Lewis, Professor at the United States Naval Academy; J. D. Eggleston, President of Hampden-Sydney College; Dr. E. G. Swem, Librarian of William and Mary College; Dr. W. H. T. Squires; Benjamin Morton; my cousin, Lucy Atkinson McIlwaine; my mother's old friend, Miss Emma C. Venable.

For courteous response to my various inquiries I wish to thank Mrs. Littleton Fitzgerald, granddaughter of Matthew Fontaine Maury; R. F. Nelson, of the Virginia State Chamber of Commerce; Captain L. R. Leahy, of the Hydrographic Office in Washington; Mrs. Mary Lee, a Williamsburg "hostess"; Joseph W. Krutch; Rebecca Johnston, and Robert A. Lancaster, Jr., of the Virginia Historical Society; Matthew Page Andrews, and John Corbin; and to Sam Woolf for the quotations from his interviews with Bill Robinson and with Senator Carter Glass.

I am most appreciative of the kindness of Mr. S. Bywater and Mr. Boughey Bywater, through whom I have obtained valuable information about the Church of St. Sepulchre in London, where Captain John Smith is buried. And to Mr. Boughey Bywater I am indebted for a letter from the head of the College of Arms in London; in which he states that the grant of Arms to John Smith is there "recorded in full and there is nothing to suggest that the original was not a genuine document."

I am again grateful to the staff of the American History Department in Room 300 of the New York Public Library, for their co-operation throughout my many months of research.

In the preparation of the volume I have been fortunate in having the use of Mr. George Arents's unique collection of books relating to tobacco.

And, as always, on the completion of a book I am deeply grateful for the encouragement of my brother, Henry I. B. Rice, and of my husband, Robert Niles.

# Sources

As a river has its source and its destination, so, also, has the story of the river. And in the teller of every tale there flows a life-stream which inevitably influences the narration of the tale.

It happens that I approach the James River story—the Virginia Venture—with my own sources springing from the early years of the seventeenth century when the story begins; for my ancestors then came out from England to settle in the new colony.

Born and raised on my father's plantation in southside Virginia, the setting of the story is cut deeply into my being. Fate took me later to Europe, Asia, Mexico, Central and South America, and to islands of the far seas; until I now behold Virginia through eyes that are at the same time familiar and new, in which intimacy is combined with perspective.

But it was necessary to prepare myself through research. As I read—and remembered—the tale assumed so clear a pattern in my mind that there gradually came to be no question which people and which events should be included; the story itself selecting what seemed most dramatic, most characteristic, and most significant.

It is not possible to list here all the books in which I sought to recover the life that had flowed out of Virginia's past into its present. I can mention only those books which I found of greatest value.

Research divides itself into eyewitness narratives, accounts received directly from eyewitnesses, and such studies as are based upon authentic records.

The most important material concerning the life of the story's first century—the seventeenth century—is found in the chronicles of the Venturers themselves: in the *Works of John Smith,* as collected and edited by Edward Arber; in the records assembled by Richard Hakluyt, and by Samuel Purchas; in the seventeenth century records published by Alexander Brown in *The First Republic* and in his *Genesis of the United States of America;* the volumes of Force's *Historical Tracts;* in Henings *Statutes: Records of the Virginia Company in London,* compiled by Dr. Susan M. Kingsbury.

The basis for the story of John Smith and Pocahontas is found in the chronicles included in Arber's edition of the *Works of John Smith.* The story of Pocahontas and John Rolfe is given by Ralph Hamor, who knew them both, in his *True Description of the Present State of Virginia.* Other books relating to the early days are E. D. Neill's *Virginia Carolorum,* and his *Virginia Vetusta.* Robert Beverley and the Reverend William Stith provide valuable early histories of the first century of the British colony in Virginia. Of the later historians, I found useful *Social Life of Virginia in the 17th Century,* by Philip A. Bruce, and by the same author, *Economic Life in Virginia in the 17th Century; Old Virginia and Her Neighbors,* by John Fiske; T. J. Wertenbaker's *Planters of Colonial Virginia* and *The First Americans;* the *History of Virginia,* by Charles Campbell; J. C. Ballagh's *White Servitude in the Colony of Virginia;* and the John Smith-Pocahontas controversy as treated by the various writers on the subject.

I have given that story as it appears to me personally, after a study of the records of eyewitnesses and of critical historical opinion; seeing it also in the light of some experience with primitive peoples.

Coming over into the eighteenth century—into the colonial period—there is abundant firsthand material.

The writings of William Byrd, edited by J. S. Bassett, give a vivid eyewitness picture of the early part of the century. *The Present State of Virginia*, by the Reverend Hugh Jones, is invaluable. Travelers record observations made in those far-off days in such books as: *Travels Through the Middle Settlements in North America*, by Andrew Burnaby; the *Journal* of Philip V. Fithian, tutor in the family of Robert Carter of Nomini Hall: the travels of the Marquis de Chastellux, of Thomas Anbury, J. D. Schoepf, and the Abbé Robin.

The picture which I have given of George Washington is based upon his own writings, public and personal: the "Rules of Civility and Decent Behaviour in Company and Conversation," copied in his early notebooks: the volumes of his *Diaries*, as collected and annotated by John C. Fitzpatrick; the general *Writings* and letters assembled by Fitzpatrick; the *Writings* as collected and annotated by Worthington Chauncey Ford; the *Letters to Washington*, assembled by S. M. Hamilton; the *Life and Correspondence of Joseph Reed; Sally Cary*, by Wilson Miles Cary, edited by Fairfax Harrison.

Richard Bland's *Inquiry into the Rights of British Colonies* is prophetic of what was to be the future of such colonies in the empire. The *Journal of a Young Lady of Virginia*, by Lucinda Lee, edited by Emily Mason, is a sparkling intimate glimpse into the life of a young girl in colonial Virginia. A picture of the commercial life of the period may be drawn from *John Norton & Sons, Merchants of London and Virginia*, edited by Frances Norton Mason. And the old files of the *Virginia Gazette* are illuminating. For those who have not the opportunity to all these files, I recommend *Williamsburg in Colonial Times*, by J. A. Osborne who has here made a collection of extracts from the *Gazette*.

Other eyewitness material on the eighteenth century is found in Thomas Jefferson's *Autobiography*, in his *Notes on the State of Virginia,* and in his *Works* collected by W. C. Ford.

So much for firsthand accounts. Valuable secondary books are: George Sidney Fisher's *The True Revolution* and *The Struggle for American Independence; Washington after the Revolution,* by William S. Baker; Charles Moore's *Family Life of George Washington;* John Corbin's *The Unknown Washington,* an original and stimulating biography; Gilbert Chinard's *Thomas Jefferson;* H. S. Randall's *Life of Jefferson; Jefferson,* by James Truslow Adams; *The Revolution, with discussion of the documents relating to the writing of the Declaration of Independence,* by John C. Fitzpatrick. Mr. Fitzpatrick, formerly of the Manuscript Division of the Library of Congress, writes with the authority of a personal study of documents. In the April, 1927, number of *Scribner's Magazine,* he conclusively disposes of the pernicious scandals concocted to discredit Washington.

Elliot's volumes of *Debates* on the Federal Constitution, and Hugh Blair Grigsby's account of the Virginia Convention of 1788, called to vote upon the Constitution, provided the material from which I evolved the drama of the Constitution as it was enacted in Virginia.

The best material on Patrick Henry, I found in *Sketches of the Life of Patrick Henry,* by William Wirt; *Patrick Henry,* by Moses Coit Tyler; and *The True Patrick Henry,* by George Morgan.

Good general secondary books on the colonial days are: *Old Churches and Families of Virginia,* by Bishop Meade; *The Cradle of the Republic,* by Lyon G. Tyler; *Colonial Virginia,* by Mary Stanard; *Williamsburg in Virginia,* by R. Goodwin; *Historic Gardens of Virginia,* by Edith Tunis Sale; *Williamsburg Scrapbook,* sponsored by the Garden Club of Williamsburg; *Historic Virginia Homes and Churches,* by R. A. Lancaster, Jr.; *The History of Bruton Parish Church,* by Dr. W. A. R. Goodwin; *The Colonial Period of American History,* by Charles McLean Andrews;

*Virginia, the Old Dominion,* by Matthew Page Andrews; the *National Geographic Magazine,* April, 1937, contains contributions concerning the Williamsburg Restoration, by Dr. W. A. R. Goodwin and John D. Rockefeller, Jr.

For general conditions in Virginia during the nineteenth century there are: *Travels Through the United States of North America,* by Isaac Weld; *Travels Through the United States,* by John Melish; *Remarks During a Journey in America,* by Adam Hodgson; *The Cotton Kingdom,* by A. L. Olmsted, and by the same author *A Journey in the Seaboard Slave States; Retrospect of Western Travel* and *Society in America,* both by Harriet Martineau; *The Slave States of America,* by J. S. Buckingham; *A South-Side View of Slavery,* by Nehemiah Adams; *The Southern Plantation Overseer as Revealed in His Letters,* edited by J. S. Bassett; "Negroes Who Owned Slaves," by C. D. Wilson in *Popular Science Monthly* for October, 1912; *Virginia's Attitude Toward Slavery and Secession,* by Beverley Munford; and *History of Travel in America,* by S. Dunbar.

For the study of the characters featured in this volume, there are the following books: *Light-Horse Harry Lee,* by Thomas Boyd; *My Day* and *Reminiscences of Peace and War,* by my grandmother, Mrs. Roger A. Pryor. Several of the stories given in her books I have preferred to relate as she herself told them to me, being more informal than the form in which she has printed them. Of the many books on Edgar Allan Poe, Hervey Allen's *Israfel* is the most readable and valuable. I found but two lives of John Jasper; both by men who personally knew the famous old Negro preacher— William E. Hatcher and E. A. Randolph. In quoting from these authors I have occasionally simplified the spelling of the Negro dialect, for the benefit of those who do not read it easily. The only account of Maggie Lena Walker which I have been able to find is the chapter in Sadie Iola Daniel's *Women Builders.* For the story of General Pickett and his wife, read *What Happened to Me,* by LaSalle Corbell Pickett, and *The*

*Heart of a Soldier,* in which Mrs. Pickett has printed her husband's intimate letters to her.

The best biographies of Matthew Fontaine Maury are by his daughter, Diana Fontaine Maury Corbin, and by Charles L. Lewis. And in order further to see into the mind of the great Maury, I read with delight his own famous book: *Physical Geography of the Sea.*

For lives of Abraham Lincoln I recommend *The Life of Lincoln,* by Ida M. Tarbell, and *Abraham Lincoln,* by Lord Charnwood.

Of firsthand material about Robert E. Lee, nothing equals *Recollections and Letters of General Robert E. Lee,* by his son, Robert E. Lee.

After that comes *Personal Reminiscences, Anecdotes and Letters of General Robert E. Lee,* by J. Williams Jones, who was chaplain in the Army of Northern Virginia, and later chaplain at Washington College while Lee was its president. Other personal accounts of value are: *Four Years Under Marse Robert,* by Robert Stiles; *Robert E. Lee,* by Emily V. Mason; and the brief, but stirring impression of Lee by Viscount Wolseley.

Good biographies of later date are: *Robert E. Lee and the Southern Confederacy,* by Henry A. White; *Robert E. Lee, Man and Soldier,* by Thomas Nelson Page; *Lee of Virginia,* by W. E. Brooks; *Lee the American,* by Gamaliel Bradford; but the greatest of them all is that magnificent and inspiring work in four volumes, *R. E. Lee, A Biography,* by Douglas Southall Freeman.

For a general firsthand picture of life during the War Between the States there are Mary Boykin Chestnut's *Diary from Dixie* and Mrs. Roger A. Pryor's *Reminiscences.* For the war itself: *The Sunset of the Confederacy,* by Morris Schaff; *A Rebel's Recollections,* by G. C. Eggleston; *First Fight of the Iron-Clads,* by John Taylor Wood; the *Papers of Charles Marshall, Aide-de-Camp of Lee,* edited by Major General

Frederick Maurice; and Charles Marshall's *Address* before the Lee Monument Association; General George A. Forsyth, U. S. A., in *Harper's Magazine*, April, 1898, has an important article on Appomattox; and always, for the War period, Douglas Southall Freeman's biography of Lee.

In addition to the preceding list, valuable material is to be found through Swem's *Virginia Historical Index;* and in the volumes of *Southern Historical Society Papers, Old South Leaflets,* old issues of the *Southern Literary Messenger, The William and Mary Quarterly, The Virginia Historical Magazine,* Tyler's *Genealogical and Historical Quarterly, Virginia Magazine of History and Biography, Virginia Historical Collections,* and in contemporary newspapers.

In visiting restored Williamsburg I was fortunate in having my husband with me, he providing an architect's eye to supplement my intimate and historical point of view.

# Index

# RIVERS AND AMERICAN FOLK

*By*

CONSTANCE LINDSAY SKINNER

## PUBLISHERS' NOTE

Miss Skinner's essay, "Rivers and American Folk," is included at the end of this volume for the benefit of those readers who are most interested in our American heritage, and who may want to know more of the idea responsible for the Rivers of America.

WHEN American folk have troubles which do not end swiftly, they begin presently to examine their own sources as a nation and their own story as a people. They forget about these in good times. But when they are hit they remember that a new story, like no other in the world, was carried in chapters and cantos across the American wilderness on a strong rhythm and they catch at phrases to console and encourage themselves.

From Maine to New Mexico and from Texas to Oregon, old phrases are being spoken and then newly turned. There is in a number of states a very keen interest in the earlier life of those sections and efforts are being made to interpret it, or at least to make some new record of it, in literature and art. A new record, that is, which shall bring the vital past into the living present, unite them; so that it can be said "this we were and are, and there is beauty in it."

The first necessity of our times, as they relate to letters, would seem to be the retelling of the American story as a Folk Saga; if only to make the parts luminous by shedding on them the light of the whole.

There are, of course, several ways of doing it. Forms came into being for such material long ago.

The two most familiar are the epic poem, such as the Iliad in which a great poet blended fragments of history and myth, and the prose chronicle like the Icelandic Sagas told by several bards who could speak in prose as well as verse. We are conscious of rhythm as we read the Icelandic Sagas, as if thought sounded as it flowed, and the land the Saga-tellers lived in seems to rise visibly and move about the characters in the stories. The American Indians were aware—at least, their poets and dancers were—that rhythm flowed out of their beautiful land to them, bringing them thoughts, helping them to interpret Nature, their past history and their present experience.

The natural rhythm moving the pioneer life of America forward was the rhythm of flowing water. It is as the story of American rivers that the folk sagas will be told.

There are several reasons for telling the great saga along the rivers. We began to be Americans on the rivers. By the rivers the explorers and fur traders entered America. The pioneers, who followed them, built their homes and raised their grain and stock generally at, or near, the mouths of rivers. As their numbers increased they spread up the valleys, keeping close to the streams, since water is an indispensable element of the sustenance of the soil and all animal life. The rivers were the only highways of communication and commerce between solitary hamlets. Settlement expanded from the rivers. To repeat, the first foreigners on these shores began their transition from Europeans to Americans as River Folk.

Naturally enough, the effort to make a whole interpretation of a few American folk in localities has played its part in opening up the greater adventure, namely a composite study of the American Folk as a nation. This interpretative study will be issued in twenty-four volumes by Messrs. Farrar & Rinehart under the general title of *Rivers of America*.

This is to be a literary and not an historical series. The authors of these books will be novelists and poets. On them, now in America, as in all lands and times, rests the real responsibility of interpretation. If the average American is less informed about his country than any other national, knows and cares less about its past and about its present in all sections but the one where he resides and does business, it is because the books prepared for his instruction were not written by artists. Few artists have displayed to him the colors and textures of the original stuff of American life; or made him a comrade of the folk who came from the crowded civilizations of the old world and entered the vast wilderness of the new by all its shining rivers; or thrust him, as one of them, into the clash of spirit with circumstance, under the green arches of beauty, from which emerged the democratic ideal and American individuality—"rugged" truly, in its loyal strength, sacrifice and self-dependence. He has not been led to feel himself a neighbor and brother in the foreign groups which developed into separate Little Americas; evolving their own lore by blending old memories with fancies kindled by the new experience and, as the groups enlarged and mingled and occupied wide sections of river-pathed territory, spreading their imaginative compound of pioneer and Indian folkways, stories, songs and myths like a rich loam over all the seeding-ground of this present nation.

The average American has been prevented from a profound self-knowledge, as a descendant and a citizen, and deprived as an individual of the thrill and inspiration of a dramatic experience, because the epic material of America has been formulated by the scholastics instead of by the artists. This is said with full realization that we can hardly give adequate thanks for the patient researches of the scholars, and may properly say a word in censure of those budding writers who went to colleges and drowsed through the history hours without hearing even a few phrases of the great rhythm pulsing under the berceuse.

What has caused the tardy awakening? Partly, of course, the depression, and the present war of soap boxes beneath the artist's window. But the deeper reason for it is found in the recent self-assertion of the American spirit as expressed in sectional fiction and verse. There is something new in the approach which indicates that the American writer's reliance on traditional forms and methods is coming to an end. The spade striking to the root today seems to be sharper (if also wielded with less concern for surrounding growths): the horizon is often no farther off than the farm fence, the foundry wall, the end of Main Street; and there is an intensive, meticulous, and on occasions tediously thorough, searching of the particular spot and of the minds of the few characters; for the aim, whether it hit true or not, is such spiritual interrelationship of folk and scene that the ground itself shall sound under their footsteps and the shadow of their bodies never pass from the meadow or the forge where they labor.

The historical part played by rivers in the folk

life is evident but it may be a new idea to many that geography itself determined that Americans should first live on and by the rivers.

Here the map of North America unrolls, and comes into the discussion; hinting that Nature foresaw the day when old world folk would feel the need of a new world, and the new world call for inhabitants, and therefore set about her topographical modeling of the major part of the continent, between the Rio Grande and the Arctic sea, with accessibility as her chief aim. She traced large rivers in deep long lines north and south, such as Mississippi and Mackenzie, and east and west, as Rio Grande and Missouri. Others she drew with a fanciful touch; like Ohio and Columbia, which mark the map in large, irregular loops with an angle or two. There seems to be little logic in their designs yet, on their careless rambles—Columbia is more erratic than careless—they make contact with scores of smaller streams and so gather huge territories about them. The modern map is too crowded to do justice to the free beauty of the watercourses. They should be studied from the early pen-and-ink maps of the fur traders, who set down little else; since beauty wherever found is significant, and nothing is more so, and these charts show all the land traversed, and its remotest bounds linked, with rhythm, power, and grace. Philip Turnor's map, the first ever drawn of the beaver-hunters' canoe trails in the Northwest, is before me. The slender curving lines of the rivers, with the lakes set in like jewels, make a design a master goldsmith might choose for an empress's necklace.

In the heyday of the beaver trade, rivers opened

most of the territory between the Arctic coast and the Mexican border to the daring, singing voyageurs of the fur fleets. There was the famous Canadian route, traveled yearly from Montreal by the St. Lawrence, Ottawa, Great Lakes, and Lake Winnipeg to the Saskatchewan, which is commonly said to empty into Lake Winnipeg, but which, in reality, flows through its northern end and continues under the name of Nelson to Hudson Bay. From New Orleans the voyageurs went by the Mississippi and the Missouri, the true Upper Mississippi, to Montana: or ascended the Mississippi to its Minnesota headwaters, crossed into Canada by Rainy River, turned west through Lake of the Woods and English and Red rivers into Lake Winnipeg, and out again by either the Nelson, or the Hayes, thus following the whole of the water chain which connects New Orleans, La., with York Factory on Hudson Bay.

Mackenzie opened two new trails whereby traders in canoes could go from Montreal to the Pacific coast, having entered British Columbia by Peace River and to the polar ocean by Slave River, Slave Lake, and the Mackenzie. If they had a mind to go to the mouth of the Mackenzie from the mouth of the Mississippi they could do so, by water and the portages which were a part of all canoe travel.

When the trade was carried west of the Rockies, the favorite route led through the mountains from the headwaters of the Saskatchewan to that bizarre but navigable north angle of the Columbia River thrust up into British Columbia. From this point the voyageurs might choose to follow the river to Astoria at its mouth; or to swing eastward again by the passes, coming out in time on the Missouri at Three Forks and going on from there to St. Louis or New Orleans.

These were the routes of the great journeys, but the singing voyageurs found many other water trails, branching off from Ohio and Mississippi—the Arkansas, Illinois, Red, Canadian (named for them)—and all the smaller rivers lacing the western lands. They had no thought of settlement, their aims were fur and freedom, as they flashed their paddles in every navigable stream and loosed more than a thousand new songs on the air to the rhythms of new waters. Yet little as they thought it (and how much less would they have desired it!) they were opening a continent to the Folk. By the shining, running rivers, which had inspired men to sing in the wilderness, entered "a great number of weake and distressed soules, scattered, poor and persecuted," to grow strong and confident upon their banks. In which connection, let us recall that long before voyageurs caroled of "good wind and swift water," an Indian poet sang prophetically:—

Bright with flashing light the distant line
Runs before us, swiftly runs,
River runs, winding, flowing through the land . . .
Water brings to us the gift of strength.

Good reasons are found then, in geography and history, for telling the American Folk Saga beside the rivers. In this literary series, however, and it should be emphasized that the *Rivers of America* is literary, as distinct from historical, other reasons are paramount.

The special function of literature is to diffuse enchantment without which men's minds become shrunken and cold. There is a magic in rivers, beyond their gleaming beauty. They are unending rhythm; even when winter closes over them, in the mind, like remembered verse, they are still flowing. They are the motion in the still land, the vital fluid coursing through the clay body. To the first American, the Red Man, seeing them ever flowing away, yet ever there, they were mystery and wonder and beckoning—"That broad water, that flowing water! My mind wanders across it." Rivers symbolized life to him, as they have to other primitive poets in other lands. Our rivers typify for us our living link with the pioneers, who received "the gift of strength" on the banks of American rivers; who there became American Folk "naturalized" not by artificial processes of law and politics but by fearless submission of their hearts, and by honest putting of their hands to work.

The American nation came to birth upon the rivers. Has the fact colored our temperament? Are we a restless people because motion flowed by us continuously in our youth? Are we optimistic, eager, imaginative, daring, and even recklessly experimental, because of the beckoning of the tides "bright with flashing light" which ran swiftly past our known shores into domains beyond our vision? Are we in any part what we are, because of rivers? Possibly only a poet would answer yes. Poets have written of rivers and men, blending the spiritual over-tones of both: Spoon River in our time, Kubla Khan and Sorab and Rustum of an earlier period. Poets had discerned the power of Nature to influence thought and character long before the geographers of our day—more power to them!— began to contend with the economists for the soul of man. The *Rivers of America* offers a new and stirring appeal to the imagination of authors and readers. It is like a light slanted down into the depths of the American consciousness, which have become obscured from us by confusion in the shallows.

It is, of course, impossible to tell the complete story of America in any one series of books. The *Rivers of America,* also, is selective, conceived within definite limits set by the basic idea, namely the rivers and the folk. People are supreme; events are secondary. This is natural and right, because past events in America have been peculiarly an expression of the Folk of America, in striking contrast to the determining events in European history, which have been more often set afoot by monarchs and ruling classes from motives that took small account of the masses. The folk groups have increased mightily since they first planted themselves by the rivers; they occupy large sections and these various sectional groups now need a new introduction to one another. These volumes will make the inhabitants of the Columbia River country, for instance, acquainted with those who live in the Connecticut valley, the people along the Gila with the people beside the Hudson, on the basis of their common origin as River Folk.

The idea of the *Rivers of America* is original, and the plan it dictates breaks with both the old systems used thus far in American literary and historical series; i.e., the chronological plan, which divides material into periods, and the topical plan which arranges it by subjects. The periods will appear in these volumes as the intimate setting in which the folk of the times lived out their lives. The topics will be there, too, treated as larger expressions of the folk's energy, initiative, and will to life and power; which is what they were, in reality.

Instead of volumes on shipping, cattle, the fur trade, etc., stressing their economic importance, fur traders, cowboys, farmers, lumberjacks, fishermen, shipbuilders, will be shown as pioneer folk being cast in new molds by their occupations; for these labors and trades were natural and primitive, indigenous to the folk life, the soil, and the times. The church, the school, and the assembly have their place in these volumes. Civil rights, God, and the primer were held in honor on the banks of American rivers. How many state buildings, besides the Capitol, how many universities, agricultural colleges, how many temples, today lift their domes and towers above running water? A large number. We can still find some of their modest forerunners—on the Connecticut River at East Haddam, for instance, where Nathan Hale's schoolhouse remains and the chaste spire of the old church rises, radiant under the sun and, in the dusk, cloud-white. Religion, arts, crafts, and folklore will be treated in these volumes as characteristic expressions of the folk mind. Religious sects will be handled in the manner of good neighbors who show courtesy to other folks' opinions whether they agree with them or not. The plan will be carried out by the Editor, who has selected the rivers and approved the material, i.e., the special folk stories for the several books. Each volume will be fully illustrated. The series has two purposes, to kindle imagination and to reveal American Folk to one another. Its authors, illustrators, editor, and publishers are also "folks," absorbed in issuing the story they have discovered which has been, thus far, a lost version of a great saga.

Everyone, apparently, has his "revolution" today —the word makes nice large mouthing, anyway—and American writers and illustrators are entitled to theirs against the "economic interpreters" with their foolish notion that the belly is the hub of the universe and America's own bright and morning star. If, as we hear shouted from the soap boxes, the old America with its customs and ideals is on the way out, we can march to intercept it and seize its baggage for our own purposes. Before the citizen, who flees history books, and is justified, agrees to exchange the American system for some other he should at least know what he is parting with. He really has no idea: he has not met "the folks." To be sure, philosophies change and systems fall; and the present is wiser to forbid nothing to the future since the past, heady too in its time, sought to picket the present and is proved foolish. To the creative imagination, the poet—and all artists are poets whether they use words or paint—the impermanency of structures is relatively unimportant. The significant thing is the beauty they have recorded and the inspirations of that beauty which flowed by many brooks into the long river of human thought.